ned

KNOWLEDGE MANAGEMENT AND
ORGANIZATIONAL COMPETENCE

Knowledge Management and Organizational Competence

Edited by
RON SANCHEZ

OXFORD
UNIVERSITY PRESS

OXFORD

UNIVERSITY PRESS

Great Clarendon Street, Oxford OX2 6DP

Oxford University Press is a department of the University of Oxford.
It furthers the University's objective of excellence in research, scholarship,
and education by publishing worldwide in

Oxford New York

Athens Auckland Bangkok Bogotá Buenos Aires Cape Town
Chennai Dar es Salaam Delhi Florence Hong Kong Istanbul Karachi
Kolkata Kuala Lumpur Madrid Melbourne Mexico City Mumbai Nairobi
Paris São Paulo Shanghai Singapore Taipei Tokyo Toronto Warsaw

with associated companies in Berlin Ibadan

Oxford is a registered trade mark of Oxford University Press
in the UK and in certain other countries

Published in the United States
by Oxford University Press Inc., New York

British Library Cataloguing in Publication Data

Data available

Library of Congress Cataloging-in-Publication Data

Knowledge management and organizational competence / edited by Ron Sanchez
p. cm.
Includes bibliographical references and index.
1. Knowledge management. 2. Organizational learning. 3. Organizational
effectiveness. I. Sanchez, Ron.
HD30.2 .K63685 2001 658.4'038—dc21 2001034046
ISBN 0–19–924028–0

1 3 5 7 9 10 8 6 4 2

Typeset by
J&L Composition Ltd, Filey, North Yorkshire
Printed in Great Britain
on acid-free paper by
T.J. International Ltd., Padstow, Cornwall

Contents

Contents

List of Contributors

CHARLES BADEN-FULLER, Director of Research, Centenary Professor of Strategy, Department of Strategy and Marketing, City University Business School, Frobisher Crescent, Barbican Centre, London EC2Y 8HB, United Kingdom

MAX BOISOT, Professor of Strategic Management, ESADE, Avda. Pedralbes 60–62, 08034 Barcelona, Spain

TOM ELFRING, Associate Professor of Business Environment and Strategy, Rotterdam School of Management, Erasmus University Rotterdam, PO Box 1738, 3000 DR Rotterdam, The Netherlands

DOROTHY GRIFFITHS, Senior Lecturer in Organizational Behavior and Industrial Relations, and Director of Quality, Imperial College Management School, 53 Prince's Gate, Exhibition Road, London SW7 2PG, United Kingdom

PHILIPPE LORINO, Professor, Accounting and Management Control Department, ESSEC Business School, Avenue Bernard Hirsch, B.P. 105, 95021 Cergy Pontoise Cedex, France

YASMIN MERALI, Lecturer in Information Systems and Director of the Information Systems Research Unit, Operational Research and Systems Group, Warwick Business School, University of Warwick, Coventry CV4 7AL, United Kingdom

FIONA MURRAY, Visiting Associate Professor of Management of Technology, Innovation, and Entrepreneurship, MIT Sloan School of Management, 50 Memorial Drive, Cambridge, MA 02142, USA

STEFFEN P. RAUB, Adjunct Professor, HEC Geneva and HEC Lausanne, UNI MAIL, BD du Pont-d'Arve 40, CH-1221 Geneva 4, Switzerland

JONAS RIDDERSTRÅLE, Assistant Professor, Center for Advanced Studies in Leadership, Stockholm School of Economics, PO Box 6501, S-113 83 Stockholm, Sweden

RON SANCHEZ, Professor of Strategy and Technology Management, IMD, Chemin de Bellerive 23, CH-1001 Lausanne, Switzerland

PETTERI SIVULA, Leader, eRM, Satama Interactive Oyj, Henry Fordin Katu 6, FIN-00150 Helsinki, Finland

JOHAN STEIN, Associate Professor, Center for Management and Organization, Stockholm School of Economics, PO Box 6501, S-113 83 Stockholm, Sweden

FRANS A. J. VAN DEN BOSCH, Professor of Management and Chairman of the Department of Strategic Management and Business Environment, Rotterdam School of Management, Erasmus University Rotterdam, PO Box 1738, 3000 DR Rotterdam, The Netherlands

RAYMOND VAN WIJK, Assistant Professor, Department of Strategic Management and Business Environment, Rotterdam School of Management, Erasmus University Rotterdam, PO Box 1738, 3000 DR Rotterdam, The Netherlands

HENK W. VOLBERDA, Professor of Strategic Management and Business Policy, Rotterdam School of Management, Erasmus University Rotterdam, PO Box 1738, 3000 DR Rotterdam, The Netherlands

NICOLAY WORREN, Saïd Business School, University of Oxford, Oxford OX1 3UJ, United Kingdom, and Accenture, Drammensveien 165, PO Box 550 Skøyen, 0214 Oslo, Norway

PART I

MANAGING KNOWLEDGE
INTO COMPETENCE

Managing Knowledge into Competence: The Five Learning Cycles of the Competent Organization

RON SANCHEZ

INTRODUCTION

As we enter the first decade of the twenty-first century, contemporary management thinking is being profoundly reshaped by two new convictions:

(1) managing organizational knowledge effectively is essential to achieving competitive success;
(2) managing knowledge is now a central concern—and must become a basic skill—of the modern manager.

Despite wide acceptance of these premises, there exists no agreement among managers or management academics as to what exactly we mean by key terms like *organizational knowledge*, nor is there any generally accepted methodology for managers to use in managing knowledge and organizational learning. Instead, as is often the case with any emerging area of theory and practice, a great diversity of ideas is now being proposed under the banners of "knowledge management," "the learning organization," and similar labels. Many of these ideas, however, either fall into the category of abstract theoretical schema with no clear connections to the realities of managers and their organizations, or belong to the category of "practical" action-oriented steps that ignore (and sometimes contradict) insights into human cognition and organizational behavior that have been developed in psychology, sociology, and other disciplines in recent years.

This volume has been conceived to explore the vital middle ground of theoretically sound and practically implementable ideas for effectively managing knowledge and converting knowledge into increased organizational competence. The chapters in this volume draw on a number of management perspectives—strategy, technology management, marketing, information systems, innovation, accounting and control, as well as general management—to clarify the processes through which people create and use knowledge in organizations. At the same time, case studies and other action-oriented research methods are used to derive practically implementable ways to support, improve, and stimulate the creation and use of knowledge that can enhance organizational competences and bring strategic benefits to organizations.

This chapter introduces a model of the *five learning cycles* of the competent organization. The five learning cycles represent the processes through which

(1) individuals in organizations create knowledge;
(2) individuals and the groups they work in interact to create shared knowledge and to generate new knowledge;
(3) groups use their knowledge to undertake coordinated action and to jointly develop new organizational competences.

The five learning cycles model provides an integrated "bottom-to-top" and "top-to-bottom" view of knowledge and learning processes in organizations. In this chapter, we also use the five learning cycles model to show how the ideas developed in the other chapters of this volume "fit together" in an integrated, conceptually coherent view of what knowledge management consists of in the competent organization.

Conceptual coherence of the chapters in this volume has been achieved largely because the research reported in these chapters has been motivated by a set of compatible concepts about knowledge, learning, competence, management, and other foundational ideas. Further, adoption of a common vocabulary for referring to those concepts has made it possible to directly connect the ideas developed from one management perspective in one chapter with the ideas developed from other perspectives in other chapters. The result is something much more useful than the "kaleidoscope" of multiple but unconnected perspectives on a complex management problem usually offered in an edited volume. Rather, these chapters offer complementary, interrelated explanations of key knowledge creation and application processes in the five learning cycles of the competent organization.

To lay the foundation for this volume's exploration, we begin this chapter with a brief discussion of foundational concepts and terms used throughout the volume. These concepts form the building blocks of the organizational sensemaking, learning, and competence building and leveraging processes in the five learning cycles of the competent organization. After an introduction to the five learning cycles, we examine each learning cycle in more detail and highlight the contribution of each chapter in this volume to understanding the knowledge creation and application processes in each learning cycle. We conclude this chapter by building on the insights offered by the chapters in this volume to propose a set of basic principles for managing knowledge and organizational learning in each of the five learning cycles.

BASIC CONCEPTS AND TERMS

In this volume we represent learning in organizations as a collective sensemaking process that follows an identifiable progression of cognitive activities. The progression begins with individuals noticing events of potential significance for the organization, then seeking to derive meaning from those events by applying interpretive frameworks, and finally reacting to the meanings derived from events by forming new or modified sets of beliefs about the world and the situation of the organization in the world. To describe this process more clearly, we need to use a vocabulary of well-defined terms that refer to specific aspects of this sensemaking process. We therefore next define several terms that represent the essential building blocks of organizational sensemaking processes: data, information, knowledge, learning, sensemaking, and interpretive frameworks.

Data are representations of the events that people notice and bring to the attention of other people in the organization. Data consist of qualitative or quantitative descriptions of events. As descriptions, data are always incomplete representations—some aspects of an event are noticed and recorded in some way, while other aspects either are not noticed or are not included in the representation of an event. How an event becomes represented in data depends on what aspects of an event an observer notices and thinks will have significance, personally or for the organization. Just as it has been noted that "all facts are theory laden," all data are *selective representations of events*, implicit in which are some presumptions about which events and which aspects of those events are likely to have significance in some context of interest. Thus, the data entering an organization are greatly influenced by the interpretive frameworks (defined below) that determine which events are noticed and how those events are represented to the organization.

Information is the significance—or more precisely, the *meaning*—that is imputed to some data by evaluating the data in an interpretive framework. Meaning is derived through comparisons of data with other data, and the interpretive framework used to impute meaning to data determines the kinds of comparisons that are thought to be relevant for a given set of data, as well as the metrics that will be used to make those comparisons. In this sense, as Merali explains in her chapter,[1] information is essentially the difference in data that makes a difference in the way we understand some aspect of the world. When comparisons of some data suggest a significant change in the state of the world or an organization, that perceived change is the meaning or "information content" derived from the process of comparing data. Further, we can add that comparisons of data suggesting that the world or organization have *not* changed also provide information that, in effect, tends to confirm our current world view.

Knowledge is a set of beliefs about causal relationships in the world and an organization. In essence, we adopt in this volume a pragmatic concept of knowledge as some variant on a belief that "A causes B." This pragmatic concept of knowledge is appropriate—and perhaps even essential—for studying knowledge management, because the basic objective of management is to help organizations *do things* more effectively and efficiently. In essence, we are concerned in our discussion of knowledge management

---

[1] All references in this chapter that mention only an author's last name refer to that author's chapter in this volume. Other references are made in the standard Harvard format, which indicates the year of publication of the reference after the author's name.

with forms of knowledge that can be used to cause things to happen. This concept of knowledge helps to make an important distinction between simply being aware of something, which means having data or information in our framework, and having knowledge, which implies actually knowing how to do things or to cause things to happen. Thus, our theoretical conception of knowledge is one that is rooted in the action-oriented world of managers. Finally, although we will assume that knowledge ultimately resides in the minds of individuals, we shall also refer to *organizational knowledge* that exists when individuals in an organization share sets of beliefs about causal relationships that enable them to work together in doing something.

Learning is the process that results in a change in knowledge—i.e. a change in our beliefs about causal relationships in the world and our organization. Learning makes us believe that new things can now be done, that familiar things can no longer be done, or that familiar things will have to be done in new ways. Because learning changes the web of interrelated causal relationships that make up our knowledge base, learning results in new or modified interpretive frameworks for making sense of the world and taking action in it. We assume that learning fundamentally occurs in the mind of an individual, but we also recognize that the learning processes of individuals are greatly affected by their interactions with other individuals in the groups they participate in, and by the interactions of their groups with the overall processes of the organization.

Sensemaking is the process of perceiving events, looking for similarities or differences between current events and past events, and forming expectations about the significance of current events based on their similarities or differences with past events. In the terms we have just defined, sensemaking is the process of gathering and interpreting data to create information that is then used to formulate a set of beliefs about important (causal) relationships in the world and an organization. Sensemaking may therefore lead to two forms of learning: reinforcement of our current beliefs about causal relationships, or modification of those beliefs.

An *interpretive framework* is an existing set of beliefs about causal relationships, against which we compare current events in our sensemaking process. Our current interpretive frameworks greatly influence what we notice in the world around us. An interpretive framework draws our attention to certain events and colors our perceptions of those events, while also acting as a cognitive filter that leads us to ignore or discount the importance of other events. When what we notice about current events does not appear to be consistent with the beliefs about causal relationships that make up our interpretive framework, we may modify our beliefs to become more consistent with our observations of events, thereby making current events more "understandable." In this regard, interpretive frameworks are both the means for our sensemaking and the result of our sensemaking. Because modifying an interpretive framework may require significant cognitive effort, however, sometimes people may prefer to ignore events that are not consistent with their current beliefs, may pay greater attention to other events that tend to corroborate a current interpretive framework, or may simply choose not to worry about the inconsistency of current events with a current interpretive framework.

The foregoing terms will be used in this volume's analysis of individual and organizational sensemaking processes. From a management perspective, however, sensemaking is not a goal *per se* for an organization, but only a means to achieve the goals of the organization. To achieve its goals, an organization must be able to integrate its sensemaking activities into processes for competence building and leveraging. In essence, sensemaking must support effective action taking. We therefore next introduce some key concepts and terms for investigating an organization's processes for building and leveraging competences. We consider the interrelated concepts of assets, resources, skills, competencies, capabilities, and competences.[2]

Assets are anything tangible or intangible that an organization could use in the pursuit of its goals. *Resources* are any assets that are actually available to an organization to use in pursuit of its goals. Resources may be either firm-specific assets internalized within a firm or firm-addressable assets that are outside the boundaries of the firm but that can be accessed by the firm when needed.

Skills are the abilities an individual has to do things. *Competency* is the set of skills that an individual can use in doing a given task. *Capabilities* are repeatable patterns of action that an organization can use to get things done. Capabilities reside in groups of people in an organization who can work together to do things. Capabilities are thus a special kind of asset, because capabilities use or operate on other kinds of assets (like machines and the skills of individuals) in the process of getting things done.

Competence is the ability of an organization to sustain coordinated deployments of assets and capabilities in ways that help the organization achieve its goals. Note that this concept of competence has three essential elements: (i) *coordination* of assets and capabilities; (ii) *intention* in deploying assets and capabilities to specific purposes; and (iii) *goal-seeking* as the driver of organizational action. Competence is thus a property of an organization that depends on three essential inputs from managers: articulating the general goals of the organization, defining specific actions that will help the organization achieve its goals, and coordinating the use of resources in carrying out those actions.

Organizations try to achieve their goals by building, leveraging, and maintaining competences. *Competence building* is the process of creating or acquiring new kinds of assets and capabilities for use in taking action and/or of learning how to coordinate assets and capabilities in new ways in taking action. *Competence leveraging* is the coordinated use of an organization's current assets and capabilities in taking actions. *Competence maintenance* is the maintaining of an organization's current assets and capabilities in a state of effectiveness for use in the actions which the organization is currently undertaking.

With these concepts and definitions in place, we can now turn to a more detailed investigation of the central question of this volume: How can organizational knowledge be created and managed so as to improve the building, leveraging, and maintaining of an organization's competences? To answer this question, we now identify and investigate five learning cycles that drive the sensemaking and competence building and leveraging processes of an organization.

---

[2] These definitions were first developed in ch. 1 of *Dynamics of Competence-Based Competition* (Ron Sanchez, Aimé Heene, and Howard Thomas (eds.), Oxford: Elsevier Pergamon, 1996).

THE FIVE LEARNING CYCLES OF THE COMPETENT ORGANIZATION

We start our discussion of the five learning cycles of the competent organization by making plain two key presumptions of this volume:

(1) no one can manage something that is not defined;
(2) no one can manage well something that is inadequately defined.

Our first step in understanding the process of managing knowledge must therefore be to identify the various forms of knowledge in an organization that must be interrelated and integrated in processes of organizational action taking.

There are many ways one can begin to define categories of knowledge, but the most important characteristic of knowledge for the purposes of creating organizational competences is whether some knowledge (i) exists only in the mind of an individual, (ii) is shared among participants in a work group, or (iii) is recognized and used at the level of the overall organization. These three distinctions are represented by the Individual, Group, and Organizational Learning Cycles shown in Figure 1.1.

As suggested by the large Individual Learning Cycle at the bottom of Figure 1.1, the foundation of organizational knowledge is the knowledge (beliefs about causal relationships) that individuals develop through their own personal sensemaking processes. In essence, it is individuals within an organization that are the sources of beliefs that become incorporated in interpretive frameworks used by the organization. It is also individuals who may have the imagination to generate alternative interpretive frameworks that complement or challenge existing organizational frameworks. Ultimately, the meanings that are derived from comparisons of data within an organization depend on the kinds of comparisons that each individual member makes and on the deductive and inferential powers that each individual can draw on in making those comparisons. Thus, the wellsprings of organizational sensemaking are the dual capacities of the individuals in an organization to apply interpretive frameworks effectively and to generate new interpretive frameworks that improve or extend the sensemaking capabilities of existing frameworks. The Individual Learning Cycle in Figure 1.1 represents the individual sensemaking process. The "inventory" of interpretive frameworks of all individuals in an organization and their cognitive capacities for generating modified or new cognitive frameworks is represented at the center of the Individual Learning Cycle.

Some knowledge possessed by an individual may be applied directly to performing his or her assigned task, but much individual knowledge must be shared with other individuals in a group before that knowledge can become the basis for taking action. Thus, a critical organizational learning process is one through which individuals both share knowledge with other people in the group they work in and receive knowledge from their coworkers. This critical "up/down" learning cycle joining individuals and the other people in their work groups is shown as the Individual/Group Learning Cycle in Figure 1.1. At the center of the Individual/Group Learning Cycle is the repertoire of modes of interactions through which people within a given group share their individual knowledge with others in their group.

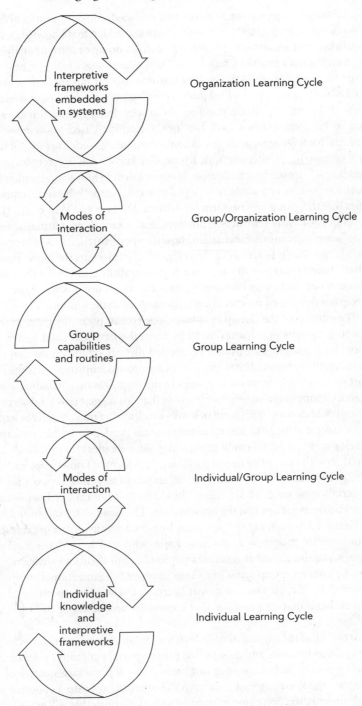

Fig. 1.1 *The five learning cycles of the competent organization.*

Individuals in groups must have some knowledge in common in order to perform tasks in a coordinated fashion, but they may also add to that knowledge. In performing individual and group tasks, people may learn by doing or learn by analyzing. Learning by doing creates practical, hands-on, "know-how" knowledge of how to perform a given task consistently—the kind of learning that creates the "repeatable patterns of action" that we refer to as *capabilities*. Learning by analysis helps to develop more theoretical "know-why" understanding about why doing certain things enables a given task to be accomplished (Sanchez 1997). Routine-based know-how knowledge is essential for leveraging an organization's competences—doing more of the same thing in a consistent, predictable way. Know-why knowledge is essential for competence building—learning how to do new things or learning how to do familiar things in new ways. Know-how knowledge developed by a group usually becomes embedded in routines that the group can perform on demand (Nelson and Winter 1982). Groups that develop know-why knowledge, however, may establish an additional set of "double-loop" learning routines for changing how they perform their tasks (Argyris and Schoen 1978). The Group Learning Cycle in Figure 1.1 represents the know-how and "know-what" driven processes through which groups apply and extend their knowledge. At the center of the Group Learning Cycle is the repertoire of know-how routines that a group has developed for executing tasks assigned to the group.

The outputs of the Group Learning Cycle consist of one or more of three forms of learning. Groups may learn how to perform their current tasks better. This form of know-how learning can usually be applied directly by the group that generated the learning, though sometimes implementing process improvements may require support and resources from other groups in the organization (including groups of managers). Groups may also generate learning that can suggest new kinds of capabilities the group could develop. This form of know-why learning must usually be explained to the organization at large to attract new resources needed to build new capabilities and develop new routines. Finally, groups may generate ideas for new kinds of things they could do with current or new capabilities. This form of know-what learning (Sanchez 1997) must also be shared with the organization to gather support for the group to undertake new kinds of activities. Thus, a second critical up/down learning linkage exists between groups and the organization. The Group/Organization Learning Cycle in Figure 1.1 represents the processes by which groups in an organization interact, communicate their new know-how, know-why, or know-what knowledge to other groups, acquire the other resources required to put their knowledge into action, and thereby convert group knowledge into improved organizational competence. At the center of the Group/Organizational Learning Cycle is the repertoire of communication and explanation processes that a given group can use in this up/down learning linkage.

At the top of the five learning cycles is the Organization Learning Cycle. In this learning cycle, individuals and groups that play important cognitive roles in the organization (generally including—but not limited to—top management) look for ways to integrate the knowledge of groups in the organization into a coherent vision of the goals the organization could or must pursue, the actions that will give the organization its best possibilities for achieving those goals, and how those actions should be coordinated. In essence, the Organizational Learning Cycle is the process that draws on and tries to integrate the knowledge in the organization to develop a *strategic logic* for the organization (Sanchez, Heene, and Thomas 1996).

Note, however, that the Organizational Learning Cycle is not the exclusive concern of top managers in an organization, but rather is a process in which work groups and even key individuals outside top management may play a role. Indeed, top managers as a group may be only one of many groups whose sets of beliefs about causal relationships in the world are competing for followers in shaping the strategic logic of the organization. Nevertheless, top managers have some important "top-down" levers of influence, because they can decide which interpretive frameworks will be institutionalized as the official or recognized frameworks for sensemaking in the organization. These frameworks usually become embedded in organizational systems and processes. Although establishing interpretive frameworks endorsed by top management by no means assures that all individuals in the organization will subscribe to those frameworks, such frameworks in effect establish a "cognitive orthodoxy" which alternative interpretive frameworks must compete against in processes for defining the strategic logic of the organization. The Organizational Learning Cycle is the process through which an organization selects and formalizes its embedded interpretive frameworks. At the center of the Organization Learning Cycle are the interpretive frameworks that have been embedded in an organization's systems and processes and thereby shape its strategic logic for action taking.

It is important to understand that the array of five learning cycles in Figure 1.1 does not represent an ascending authority hierarchy, with the ideas of individual workers at the bottom and the ideas of top management at the top. As explained above, the critical distinction in this array of learning cycles is whether some knowledge is held by an individual, is shared by a group of people, or has become part of a strategic logic embraced widely within an organization. Thus, in the five learning cycles model of organizational sensemaking and competence building, the ideas of the production-line worker and the ideas of the CEO of an organization begin in fundamentally the same position: the mind of an individual. Though a CEO may have certain advantages over the front-line worker in propagating his or her ideas within the organization, both individuals face essentially the same challenges if they are interested in having their beliefs accepted by their work groups and ultimately by the organization at large. All individuals with beliefs that they want to propagate within an organization must find a way to clear the cognitive hurdles of group acceptance and organizational endorsement in order to manage those beliefs "into good currency" within the organization (van de Ven 1986).

In the competent organization, managers will understand the dynamics that drive all five learning cycles and will devise knowledge management practices that stimulate both the generation of new ideas by individuals and the progression of those ideas upwards and downwards through the five learning cycles. We next draw on the insights developed by the authors of the chapters in this volume to elaborate the key progressions of ideas through the five learning cycles of the competent organization.

THE INDIVIDUAL LEARNING CYCLE AND INDIVIDUAL/GROUP INTERACTIONS

How people learn is a question that will no doubt be studied for decades to come, yet we do know some important things about learning. We know, for example, that learning fundamentally occurs in the minds of individuals as they evolve their personal interpretive frameworks for making sense of the world. As Stein and Ridderstråle describe it, learning occurs through a process of "internal simulation" that draws on past experiences in trying to understand the significance of current events and to predict future events and circumstances. This internal simulation is an exploration of possible cause-and-effect relationships carried out within the current content and limits of each person's interpretive framework.

Each individual's sensemaking process is carried out within a *cognitive infrastructure* that influences the content and evolution of his or her interpretive framework. Merali explains that this cognitive infrastructure is inherently social and leads each individual to try to achieve "cognitive congruence" in his or her social interactions. The basic mechanism in each person's sensemaking process is an action-perception cycle: People act on the basis of their current beliefs, then evaluate the effects of their actions on the people in their social context. Through their social interactions, each person evolves a "self-concept" or identity that he or she expresses by following a "script" that defines values, norms, and behaviors consistent with that self-concept. Each person's script leads them into specific kinds of relationships with the people they interact with, collectively creating a unique "schema" of relationships and social interactions for each person. The desire to make sense out of one's life process and to achieve a measure of compatibility with the people one interacts with leads people to seek a cognitively congruent schema—a schema for which the beliefs and resulting scripts are compatible with the scripts of other people in their social context. An individual's basic means for seeking cognitive congruence is the process of "intersubjective sensemaking"—adjusting his or her self-concept and script until they come into congruence with the important relationships in his or her social context.

What Merali's cognitive congruence framework for understanding individual learning processes helps us to understand is that each individual's sensemaking process is one that is fundamentally equilibrium seeking. As humans, we want the world to make sense, and we want to feel compatible with our immediate social context. The way we seek to achieve sense and compatibility is through adjusting our beliefs to come into a kind of cognitive equilibrium with our immediate social environment. This equilibrium-seeking view of human sensemaking has at least two practical implications for managing individual/group learning interactions.

First, left to its own, the desire of individuals for cognitive congruence can create cognitive stasis in work groups. Individuals will tend to converge towards a set of individual beliefs, self-concepts, and scripts that are mutually compatible, and will prefer to stay in a state of cognitive compatibility once an equilibrium is achieved. In effect, each individual's desire to achieve cognitive congruence with his or her social context can be a source of rigidity in beliefs and of resistance to change once

congruence is achieved. Stimulating individual learning processes in an organization may therefore require intervening at the work group level to upset established
cognitive equilibria. Second, simply changing the processes that a group carries out
will not lead to changes in the knowledge and skills that people in that group
develop. As Merali argues, managers trying to effect organizational change by
redesigning an organization and adding "a high degree of rationalized process congruence" will find that changing processes *per se* will not lead to a shift in the cognitive equilibrium of a work group. Rather, work groups may need to be exposed to
new environmental conditions that make it impossible for the existing group cognitive equilibrium to continue. Further, once a group's cognitive equilibrium is dis-
turbed, the drive to re-establish cognitive congruence must be guided in the right
direction, with clear indications of the new values and norms desired from group
members. This suggests that if one or a few key members of a group can be converted to some desired new values, norms, and beliefs, other group members' drives
to achieve cognitive congruence with the converted group members may work to
align the group as a whole around a new cognitive equilibrium consistent with the
change objectives for that group.

What then determines the kinds of new knowledge that individuals and groups of
individuals will be motivated to develop? Sivula, van den Bosch, and Elfring illuminate
some important aspects of this issue through their study of how consulting firms gain
knowledge through client relationships. Sivula *et al.* argue that learning about the
kinds of problems that need to be solved is just as important as learning about possible
solutions to problems. As Simon (1982) and others have noted, most human learning
occurs in problem-solving, and identifying new problems is perhaps the primary
stimulus for creating new knowledge that can subsequently be used to solve those
problems.

The kind of learning that occurs in problem-solving will be determined by the
extent to which a problem is perceived to be widespread versus specific to a given context. As Sivula *et al.* point out in the context of consulting firms solving problems for
clients, when a problem is perceived to be widespread, so that an appropriate solution
would have the potential to be leveraged widely, there will be a greater incentive to
devise a general solution that will work in many or all contexts. Devising general solutions requires people to learn at higher levels of abstraction than inventing *ad hoc* solutions useful only in specific contexts. In addition, the perception that a problem is
widespread creates an incentive for knowledge that is useful in solving such problems
to be articulated and made explicit so that the knowledge can be transferred readily and
applied in many situations. A clear lesson from this analysis is that if an individual or
group is concerned only with context-specific problems, any new knowledge developed through problem-solving is likely to be context-dependent and to remain in tacit
form. To encourage learning of a more generalizable nature, managers should therefore help work groups become aware of related problems in other groups and find ways
and create incentives for individuals and groups to leverage their learning beyond their
own context.

Groups of people will work together more effectively when individuals are willing to share knowledge with coworkers in their group. The sharing of knowledge by individuals with others in their work group is investigated by Stein and Ridderstråle, who identify three basic problems that may arise in this process:

(1) people may know more than they say (i.e. individuals may prefer to keep some knowledge in personal tacit form);
(2) people may say more than they know;
(3) people may hear something other than what is said.

These problems of knowledge sharing may arise because of the nature of the learning process itself, as well as for economic and social reasons.

Stein and Ridderstråle describe individual learning processes as consisting of reduction and extrapolation. Reduction is a cognitive process of grouping experiences together to establish categories of similar and dissimilar events. Causal relationships between categories of events are then hypothesized and tested by individuals as they form their beliefs about the causal relationships that characterize the world and the organization they participate in. When an individual has a new experience, he or she tries to match that experience with the established categories of events in his or her experience. When a new event is matched (more or less) with a prior event, an individual extrapolates from prior similar events they have experienced to predict the likely consequences and thus significance of the new event. Through this joint process of reducing experiences to categories of events and then extrapolating expectations for related events, the cognitive processes of individuals create meanings for the stream of events they experience on a daily basis.

Inherent in this basic sensemaking process is the potential for cognitive error, both in making statements of personal knowledge and in interpreting statements that others make. Because people rarely have a complete understanding of any situation and may be subject to various biases in what they notice or remember about a situation, individuals may group experiences together in ways that do not fully or accurately represent the "true" nature of those experiences. People also differ in the parameters of similarity or difference that they use to group experiences, with the result that different people who have experienced the same situation may place that experience in very different categories of events. Moreover, people are subject to heuristic biases in making predictions about new events. As Stein and Ridderstråle relate, people tend to try to verify rather than falsify their predictions, are likely to overgeneralize from a limited experience base, and tend to overestimate the likelihood of recurrences of events that they can easily remember. Because of these human cognitive tendencies, people may both say more than they actually know and hear something other than what has actually been expressed by another person.

Economic and social influences also affect how much knowledge people share with others as well as the accuracy of that knowledge. People may say less than they know because they fear that fully disclosing what they know may diminish their value to an organization and undermine the importance or security of their positions in the organization. People may also feel that an organization lacks an infrastructure (or the will to create an infrastructure) that would be capable of absorbing and acting on knowledge they reveal. More generally, people may believe that the marginal effort required to articulate and share their knowledge may exceed the benefits that such an effort would bring to them in their organization. People may also fear that saying exactly what they know will challenge or upset power relationships in their organizations, with negative consequences for themselves.

What people pay attention to, what new knowledge they derive from interpreting events, what knowledge they develop, and whom they choose to share their knowledge with may be influenced by the norms of professional groups that people belong to, as well as by the goals of the organizations they work for. Murray and Worren note that some key knowledge workers may attach more importance to making a valuable intellectual contribution to their professional field than to developing knowledge that is timely and effective in helping their employing organization achieve its goals. Further, as Boisot and Griffiths point out, knowledge workers may also try to build up personal professional capital by informally trading (or sometimes simply giving away) knowledge with others in the same profession, even when they are employed by competing companies.

Managers need a toolkit of methods for removing impediments to individuals sharing reliable knowledge with other individuals in their work groups and at the same time containing important knowledge within their own organization. Drawing on the experience of Ericsson and other companies, Stein and Ridderstråle explain how managers can create individual incentives for knowledge sharing and promote various socialization processes to encourage individuals to convey what they know more freely to their coworkers. At the same time, to prevent people from saying more than they know or hearing something other than what has been said, some managers have implemented group discussions of the ideas of individuals as a way to bring multiple perspectives to bear on some proffered knowledge. These discussions help to surface the unrecognized assumptions in an individual's knowledge, and provide group feedback to help individuals rethink and correct some of their beliefs. This latter process is especially important when one recognizes that people have different levels of aspiration with respect to the reliability and performance of their beliefs. In addition, by carefully defining and widely disseminating terms that represent important concepts, managers can help to create a corporate vocabulary that can facilitate more accurate communication of ideas among individuals and groups. Further, as Boisot and Griffiths advise, creating greater wealth-sharing incentives for knowledge workers is an essential step in curbing the temptation to use know-how trading to acquire personal benefits at the expense of an employing organization.

THE GROUP LEARNING CYCLE AND GROUP/ORGANIZATION INTERACTIONS

We now take a closer look at how groups learn and how groups interact with the organization at large in communicating their knowledge in processes for building and leveraging competences. We also consider ways in which creating new organizational knowledge depends on creating and accessing new kinds of group-based knowledge.

In his study of the development of new environmental competences by a Swiss retailer, Raub describes the competence building process as a set of interactions between top managers and several groups. Those interactions took place in three phases. The first phase was an *imagination* interaction between top managers (who had formed a strategic intent to improve the environmental performance of their organization) and several groups in the organization that could help the managers define specific *strategic options* for developing environmental programs. These groups helped define significant environmental issues in more detail, proposed ways of dealing with those issues, and identified specific knowledge within and external to the organization that could be used in managing those issues. These interactions helped top managers begin to act on their strategic intent and take the first steps toward defining a new strategic logic for the organization. In effect, the Swiss retailer's "corporate imagination" was stimulated by an interplay of top managers' know-what knowledge that becoming more environmentally responsible would help the organization achieve its goals. Several other groups then contributed more detailed know-what knowledge that could define specific change objectives and applied their know-why knowledge to design appropriate processes for accomplishing those changes.

The second phase in the Swiss retailer's competence building process was an *integration* interaction between the groups and the rest of the organization. A "coordination team" was created to promote communication between top managers and various groups and to facilitate exchanges of knowledge and information between groups and individuals who would be involved in the competence-building process. The coordination team helped allocate specific areas of activity and responsibility to involved groups, established organizational structures for transferring knowledge among groups, and led a process of codifying relevant knowledge to improve its visibility and accessibility by groups within the organization. Specific groups then applied their existing know-how knowledge in identifying the resources that could be deployed to develop specific new environmental capabilities.

The third phase in this process was an *implementation* interaction among top managers, the coordination team, and involved groups. Specific projects were evaluated in detail, selected for action, and prioritized. Strategic plans were drawn up to coordinate the various capability development projects of the involved groups and to assure that subsequent deployments of the new capabilities would in fact lead to new environmental competences for the organization.

Raub's analysis of imagination, integration, and implementation interactions highlights the importance of applying know-what, know-why, and know-how forms of knowledge at different stages in the competence-building process. To build on the know-what knowledge of the group of top managers that identified improved environmental performance as strategically important for the organization, it was necessary to draw on the know-why knowledge of middle-management groups to define specific strategic options for capability development and to design projects that could create those capabilities. The know-how knowledge of groups of lower-level managers and functional specialists in the organization was then needed to define resource requirements for carrying out the projects. Only after the organization had inter-related its available know-what, know-why, and know-how forms of knowledge could specific strategic options be identified, assessed in detail, selected, and then put into action.

What happens when an organization lacks some form of know-why or know-how knowledge needed to respond to some new know-what knowledge—e.g. a newly per-ceived strategic opportunity or necessity? Murray and Worren propose that large firms are more likely than small firms to fail to create the new know-why or know-how knowledge needed to respond to a changing environment. Large firms often have large incentives to maintain their current revenue streams by continuing to use existing know-how knowledge. Repeated patterns of usage of know-how knowledge (espe-cially in problem-solving) establish routines that become part of an organization's "core competences." These routines may also become "core rigidities," however, when a focus on competence leveraging leads to a neglect of new competence building and new kinds of know-how knowledge are not created or acquired and used (Leonard-Barton 1992). Moreover, managers of large organizations may not be able to recognize when groups that prefer to stay within the boundaries of their existing know-how knowledge may thereby be limiting the strategic options they bring to the attention of top managers of the organization.

Murray and Worren suggest that entrepreneurial managers of small organizations, on the other hand, are more likely to know when the groups in their organization lack critical forms of know-how or know-why knowledge, and are more likely to allow or even to insist on trying new approaches to problem-solving that require acquiring new forms of know-how and know-why knowledge. Murray and Worren argue that com-petence can be derived from two rather different kinds of processes for using know-ledge. An organization may create competence either by leveraging its current knowledge base into related problem-solving areas or by combining previously unconnected bits of knowledge in novel approaches to solving new kinds of problems—something Murray and Worren refer to as an "analogical transfer" of knowledge. Large firms are more likely to pursue competence building by using well-established routines to leverage their significant stocks of internal knowledge into closely related problem-solving areas. Small firms that lack extensive knowledge bases, on the other hand, are more likely to allow or encourage creative problem-solving heuristics that lead to novel combinations of their more limited knowledge with firm-addressable knowledge outside the firm.

The routines that firms develop for applying knowledge, whether internal or boundary-spanning in nature, sometimes need to be "retired" and replaced by new routines better suited to a changing environment. In their investigations of large firms, Baden-Fuller and Volberda observed that routines that are retired often do not disap-pear from an organization, but rather become part of an organization's repertoire of "dormant capabilities" that can be revived in the future. The older and more complex an organization, the larger the repertoire of dormant capabilities it may have accumu-lated. Dormant capabilities may provide managers—especially at the middle levels of an organization—with attractive strategic options, since reviving prior routines may be relatively quick and efficient compared to developing new routines. From this perspective, organizational processes for unlearning old routines should be managed so as to add to an organization's stock of dormant capabilities, rather than resulting in complete loss of prior capabilities.

Baden-Fuller and Volberda's studies also show that capabilities are often "organizationally separated" in large complex organizations, creating opportunities for changing the capabilities of one part of the organization by transferring capabilities from another part of the organization. Often this transfer may be accelerated by rearranging organizational boundaries to consolidate the capabilities needed by one group with another group that already has those capabilities. To make sure transferred capabilities "take root" and are implemented effectively in a new group, however, managers may also have to transfer new strategic logics and methods of coordination that enable a group to integrate the new capability with their other capabilities in creating a new organizational competence. Transfers of managers who have been following a given strategic logic and using supporting coordination methods may therefore accelerate the building of new competences. Baden-Fuller and Volberda also note that groups receiving new capabilities are often encouraged to absorb and use new capabilities when they know that unfamiliar ways of working based on those capabilities have actually worked well in another part of the organization.

THE ORGANIZATION LEARNING CYCLE

Knowledge moves upwards through the five learning cycles as the knowledge of individuals becomes understood and adopted by their work groups and as the knowledge of one work group is shared with other groups. Although visionary or persuasive individuals may have profound impacts on what an organization comes to believe and accept as knowledge, the research reported in this volume strongly suggests that the knowledge of individuals must first pass the test of acceptance by formal or informal groups of people within an organization. Thus, in our five learning cycles model, the creation of organizational knowledge occurs when the knowledge of one or more groups is accepted as valid and adopted widely throughout an organization. The Organizational Learning Cycle is the process through which the knowledge of various groups is evaluated, selected, and integrated within an organization at large. In this process, managers occupy a privileged position that gives them significant—but not exclusive—influence on the ideas that become accepted as knowledge in an organization. Our exploration of the Organization Learning Cycle therefore highlights several key aspects of managers' roles in shaping organizational learning.

The role of managers as knowledge evaluators and integrators is explored by van den Bosch and van Wijk. Reflecting many of the findings of Raub's study of how managers manage knowledge in building new organizational competences, van den Bosch and van Wijk characterize managers as ultimately responsible for orchestrating the knowledge identification, evaluation, and integration processes that lead to the formation of an organization's strategic logic. In their analysis, managerial knowledge is fundamentally about knowing "how to get things done through and with people." Knowing how to get things done in turn requires developing managerial know-how, know-why, and know-what forms of knowledge at various levels of an organization. Managers with responsibilities at lower levels of an organization must acquire know-how forms of knowledge that enable them to help employee groups accomplish their tasks. Managers at the mid-level of an organization must develop the know-why forms of knowledge that enable them to design new organizational processes and to improve current group capabilities. To perform this task, however, mid-level mangers must have an adequate understanding of what various groups in the organization are currently capable of doing and what new capabilities they could reasonably be expected to develop. Managers at the highest levels of an organization should be primarily concerned with developing know-what forms of organizational knowledge. In essence, top managers as a group should evaluate the strategic environment of the organization, assess possibilities for new and improved value-creating activities suggested by mid-level managers, and derive from those possibilities a coherent strategic logic that offers the best feasible plan of action for achieving the organization's goals.

In these management processes, managers may foster the development of new organizational knowledge in three ways. Managers may support individuals and groups in identifying and absorbing knowledge located outside the organization. They may recognize and exploit opportunities to transfer knowledge internally from one group to another (as observed in Baden-Fuller and Volberda's study). Managers may also identify possibilities for combining the knowledge of different groups in new ways and for integrating that knowledge through new organizational processes.

Van den Bosch and van Wijk also remind us that managers may use the knowledge they develop as individuals in two ways. Managers may apply know-how or know-why forms of knowledge directly in problem solving, or they may absorb know-what forms of knowledge that help to form mental models of organizational situations and strategic possibilities. This latter process shapes the evolution of a manager's style of managing and greatly influences the way he or she perceives the competitive environment, reacts to possibilities for new capability development, determines the set of feasible strategic logics available to an organization, and selects the strategic logic an organization ought to pursue. Thus, in their role as key contributors to organizational knowledge, managers must sustain learning on two fronts. Managers must acquire new know-how or know-why forms of knowledge that can be used in practical problem-solving within their immediate area of responsibility, but managers must also absorb new know-what knowledge in the form of new ideas and theories that enrich the managerial imagination and suggest new possibilities for organizational goal-setting and action-taking.

Perhaps the most profound influence that managers have on what comes to be accepted as knowledge in an organization is their ability to define and institutionalize the control systems an organization uses. Control systems are the formalized processes an organization uses to coordinate its activities, including accounting and other information systems for monitoring, measuring, and assessing those activities.

Control systems therefore largely determine the kinds of data that are generated by an organization and how those data are interpreted formally within an organization to create information. Through their influence on what is "officially" accepted as information in an organization, control systems constitute *de facto* interpretive frameworks that greatly shape managers' and other employees' perceptions of environmental stability and change, as well as organizational success and failure. These perceptions in turn shape what is regarded as useful knowledge and important learning opportunities within an organization.

The impact of control systems on organizational sensemaking and competence development is investigated by Lorino through his study of a leading French computer company in the 1980s. To illuminate the role of control systems in organizational sensemaking, Lorino applies Charles Peirce's (1954) theory of triadic interpretation. Managers' interpretive frameworks become embodied in the control systems they design for their organization. Once one group of managers' interpretive frameworks become institutionalized in control systems, those systems become "symbols" or "artifacts" that other members of an organization must interact with regularly. Those interactions then shape the perceptions and sensemaking processes of others in the organization as they develop their own individual interpretive schemes. In this role, control systems help to create shared mental models that "ensure at least a minimum level of coherence between multiple kinds and levels of interpretation processes within an organization." Thus, control systems are instrumental in bringing about sufficient alignment of individuals' sensemaking processes to achieve efficient coordination of activities within an organization.

At the same time, control systems may have a constraining influence on organizational learning. Institutionalizing certain interpretive frameworks creates a kind of organizational inertia that pressures individuals to adjust their personal interpretive frameworks to conform to the view of "reality" embedded in the institutionalized framework. This pressure both constrains the sensemaking processes of individuals and groups within the organization and shifts "the burden of proof" in arguing for new or modified interpretive frameworks onto those seeking change. Thus, institutionalizing interpretive frameworks in control systems may help to improve efficiency in coordinating an organization's use of its current knowledge, but it also tends to impose boundaries on—and even to create disincentives for—the development of new kinds of organizational knowledge and interpretive frameworks. Managers must therefore design control systems that achieve requisite levels of organizational coherence, while at the same time providing what Lorino terms an "inquiry procedure" for challenging and changing an organization's control systems and their implicit interpretive frameworks.

Echoing van den Bosch and van Wijk's findings, Lorino draws on Dewey's (1938) pragmatic concepts of learning in observing that managers may experience two forms of learning in managing through control systems. Through designing and using control systems, managers develop representations or "logical models" that become part of their individual interpretive frameworks. These logical models may provide generic solutions useful in solving specific problems of coordination, or they may contribute to the development of norms ("universal forms") for designing and validating inquiry procedures that can change the generic solutions a manager uses.

Boisot and Griffiths investigate several further issues related to the creation of systems for the dissemination of knowledge within an organization. They observe that in a fundamental sense only data can be disseminated within an organization, because information and knowledge are derived from interpretive frameworks ("belief systems") that are ultimately personal in nature. To achieve a requisite measure of coherence ("resonance") among individuals' activities, managers create systems for structuring data in ways that will encourage convergence of individual interpretive frameworks. When managers structure data, they try to abstract from the many aspects of the organization and its environment the essential categories of entities (customers, suppliers, defects, etc.) and events (sales, purchases, complaints, etc.) the organization must pay attention to, manage, and learn from. The categories of data institutionalized in an organization then shape individuals' perceptions and encourage formation of a (more or less) common base of experience, learning, and knowledge.

Boisot and Griffiths also observe that in the modern economy firms and economic organizations are no longer coextensive. In other words, the knowledge a firm needs to create economic value is not likely to be wholly internal to the firm, but rather is likely to reside in a number of people and organizations beyond the boundaries of the firm. The Internet and other kinds of information systems now make it possible to draw on the knowledge of many people and organizations beyond the boundaries of the firm. Thus, directly owning knowledge is becoming less critical than being able to access and use knowledge. In the Internet age, the increased interconnectivity of people and organizations around the globe provides a powerful new means for making new knowledge and new interpretive frameworks available to an organization.

In the Internet-driven "knowledge economy," however, more and more of the knowledge a firm needs to create economic value will be possessed by individuals who know that the knowledge they have is valuable and who can convey that knowledge to other people or organizations—if they choose to do so. These key knowledge workers may, in effect, seek to establish an ongoing bargain with the organizations they are employed by, providing to their work groups or the organization at large only the amount of knowledge they feel they are being justly compensated for. If a knowledge worker feels inadequately compensated for his or her knowledge, or if he or she wants to improve their standing in their professional community (and thereby enhance their options to obtain a better employment relationship in other organizations), they may engage in informal know-how trading with their counterparts in other firms. Thus, an important challenge in managing knowledge today is creating economic incentives for knowledge workers to keep their knowledge within the firm. To provide adequate incentives, managers will increasingly have to treat key knowledge workers more like residual claimants (shareholders) than employees.

Ultimately, Boisot and Griffiths advise, managers must choose either protection or speed as a basic strategy for managing knowledge. In the protection strategy, much knowledge may be kept in tacit form to prevent its diffusion outside the firm, and significant effort will be made to control knowledge legally and contain it within the firm.

Because tacit knowledge is harder and takes longer to transfer from one person to another in an organization, however, the essence of the protection knowledge management strategy is controlled—but relatively slow—knowledge leveraging. By contrast, the speed strategy for managing knowledge emphasizes the creation of incentives for knowledge workers to articulate their knowledge into explicit form. The speed strategy also invests in information systems for rapidly disseminating explicit knowledge to all parts of the organization, and seeks thereby to stimulate the use of existing knowledge and the rapid development of new knowledge throughout the organization. In essence, by focusing on facilitating articulation and dissemination of knowledge rather than trying to control leakage of knowledge beyond the organization, the speed strategy seeks to create an engine of learning and knowledge leveraging that can outpace competing firms with less high-powered knowledge management systems.

The use of product and process architectures as organizational frameworks for managing knowledge articulation and dissemination and for strategically guiding organizational learning is investigated by Sanchez. An architecture is the way a product or process design is decomposed into its component parts and the way the interactions of component parts are controlled through interface specifications. The way an organization decomposes its product designs largely determines the way the organization can structure its process designs. When the component parts of a product are closely and complexly interrelated—i.e. "tightly coupled"—in a product design, the component parts of an organization's processes for developing, producing, distributing, and supporting that product will also have to be tightly coupled. When the component parts of a product are designed to be modular (or "loosely coupled"), so that various component designs are "plug and play" compatible with other component designs within the product as a system of components, the processes for developing and producing the components can also become loosely coupled (i.e. autonomous).

Sanchez explains a number of ways in which using modular architectures can improve an organization's ability to develop and leverage technical and market knowledge. On the supply side, the technical knowledge an organization creates through its technology and product development processes tends to become clustered around the major components in its product and process designs. This clustering of knowledge occurs because development groups generally work on specific components and then develop in-depth knowledge specific to that component. The result of this clustering of knowledge around components is that the product architectures an organization uses will determine, in effect, the architecture—i.e. the content and the structure—of the technical knowledge the organization develops.

The loose coupling of components within a modular architecture is achieved through the standardization of component interface specifications. Standardizing component interfaces also creates a stable and fully defined technical infrastructure for the product that allows component development tasks to be performed independently by autonomous component development groups. Thus, creating fully specified modular architectures greatly improves the ability of an organization to manage global networks of component developers and thereby to access important sources of technical knowledge beyond the boundaries of the organization.

On the demand side, modular architectures enable new approaches to learning about evolving market preferences. When modular product architectures are decomposed so that there is a "one to one" mapping of specific customer benefits into specific components, the mixing and matching of modular component variations expands the product variety an organization can offer and increases the speed with which it can bring new product variations to market. Thus, modular architectures make it possible to engage in "real-time market research" that accelerates learning about consumer preferences by offering a changing array of new product variations and letting customers select "in real time" the product variations they like most. Modular architectures are also the basis for mass-customization and product-personalization strategies that let individual customers select the combinations of components they prefer in a given product. Letting customers select preferred components from a menu of modular components enables an organization to develop deeper and more precise insights into exactly which component-based functions, features, and performance levels various customers prefer. Such insights can then suggest which components should be targeted for improvement through further technology development, thus providing a more direct, component-based linkage between marketing research and technology development.

Further, Sanchez argues that the use of modular architectures can help an organization to "know what it knows." When an organization creates a modular architecture that can accommodate a range of plug-and-play modular components, the range of product variations that can be leveraged from the modular architecture defines, in effect, the new products the organization knows how to bring to market in the near-term. Moreover, when a firm plans its future product strategies by defining future generations of modular architectures, new kinds of components needed to bring new functions, features, and performance levels to its products can be identified more clearly. If an organization determines that it is not capable of developing such components today, it can focus its technology development and other organizational learning efforts on creating the new capabilities it will need to develop new kinds of components for future product architectures.

As described by Sanchez, product and process architectures may be used as formal systems for articulating, codifying, and leveraging technical and market knowledge in supporting the speed strategy for managing knowledge proposed by Boisot and Griffiths. The architectures an organization uses also function as control systems, in the sense explained by Lorino, because they both define an organization's technical representation of its products and the way an organization relates its technologies and products to its markets. Sanchez therefore proposes that when managers think about product strategies in terms of architectures rather than individual products, the complexity that managers must deal with in formulating product strategies can be significantly reduced, suggesting that architectures are the "right logical increment" for analyzing and managing strategic change in dynamic technology and market conditions.

MANAGING KNOWLEDGE INTO COMPETENCE THROUGH THE FIVE LEARNING CYCLES

The five learning cycles of Figure 1.1 represent the basic processes through which an organization receives, evaluates, absorbs (or rejects), and deploys new knowledge. The overall dynamics of the five learning cycles are suggested in Figure 1.2. In an organization that is an effective knowledge processor, new knowledge first appears in the organization (at the bottom of Figure 1.2) when individuals critique existing organizational

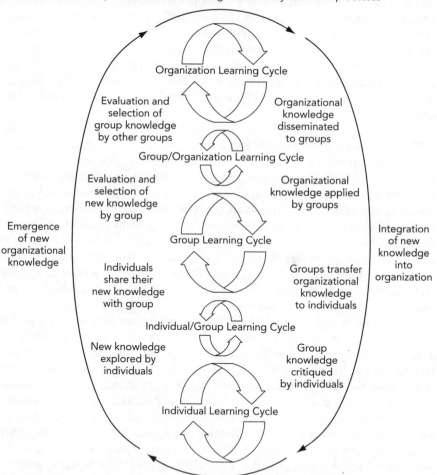

Managers select and embed new knowledge
and interpretive frameworks in organization's systems and processes

Organization Learning Cycle

Evaluation and
selection of
group knowledge
by other groups

Organizational
knowledge
disseminated
to groups

Group/Organization Learning Cycle

Evaluation and
selection of
new knowledge
by group

Organizational
knowledge applied
by groups

Group Learning Cycle

Emergence
of new
organizational
knowledge

Individuals
share their
new knowledge
with group

Groups transfer
organizational
knowledge
to individuals

Integration
of new
knowledge
into
organization

Individual/Group Learning Cycle

New knowledge
explored by
individuals

Group
knowledge
critiqued
by individuals

Individual Learning Cycle

Individuals imagine alternative interpretive frameworks
and useful new kinds of knowledge

Fig. 1.2 *Organizational learning dynamic sustained through the five learning cycles.*

and group knowledge, imagine alternative interpretive frameworks, and explore new forms of knowledge that would play an important role in their new alternative interpretive frameworks. The new knowledge of individuals then begins to move "upward" through the five learning cycles in a process of organizational emergence as the new knowledge is evaluated and selected (or rejected) by groups, and as the newly accepted knowledge of groups is evaluated and selected (or rejected) by the organization at large.

At the top of Figure 1.2, managers play a key knowledge management role by deciding which knowledge will be institutionalized by the organization. New knowledge accepted by management is integrated into the organization by becoming embedded in its control systems, its product and process architectures, and other formal systems for representing the many aspects of the environment, the organization, and their interactions. Through an organization's system design processes, knowledge accepted by management is disseminated "downward" to groups and individuals, where the knowledge can be applied and exploited through the activities of groups and individuals. As individuals work with available organizational knowledge, their sensemaking capabilities test and critique both new and prior organizational knowledge. Some individuals may acquire new knowledge and imagine and propose alternative beliefs and interpretive frameworks, thereby closing the organization's knowledge processing loop and contributing to a new round of organizational knowledge creation and leveraging.

To create a learning organization, managers must put in place and support processes in each of the five learning cycles that will stimulate and support the critiquing and challenging of current organizational knowledge by individuals within the organization, the upward emergence of new organizational knowledge, the adoption and institutionalization of new knowledge by managers, and the downward dissemination of new knowledge through an organization's representation and interpretation systems. In this sense, the five learning cycles are like gears in an organizational engine of learning and knowledge leveraging. All five gears must function effectively for the overall learning dynamic to be sustained. A breakdown in any of the five learning cycles will cause a breakdown of learning and knowledge leveraging processes in the organization as a whole.

We now build on our analysis of the overall dynamic of the five learning cycles to derive some basic guidelines for successfully managing knowledge into organizational competence. To do this, we briefly revisit the "four cornerstones" of the competent organization—the ability of its managers to recognize, develop, and integrate the *dynamic, cognitive, systemic, and holistic* dimensions of organizational competence.[3]

---

[3] For a more complete discussion of the four cornerstones of organizational competence, the interested reader may refer to the following books and papers: Sanchez, R., A. Heene, and H. Thomas (eds.) (1996). *Dynamics of Competence-Based Competition: Theory and Practice in the New Strategic Management.* Oxford: Elsevier Pergamon; Heene, A. and R. Sanchez (eds.) (1997). *Competence-Based Strategic Management.* Chichester: John Wiley; Sanchez, R. and A. Heene (eds.) (1997). *Strategic Learning and Knowledge Management.* Chichester: John Wiley; Sanchez, R., and A. Heene (1997). "Reinventing strategic management: New theory and practice for competence-based competition," *European Management Journal,* 15 (3), 303–17.

We then consider in some detail approaches to designing and managing the five learning cycles that can support each of the four competence dimensions.

The first cornerstone of organizational competence is the ability of an organization to respond advantageously and promptly to a *dynamic* environment. The competent organization will be able to sense changes in market needs and in the technological possibilities for serving those needs. To do this, an organization must have the *cognitive* capacity to detect change in its environment and to devise strategic logics for responding effectively to those changes (the second cornerstone of the competent organization). Sensing environmental change and carrying out an appropriate organizational response requires the third cornerstone of competence—effectively managing change in an organization as an *open system* of resource flows. Managers must assure continued flows of critical resources (including new knowledge) the organization will need. As the organization evolves with its environment, managers must recognize and manage the changing interrelated economic and social interests of all its resource providers. The fourth cornerstone of the competent organization is therefore the ability of its managers to holistically define organizational goals and incentives that will bring a satisfactory level of goal attainment to each provider of critical resources.

We now consider approaches to managing the five learning circles that can improve an organization's ability to achieve each of these four dimensions of the competent organization.

Managing competence dynamics

Organizations may detect environmental change in one of two ways. Most organizations maintain formal control systems for monitoring and detecting change in the environment. As we have seen, however, the data an organization gathers and the information it extracts from those data will be greatly influenced by the interpretive frameworks embedded in an organization's information systems and other control systems. These systems may be capable of detecting change in areas of concern that are already part of embedded interpretive frameworks, but may miss completely important forms of change that lie outside the interpretive frameworks that inspired the organization's current control systems. An important second method for detecting environmental change is to draw on the sensemaking capabilities of the individual members of an organization. Only individuals have the ability to notice and ponder new kinds of phenomena, the power to imagine new causal relationships, and the ability to derive new understanding about the world. As Lorino observes, "Only [individual] actors' interpretive schemes evolve with experience and can develop perspectives that enable them to criticize and adapt or replace management systems." Therefore, the only way an organization can detect change that would not be captured by its formal monitoring systems is to regularly expose its members to new experiences and perspectives that lie outside the organization's institutionalized interpretive frameworks—and then to provide vigorous processes for disseminating, evaluating, and responding to new ideas proposed by its members.

To be sure that new ideas of individuals have every possible chance to successfully navigate upward through the five learning cycles, managers must institutionalize and support what Lorino has called an "inquiry procedure"—processes through which individuals can openly propose ideas and interpretive frameworks that question both an organization's explicitly recognized knowledge and the implicit beliefs embedded in its control systems. Only by bringing the implicit, embedded beliefs of the organization to the surface and regularly debating and testing their adequacy for representing the current environment can an organization hope to see beyond the limits of its current interpretive frameworks.

Managing cognitive processes in the competent organization

Although rarely portrayed as doing so, managers and other members of an organization are continually formulating and testing "local theories" about what kinds of actions can solve various kinds of problems or take advantage of certain kinds of opportunities (Mahoney and Sanchez 1997). In this process, managers and others interested in developing useful knowledge must address fundamentally the same ontological and epistemological issues that scientists deal with in their efforts to develop more general theories about the world. Managers, like scientists, must first determine the ontological foundations of their ideas—i.e., the entities and events that they will try to understand, explain, and (if possible) predict. Managers make important ontological determinations, for example, when deciding which categories of data an organization will gather and interpret. These data categories establish the entities and events that managers and others in an organization will study in their effort to devise insights into (or theories about) important cause-and-effect relationships affecting the organization.

Managers and organizations also develop epistemologies—ways of hypothesizing causal relationships and then testing them to see if they can be validated and accepted as knowledge, either generally or in some specific context or situation. In this regard, managers must be careful to observe a critical norm of the scientific process: Any theory can be replaced by a better theory. In effect, managers must assure that all theories in use in an organization—no matter who originally proposed them—are open to questioning and to being replaced by new theories that have a greater ability to produce desired outcomes for the organization.[4]

A key insight that has emerged from our analysis of the five learning cycles is that much of an organization's strategically important knowledge will be embedded in its systems, procedures, and distinctive ways of working. In essence, as Murray and Worren observe, much of an organization's critical knowledge will be contained in the structure of routines the organization follows, rather than in its stocks of information. The embedded nature of much organizational knowledge means that many of the beliefs that have the most profound impact on an organization are often not

---

[4] In this discussion, theories are treated simply as proposed explanations of why certain things happen. The "knowledge" an individual has is then the collection of theories that that individual has chosen to believe in and rely on in his or her effort to understand how things happen in the world.

recognized or discussed explicitly, but remain deeply woven into the procedural fabric of the organization and its routine sensemaking activities. Once a set of beliefs has become embedded in organizational systems and processes, the organizational memory of the circumstances that originally gave rise to those beliefs may start to fade. In due course, an organization can lose all awareness of the prior beliefs that have become embedded in its systems and thereby continue to exercise a profound influence on the organization's current sensemaking processes.

To help surface the implicit beliefs of an organization and to expose them to questioning and improvement, managers can adopt practices that carefully document the know-how, know-why, and know-what knowledge that underpins and becomes embodied in an organization's systems and routines. Implicit in the designs of any organization's systems and routines is some form of know-how knowledge that has led some mangers to believe that taking certain actions will lead to certain results. The specific know-how knowledge behind a given system or routine—i.e. the belief that doing A will cause B to happen—should be carefully documented so that future members of the organization can readily determine the beliefs on which a system or routine has been based. In addition, the know-why and know-what knowledge of managers that motivates the design of the system or routine should be documented. Know-why knowledge in this case refers to the beliefs of managers as to why the design chosen for a system or routine will be more effective than alternative designs. Know-what knowledge is the belief of managers as to why the task that a system or routine is intended to support is an important objective for the organization to pursue.

Documenting and disseminating the three kinds of knowledge underlying each institutionalized system and routine can help everyone in an organization to be aware of, to critique, and ultimately to improve the interpretive frameworks of managers (past and present) that led to the creation of the systems and routines the organization currently uses. In effect, documenting the know-how, know-why, and know-what knowledge behind the way an organization works is knowledge management's way of opening the "black box" of the firm and illuminating the intellectual processes that motivate organizations. In addition, documenting the reasons why an organization has created each of its capabilities can help managers to decide which capabilities that are currently "dormant" or "organizationally separated" (in Baden-Fuller and Volberda's terminology) could usefully be revived or imported from other organizational units.

Debating and improving interpretive frameworks within an organization is problematic when members of an organization use many different words to refer to a single concept or, even worse, use one word to refer to what are actually significantly different concepts. Lack of clear definitions within an organization for key terms such as "quality," "customer satisfaction," "performance," "innovation," and the like can easily lead well-intended people into lengthy but fruitless debates. Discussions of important ideas in an organization can become much more constructive when everyone in an organization is able to communicate unambiguously with each other. To facilitate clear communication, managers can begin to establish a corporate language of key terms supported by clear definitions and fully explained concepts. Establishing a well defined corporate language can create a highly visible system of representation and meaning within an organization, and is very likely to stimulate much useful discussion of beliefs and interpretive frameworks within the organization. Of course, once established as a basic system of representation and meaning, a corporate language should always be subject to regular discussion, modification, and extension as the organization and its environment evolve.

Our analysis of the role of product and process architectures in the five learning cycles also makes plain the benefits of finding better ways to define and represent what an organization currently knows. Carefully defining its product and process architectures can help an organization to surface, document, disseminate, and debate any beliefs about its products and processes that have become accepted (implicitly or explicitly) as group or organizational knowledge. Critiquing such knowledge will not only help to improve that knowledge, but also helps an organization to see more clearly the limits of its knowledge. Thus, using architectures and other frameworks to define, structure, and document what an organization currently knows can greatly improve the ability of everyone in an organization to identify new forms of knowledge that could bring significant new understanding and capabilities to the organization. In effect, as members of an organization, we need to know what we already know before we can know what else we need to know.

It is by now generally understood that much organizational learning takes place through a "double-loop" process (cf. Argyris and Schoen 1978). At the most fundamental level, people in organizations "learn by doing." This form of learning leads to incremental extensions to knowledge gained through practical experience in applying existing knowledge. This incremental learning changes *how* an organization does what it does. Organizations need a second learning loop, however, that leads to changes in *what* the organization does. This learning loop is largely driven by managers' strategic decisions about which value-creating activities offer the best chance for attaining the organization's goals. Managers' strategic decisions are, in turn, driven by their analysis of the organization and its environment within their existing interpretive frameworks.

Our analysis of the five learning cycles suggests that there is a critical third learning loop in which managers play a further essential role—organizational processes through which people in an organization change their interpretive frameworks. As we have noted, this form of learning can occur in the mind of any individual in an organization, not just in the minds of its managers. However, because managers play the critical role not just in deciding what an organization will do, but also in determining which interpretive frameworks become embedded in an organization's systems and processes, managers face a special intellectual challenge. Foremost among all members of an organization, managers must be able to manage change in their own interpretive frameworks—i.e., in the way they think about and analyze the organization, its environment, and its opportunities for undertaking value-creating activities. Thus, in managing knowledge through an organization's five learning cycles, managers face an especially demanding cognitive challenge—the need to sustain ongoing changes in their own interpretive frameworks as the world and the situation of their organization evolve.

Managing competence systemics

Within the competence perspective, the task of strategic managers is fundamentally organizational goal setting and designing of systems that enable an organization to achieve those goals (Sanchez and Heene 1997). In this capacity, strategic managers must maintain what Derek Abell (1993) has described as "dual strategies." One strategy is focused on *running* the current organization efficiently, while the other strategy is concerned with simultaneously *changing* the organization to become more effective in creating value and thereby achieving the goals of its stakeholders. A central management activity in managing knowledge into competence is therefore designing and maintaining organizational systems that both support efficient application of existing organizational knowledge and effectively manage change in the knowledge base of the organization. Our analysis of the five learning cycles suggests that these two kinds of systems should be designed to function *concurrently* in an organization. Let us take a closer look at why this is the case, and consider how managers can approach the task of designing systems that can concurrently leverage existing knowledge and create new knowledge.

Basically, managers have two choices in designing systems for leveraging and for creating knowledge—to create two systems that work sequentially or concurrently. The sequential approach creates primary organization systems focused on applying current organizational knowledge efficiently within the organization's existing interpretive framework, and occasionally uses a second process to effect periodic changes in an organization's knowledge base and associated interpretive frameworks. This "punctuated equilibrium" approach (Tushman, Newman, and Romanelli 1986) essentially assumes that an organization will have relatively long periods of equilibrium in which its processes can be focused on performing current tasks efficiently. During these periods, the organization can be relatively unconcerned about forms of organizational learning other than incremental extensions to existing knowledge achieved through learning by doing. Periodically, however, managers may recognize a need to change the knowledge base and interpretive frameworks of the organization because of changes in the competitive environment. A second set of systems or processes for creating new knowledge and interpretive frameworks would then be brought into play in an effort to "retool" the organization's knowledge base and achieve better alignment of organizational capabilities and interpretive frameworks with new environmental imperatives.

The case against relying on sequential systems to manage an organization's knowledge base largely rests on the fact that the punctuated equilibrium approach is very difficult to manage in practice and tends to result in bouts of organizational disruption, trauma, and in the worst cases, organizational failure. The seeds of these difficulties are sown during an organization's relatively long periods of equilibrium, when people—including managers—whose individual knowledge bases and interpretive frameworks are compatible with those currently in use by the organization will "self select" into the organization. During periods of equilibrium, the self selection process creates an organizational population of people who think in rather similar ways. As time goes by, increasing cognitive convergence within the organization leads to a progressively reduced ability of managers and others in the organization to recognize the need for major changes in its knowledge base and interpretive frameworks.

If efforts are made to force cognitive changes onto the organization (for example, by the actions of its board of directors), the fear or threat that current members of the organization will withdraw their support for the organization's ongoing value-creating processes may prevent the activation of the second process intended to change the organization's knowledge base and interpretive frameworks. The outcome is then likely to be a cognitive catch-22: The organization will fail externally if it does not change its knowledge base to achieve better alignment with its environment, but it will fail internally if efforts are made to force a change in knowledge base on the current members of the organization.

A common tactic for trying to avoid this catch-22 is to bring a new set of interpretive frameworks into the organization by changing top management. Yet as the five learning cycles make plain, managers constitute just one group of individuals in an organization, and changing managers is not equivalent to changing organizational knowledge, especially not the knowledge and interpretive frameworks that have become embedded in the organization's control systems and ways of working. For new managers to design and implement new control systems and processes that embed new interpretive frameworks can take considerable time, and there are many opportunities for people who do not want to change to defeat new systems and processes at the working level of the organization. Thus, while any organization may face a need to significantly change its knowledge base and interpretive frameworks if its environment changes suddenly, relying on sequential systems to drive organizational learning is a risky, crisis-prone knowledge management strategy.

The alternative to the punctuated equilibrium change strategy is continuous leveraging *and* changing of an organization's knowledge base and interpretive frameworks. This strategy calls for the codesign of systems that concurrently support applications of existing organizational knowledge and institutionalize what Lorino terms an organizational "inquiry procedure" for questioning and changing current organizational knowledge. The challenge to managers in designing and using dual systems for concurrently leveraging and changing knowledge is to create and sustain a *dynamic cognitive equilibrium*. This dynamic form of organizational equilibrium maintains the minimum level of cognitive coherence needed to carry out the organization's current value-creating activities, while also intentionally creating sufficient cognitive diversity to stimulate new conceptualizations of how the organization does or could create value. In effect, concurrent dual systems for managing knowledge will place as much emphasis on asking whether the organization is "doing the right things" as on checking whether the organization is "doing things right." While understanding how to design and manage such dual systems will no doubt occupy managers and management researchers for some time to come, our analysis of the five learning cycles does suggest some basic principles that can guide their design today.

In learning organizations with concurrent dual systems for managing knowledge, managers at all levels will be concerned not just with gathering and disseminating data within an organization, but also with generating and evaluating alternative frameworks for interpreting data. As Stein and Ridderstråle have observed in some companies now developing such systems, the design of information systems shifts from a prior focus on "pushing (specific) data" to people with a predetermined "need to know" to providing "pull systems" that make both a broad range of data and alternative frameworks for interpreting data readily available to anyone in an organization who wants or "needs to find out" something. The system design principle to keep in mind in this regard is that the *structure* of an organization's information systems will essentially determine the *content* of the information—i.e. the meanings—the systems disseminate.

When information systems are designed to channel only certain data and single interpretations of data to certain people, such structures for processing data will constrain the development—and eventually cause the convergence—of the interpretive frameworks of individuals who are required to use those data and interpretive frameworks in performing their tasks. When all (or nearly all) data available to an organization can be accessed freely and alternative ways of interpreting data can be proposed by any interested member of an organization, such an "open-access" information system structure can stimulate development within the organization both of new concepts of what constitutes "relevant data" and of new interpretations for available data. In this regard, our analysis of the five learning cycles suggests not only that "we manage what we measure," but further that the measurements of data available within an organization will fundamentally determine the *ideas* that managers develop and use as they manage.

Dual systems that concurrently leverage and create knowledge can also institutionalize an expectation that the knowledge bases of individuals, groups, and the organization at large will be in a state of constant—though managed—change. Concepts of continuous improvement or "kaizen" have already taken root in many organizations, but are today usually applied to improving the physical processes of the organization, such as production, distribution, customer service, and the like. Concurrent dual systems for managing knowledge must also design continuous improvement into the *intellectual processes* of the organization. Just as some retailers constantly renew their product mixes by regularly replacing the least profitable ten percent of goods with new items, learning organizations must design systems that periodically renew the mix of ideas the organization uses. Such systems must identify the core ideas currently used by individuals, groups, and the organization at large in performing tasks, regularly assess the effectiveness of those ideas for creating value, and replace the poorest performing ideas with new ideas that may prove more effective in creating value. Regularly retiring and replacing an organization's least effective ways of thinking (as well as doing) can create a "pull system" that regularly draws new ideas and interpretive frameworks into an organization.

Systemic cognitive interventions of this sort are necessary to prevent cognitive stasis in groups (including groups of managers). As Merali shows in her analysis of cognitive interactions between individuals, their work groups, and the organization at large, sensemaking is as much a social process as it is an intellectual process. Each person's desire to achieve a measure of cognitive equilibrium with other people in his or her environment draws everyone into a social process that seeks cognitive convergence, especially within work groups of frequently interacting people. Unless processes are institutionalized to induce change in interpretive frameworks, the "natural" social dynamic in groups is to seek a cognitive equilibrium and, once equilibrium is achieved, to maintain a stable interpretive framework.

Perhaps the most important principle in designing concurrent dual systems for managing knowledge, however, is the need to focus management attention on improving the systems an organization uses, rather than trying to manage the problems created by unrecognized design flaws in the organization's current systems. Understanding the difference in these two levels of management activities is critical to creating and sustaining a continuously learning organization. Toyota's approach to creating production systems with world-class quality illustrates this difference (Spear and Bowen 1999). When a part or process is discovered to be faulty during assembly of a Toyota vehicle, the problem is immediately analyzed to determine why the fault occurred. The analysis *must* lead to one of two outcomes. Either the design of the process that created the problem will be found to have a previously unrecognized potential for error, in which case the process design will be changed to assure that that kind of error does not occur again, or the person performing the task will be found to lack the skill required to adequately perform the task as designed, in which case the person will be provided with additional training to acquire the skills needed to perform his or her assigned task. By following this simple rule for correcting the systemic cause of the problem rather than simply repairing each problem that occurs, Toyota has institutionalized a management process that continuously focuses management attention on improving the organization's value-creating systems. In this volume, Sanchez describes an analogous architectural management process of systematically embedding knowledge gained from analyzing product and process failures in improved component and interface specifications.

Organizational learning requires individual, group, and organizational processes that work together as a system, and the challenge to managers of learning organizations is to design, support, and continuously improve processes that make learning a *systematic,* rather than sporadic, organizational activity. In the design of concurrent dual systems for organizational learning, all of the five learning cycles must be designed to support both the upward emergence and the downward dissemination of new knowledge and interpretive frameworks, as suggested in Figures 1.1 and 1.2. If any of the five learning cycles is weak or dysfunctional, the organization's learning loop will be broken and its learning dynamic lost.

Managing competence development holistically

To build and leverage organization competences, managers must recognize and serve the many interrelated economic and social interests of the providers of resources that the value-creating processes of an organization depend on. In this sense, as the competence perspective has emphasized (Heene and Sanchez 1997), managers must be as concerned with developing effective strategies for *distributing* the value created by an organization as they are with devising strategies for *creating* value.

As Boisot and Griffiths have noted about the knowledge economy, knowledge workers who understand the importance of their current knowledge and learning capacity to an organization—and who also understand the market value of both—are becoming less like traditional employees who simply receive a salary and more like residual claimants who expect to share in the economic value that their knowledge helps an organization to create. Managers who want to attract the most capable knowledge workers to their organization's value-creating processes must therefore devise new incentive structures that are effective in sharing the wealth an organization creates with those people whose knowledge and learning contribute significantly to the organization's wealth-creation capabilities.

Knowledge workers who are capable of generating new knowledge and improved interpretive frameworks, however, commonly expect more than just financial incentives from the organizations they work for. Today the most creative knowledge workers increasingly expect their employing organizations to provide them with superior opportunities to sustain their individual learning processes. In the knowledge economy, knowledge workers are as concerned with building new personal knowledge assets as they are with being compensated for the use of their current knowledge assets.

In the knowledge economy, the traditional divides between various disciplines and functions are rapidly eroding, and the knowledge that is critical in value-creating processes increasingly spans across many traditional areas of specialization. Knowledge workers who understand that this is occurring place growing value on the opportunities an organization can offer for "horizontal" learning in related knowledge areas outside their immediate area of current expertise. As van den Bosch and van Wijk point out, it is the ability of managers to identify and sustain ongoing processes for knowledge development and integration that determine the learning opportunities available to a firm and its knowledge workers. The increasing use of projects as a virtually permanent part of organizational processes offers an important way to create and share valuable learning opportunities for knowledge workers. As Raub's study of organizational competence building suggests, organizing new competence-building projects that are open to participation by interested knowledge workers within and external to an organization can be an effective way to extend the knowledge base of the organization in building new competences. As the experience of 3M and other companies has also shown, giving knowledge workers a significant degree of freedom to migrate to projects they find interesting and intellectually challenging can also be an effective way to offer valued horizontal learning opportunities to those workers.

CONCLUSION

This volume's investigations of the various processes that make up the five learning cycles of the competent organization lead us to a new perspective on what managers do in learning organizations and how managers add value in the knowledge economy. We now offer some concluding comments on this new perspective.

Nearly a century ago, the pragmatic American philosopher William James (1907) advised that "truth lives on credit." What we believe to be true—or in other words, what we think we "know"—must always be subject to ongoing testing and validation, and we must be willing to replace old beliefs, old knowledge, and even old interpretive frameworks when new ideas seem more capable of explaining and predicting events in the world—and thus are more deserving of our "credit." As Lorino has suggested in elaborating on James' insight, "knowledge is always experimental and procedural." Only by continuously testing the validity of knowledge by applying it through organizational processes can we determine the ability of any knowledge to help us accomplish our goals as individuals and organizations.

Managers of learning organizations play a privileged—but by no means exclusive—role in processes for testing and validating organizational knowledge. As we have sought to explain through the five learning cycles model, managers as individuals and as a group occupy cognitive positions that are fundamentally similar to those of other individuals and groups in the organization. An individual manager, like anyone else in an organization, must first convincingly explain his or her ideas to other managers before those ideas will become accepted as creditable knowledge by managers as a group. A group of managers must then explain and provide convincing validation for their ideas to other groups in an organization before those ideas will be accepted as creditable knowledge by members of an organization at large. The privilege that managers enjoy in organizations, however, is the discretion to choose which sets of beliefs—or interpretive frameworks, as we have called them—become embedded in an organization's formal systems and processes. If managers in essence abuse that privilege by trying to impose their beliefs on an organization without first earning "credit" for those ideas from the other groups in an organization, severe—perhaps even fatal—organizational cognitive paralysis or revolt can follow.

The essential role of managers in knowledge management that emerges from this study is therefore one of stimulating and supporting—not imposing—sensemaking processes throughout an organization. Stimulating sensemaking processes means, among other things, allocating organizational resources to exposing individual members of an organization to broad new interpretive frameworks, not just to specific new knowledge useful in their current activities. In other words, managers must support individuals in learning processes that can help to test, challenge, and renew the interpretive frameworks of the organization, and not just invest in training to improve individuals' skills that are deemed useful within the organization's current interpretive frameworks. Supporting sensemaking processes also means that managers must have the wisdom to recognize that their own personal beliefs are only part of the "gene pool" of ideas available to the organization. In addition, managers must have the courage to let their own ideas compete side by side with the ideas of everyone else in earning the cognitive credit that pulls ideas upward through the five learning cycles to take their place in the evolving interpretive frameworks of the organization. In learning organizations, managers must lead through the power of their ideas, not the power of their positions.

In the knowledge economy, the lion's share of economic wealth will be created and captured by the organizations that are most capable of evolving new interpretive frameworks for discovering emerging value-creation opportunities. The evolution of interpretive frameworks, like the evolution of species, occurs through the processes of variation, selection, and retention. Managers of learning organizations must learn not just to let cognitive variations "happen" in their organization, but to actively encourage the emergence of new interpretive frameworks. Natural selection of better variations occurs through competition between variations. Managers of learning organizations must therefore give new interpretive frameworks their chance to compete and to discover whether or not they are more capable of creating value than established interpretive frameworks. To support such processes of cognitive intrapreneuring, managers must be willing to accept failures as a normal part of the testing and validation process for determining which ideas are deserving of the organization's credit. Retention occurs when a variation is found to be better adapted to the requirements of its environment and is retained by the species through the natural selection process. Managers of learning organizations must be willing to accept and adopt new interpretive frameworks that outperform established frameworks, and to support their dissemination and retention by the organization. In the knowledge economy, managers will add value by facilitating a never-ending evolutionary process through which their organization develops, tests, and adopts better frameworks for identifying and responding to value creation opportunities.

These and other aspects of this volume's analysis of how knowledge can be managed into new organizational competences draw into sharper focus and add depth to the modern reconceptualization of managers as facilitators rather than controllers. The historic transition from command-and-control management theory and practice to a new concept of management based on knowledge creation and competence building will doubtless go on for some time, but it is our belief that this volume illuminates some of the critical next steps to be taken on that exciting journey.

REFERENCES

ABELL, D. F. (1993). *Managing with Dual Strategies: Mastering the Present, Preempting the Future.* New York: The Free Press.

ARGYRIS, C. and D. SCHOEN (1978). *Organizational Learning: A Theory of Action Perspective.* Reading, MA: Addison-Wesley.

HEENE, A. and R. SANCHEZ (eds.) (1997). *Competence-Based Strategic Management.* Chichester: John Wiley.

JAMES, WILLIAM (1907). *Pragmatism.* London: Longmans Green.

LEONARD-BARTON, D. (1992). "Core capabilities and core rigidities: A paradox in managing new product development," *Strategic Management Journal,* 13 (Summer Special Issue), 111–25.

MAHONEY, J. T. and R. SANCHEZ (1997). "Competence theory building: Reconnecting management research and management practice," in A. Heene and R. Sanchez (eds.), *Competence-Based Strategic Management*. Chichester: John Wiley, 43–64.

PEIRCE, C. S. (1932–54). *Collected Papers of C. S. Peirce*. Boston, MA: Harvard University Press.

SANCHEZ, R. (1997). "Managing articulated knowledge in competence-based competition," in R. Sanchez and A. Heene (eds.), *Strategic Learning and Knowledge Management*. Chichester: John Wiley.

—— (1998). "Strategic management at the point of inflection: Complexity, systems, and competence theory," *Long Range Planning*, 30 (6), 939–46.

—— and A. HEENE (1997). "Reinventing strategic management: New theory and practice for competence-based competition," *European Management Journal*, 15 (3), 303–17.

—— —— (eds.) (1997). *Strategic Learning and Knowledge Management*. Chichester: John Wiley.

—— —— and H. THOMAS (eds.) (1996). *Dynamics of Competence-Based Competition: Theory and Practice in the New Strategic Management*. Oxford: Elsevier Pergamon.

SIMON, H. (1982). *Models of Bounded Rationality*. Cambridge, MA: MIT Press.

SPEAR, S., and H. K. BOWEN (1999). "Decoding the DNA of the Toyota production system," *Harvard Business Review*, Sept.–Oct., 97–106.

TUSHMAN, M., W. NEWMAN, and E. ROMANELLI (1986). "Convergence and upheaval: Managing the unsteady pace of organizational evolution," *California Management Review*, 29 (1).

VAN DE VEN, A. (1986). "Central problems in the management of innovation," *Management Science*, 32 (5).

PART II

INDIVIDUAL KNOWLEDGE AND INDIVIDUAL/GROUP LEARNING INTERACTIONS

2

Building and Developing Capabilities: A Cognitive Congruence Framework

YASMIN MERALI

INTRODUCTION

Notions of dynamism, regeneration, change, and innovation are often emphasized as being important in "competing for the future" (Hamel and Prahalad 1994). Recent literature on competence-based competition (Sanchez and Heene 1997; Sanchez, Heene, and Thomas 1996) and dynamic capabilities (Lei, Hitt, and Bettis 1996; Teece, Pisano, and Shuen 1997) highlights the role of knowledge management and organizational learning in strategic competition. This discussion is concerned with the cognitive infrastructure of an organization that underpins the development and leveraging of organizational capabilities in dynamic markets.

An "information lens" is employed to develop a model for looking at issues of organizational learning, knowledge creation, and the leveraging of capabilities. The model is based on the concept of an action-perception cycle, and is used to represent an important element in the "sensemaking" processes of organizations engaged in transformational processes. Its usefulness as a descriptive and explanatory device is demonstrated through three case studies.

This discussion also elaborates on the importance of achieving *congruence* in the cumulative action-perception cycles that underpin transformative processes in organizations.

THE INFORMATION PERSPECTIVE

The importance of information in strategic management has long been recognized (e.g. Porter and Millar 1985). The view that information technology (IT) plays a key role in changing the "rules" of firm, industry, and global competition (Scott-Morton 1991) has led to the notion of "information-based competition" as a special concern within the competence-based perspective.

More recently the literature on dynamic capabilities (Lei, Hitt, and Bettis 1996;

Teece, Pisano, and Shuen 1997) and competence-based competition (Hamel and Heene 1994; Hamel and Prahalad 1994; Merali and McGee 1998a, 1998b; Nonaka and Takeuchi 1995; Sanchez and Heene 1997; Sanchez, Heene, and Thomas 1996) has highlighted the importance of organizational knowledge management for competing in dynamic contexts. The information an organization generates and uses is a fundamental part of the cognitive infrastructure that underpins organizational learning and the leveraging of capabilities (Merali 1997; Merali and McGee 1998a, 1998b).

The terms *data, information,* and *knowledge* are used with varying degrees of precision and significance in management literature. However, it is essential to work with precise definitions to achieve clarity of discourse. *Information* therefore is defined in this discussion as "that which, when received by an individual, gives new form to that individual's perception" (Merali and Frearson 1995). The essential contention in this definition is that information does not exist until it is received and internalized by a human being. The term *latent information* refers to that which would become information if received by a human being (Stonier 1990). Latent information may be thought of as a resource that has not yet been leveraged. *Information capabilities* is used in this discussion to refer to capabilities that are prerequisite for the leveraging of information—i.e., the capabilities necessary for "informing" in the sense of "giving new form" to individuals' perceptions.

THE ACTION-PERCEPTION CYCLE

Conceptualization is a primary (necessary but not sufficient) element in the identification and development of new capabilities. Similarly, action is a primary element in the leveraging of capabilities (Sanchez, Heene, and Thomas 1996). Any model of the cognitive elements that underpin an organization's capabilities must therefore represent the relationship between perception and action in developing and leveraging capabilities. For organizations competing in dynamic contexts, the "cyclical" relationship between action and perception (Figure 2.1) is particularly important. Organizations that are good at learning from their experience continually renew their perceptions of their competitive context and their organizational capabilities through their experience in undertaking action in that context. The information capabilities that underpin sensemaking and the "wisdom of action" (explained below) are of particular importance in the relationship between perception and action in leveraging capabilities.

Perception is a way of "seeing" the world, and sensemaking processes in an organization include developing ways of "seeing." An organization's activities of *evaluating, selecting,* and *planning* for action in dynamic contexts are all grounded in individual and collective perceptions of the world. In the strategy literature, these are recognized as cognitive capabilities required to formulate and enact dominant logics (Prahalad and Bettis 1986, 1995) or strategic logics (Sanchez, Heene, and Thomas 1996) which govern the leveraging of organizational capabilities. As Prahalad and Bettis (1995) note:

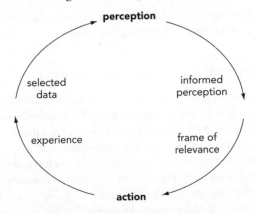

FIG. 2.1   *The action-perception cycle.*

. . . the dominant logic is an information filter. Organizational attention is focused only on data deemed relevant by the dominant logic. Other data are largely ignored. "Relevant" data are filtered by the dominant logic and by the analytic procedures managers use to aid strategy development. These "filtered" data are then incorporated into the strategy, systems, values, expectations, and reinforced behavior of the organization.

The *wisdom of action* is a term used here to refer to the notion of knowing what the appropriate thing to do is in the "here and now" of a given organization. Individual wisdom of action is observable in retrospect, as "wise" moves lead to a position of sustainable viability for an actor and contribute to building and maintaining an intact *self-concept* (discussed below). Similarly, in organizations, whilst action is directed towards strategic business outcomes, what are viewed as "appropriate" or wise actions in pursuit of a strategy depend on their impacts on the viability, sustainability, and persistence of the organizational identity. The information capabilities supporting the wisdom of action in an organization are the communication capabilities that inform individual perceptions and align and galvanize the owners of the perceptions to act appropriately and congruently in the context of the organizational existence. The term wisdom of action therefore also embraces notions of organizational recipes and routines (Nelson and Winter 1982) that maintain the *internal* congruence of the organization. Thus, the prevailing wisdom of action in an organization is concerned with maintaining congruence between an organization's identity and its external spatio-temporal context.

CHARACTERIZATION OF LEARNING AND KNOWLEDGE MANAGEMENT

The action-perception cycle in Figure 2.1 is a generalized representation of organizational *being*—i.e. what the organization is about and what it does. In essence, learning occurs through refreshment of the action-perception cycle. This section relates some existing models of learning and knowledge management to the leveraging of organizational capabilities through the action-perception cycle.

Adaptive and generative learning characteristics

Argyris and Schon (1978) showed that in order to understand learning in organizations, it is useful to look at the relationship between the *espoused theory* of an organization and the *theory-in-use* in the organization. The espoused theory defines the norms that organizational endeavor is supposed to conform to and that are reflected in the explicit strategies of the organization. The theory-in-use refers to what actually goes on in the organizational context; it is implicit in the strategies, norms, and assumptions that govern the actual patterns of task performance. In single-loop learning, changes and improvements drive adaptive forms of learning directed towards "doing what you do better" and do not threaten the *status quo* of an organization's espoused theory. In double loop learning, learning that results from changes in the theory-in-use are fed back into the model of the espoused theory and can result in its modification. Double loop learning therefore challenges the espoused norms and is *generative* in nature—i.e. it is about "doing something *different*" or "*being* something different."

Knowledge management characteristics

Organizations have distinctive characteristics associated with their role in promoting knowledge dissemination and learning across an organizational context (Boisot 1987). The "phases" from Boisot's organizational learning cycle are used here to characterize organizational learning characteristics (see Figure 2.2). (The case discussion later in this chapter employs a simplified version of Boisot's model of organizational learning to illustrate the relative strengths of each organization studied in orchestrating its learning process.)

Scanning is concerned with obtaining information to develop a map of the organizational and external environment. Scanning involves developing a map of "what is" within that environment and identifying any problems or opportunities that are presented by the environment.

Knowledge creation is concerned with "know how" and insights obtained from dealing with or solving a perceived opportunity or problem. The knowledge gained at this stage is new knowledge for the organization, will be confined to the knowledge base of the problem solver(s), and is likely to be in the form of tacit knowledge.

Codification is concerned with codifying the new, tacit knowledge so that it can be communicated to those in the organization beyond the original problem solver(s). Codification may consist of verbal articulation of what is known by the problem solver, or it may be made manifest through the demonstration of a procedure or action by the problem solver(s). Knowledge at this stage becomes explicit (cf. Sanchez 1997).

Diffusion is concerned with communicating and spreading codified new knowledge through the organization. Successful diffusion results in the incorporation of new

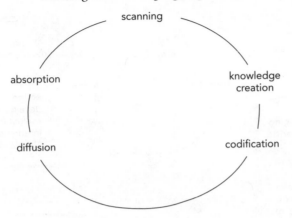

FIG. 2.2   *The model for organizational learning.*
Source: Boisot, 1987.

knowledge into the regular patterns of task performance beyond the problem solver(s).

Absorption occurs when the new knowledge has become so embedded in organizational recipes and routines that it is an implicit part of "how things are done around here." What started out as "new knowledge" has been transformed from tacit *individual* knowledge to an integral part of the tacit *organizational* knowledge base.

Some implications of this model for the creation and leveraging of organizational knowledge and capabilities are illustrated in Figure 2.3 (from Merali 1998).

The "knowledge creation" and "codification" phases shown in Figure 2.3 are important in building new organizational capabilities. The management perspective in these phases is often relatively introspective and concerned with issues related to internal processes of knowledge creation and the intrinsic "quality" of the knowledge being created.

The codification, diffusion, and absorption phases are directly concerned with leveraging knowledge. They are concerned with transforming individual knowledge into organizational knowledge and with incorporating the knowledge into behaviors and actions of the organizational being. In leveraging knowledge, the focus moves from issues of intrinsic quality to issues of the "utility value" of the knowledge to the organization. This may be established through

(1) application of the knowledge to develop a new capability or to exploit existing capabilities in an innovative way; or
(2) use of the knowledge as a basis for developing more knowledge.

In terms of the resource-based view (Penrose 1959; Peteraf 1993; Wernerfelt 1984), the "value" of knowledge depends on the rents that can accrue from exploiting the knowledge. Notions of value can only be realized in the external context, which is why the leveraging of capabilities requires organizational schemata to support mapping of the external environment.

Yasmin Merali

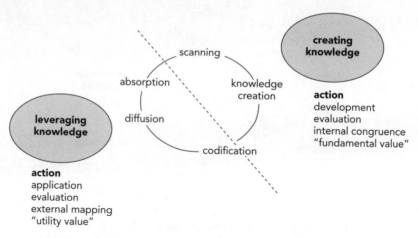

Fig. 2.3 *The leveraging of capabilities in the context of the learning cycle.*
Source: Merali, 1998.

COGNITIVE INFRASTRUCTURES: A FRAMEWORK

Much of the literature on organizational learning and learning organizations (Argyris and Schon 1978; Boisot 1987; Nonaka and Takeuchi 1995; Senge 1990) highlights both the transformation of personal knowledge into organizational knowledge (or vice versa) and the transformation of tacit knowledge into explicit knowledge (or vice versa). These transformations in knowledge (between tacit/explicit and personal/organizational) happen through the social interactions in which individuals communicate, share activities, and exchange ideas. The mechanisms for these transformations are rooted in intersubjective sensemaking processes. Two aspects of an intersubjective sensemaking process are similar to Argyris and Schon's (1978) process of organizational double loop learning. One aspect underpins the development of new organizational capabilities and generates ideas about the innovative deployment of existing capabilities. A second aspect legitimizes and communicates notions of the relevance (in terms of purpose and value) of new knowledge and their domains of useful application. This latter aspect underpins the organizational approval of actions to leverage new capabilities.

Intersubjective sensemaking can thus be seen as the key mechanism for maintaining congruence between the actions and perceptions of the action-perception cycle (Figure 2.1). An understanding of the cognitive infrastructure that both feeds and is fed by intersubjective sensemaking provides insights into the way organizations develop and leverage capabilities. The components of a cognitive infrastructure and their primary interactions are defined below. (Figure 2.4 is a schematic representation of these components and their interactions.)

Components of the cognitive infrastructure

Self-concept. The organizational self-concept is of fundamental import in the development, realization, and leveraging of distinctive capabilities. Self-concept operates at a fundamental cognitive level and is a perception of that which we call our *identity* (see Weick 1995 for a treatment of identity). Weick (1995: 160) highlights the importance of identity as a focus for sensemaking and as a basis for congruent action in organizations:

Each . . . organization chooses who it will be by first choosing what actions, if any, it needs to explain, and second, by choosing which explanations for these actions it will defend. An inability or unwillingness to choose, act, and justify these leaves people with too many possibilities and too few certainties. Binding decisions affect the tasks we are attracted to, the reasons that move us, the values we try to realize, the plans we admire, and the people we seek out. Avoidance of such decisions slows the development of attractions, reasons, values, plans, and associates.

This quotation from Weick illustrates a key relationship between action and perception. For an organization that is operating in a dynamic environment and for whom knowledge acquisition and evaluation are significant activities, the establishment and understanding of its own identity is particularly important. Self-concept arises from this sense of identity and in turn gives rise to action.

Whilst Weick suggests the primacy of perception as a driver of action, in dynamic contexts there is a "cyclical" relationship between action and perception: self-concept and identity shape action which in turn informs perception, as suggested in Figure 2.1.

Relationships. Relationships between individuals determine the content and structure of intra- and interorganizational knowledge networks. At the individual level, the relationship acts as a relevance filter. The value attached to a piece of information by the recipient of the information is affected or "filtered" by the credibility that he or she attributes to the informant. The recipient's investment of credibility in an informant may be rooted in any number of factors, including the informant's position in the organizational power structure, his track record in dealings with the recipient, his wider reputation, his technical/academic/professional credentials, his ideology, and even the informant's and recipient's interpersonal "chemistry." Extended to the organizational level, relationship networks are important mechanisms for the sharing and diffusion of ideas and the resulting intersubjective realization of the organizational self-concept.

The Script. In considering how relationships generate mutual perceptions and shared learning, it is useful to characterize the roles of the participants in the relationship. Each relationship is distinctively mediated through, and evidenced by, its transactions. Transactions are influenced by the perception of each participant about himself or herself in relation to the other participants. These perceptions are analogous (see Merali and McGee 1998a) to *scripts* in *transaction analysis* (Berne 1961):

An individual's script is an internal conceptual structure containing a set of rules and norms and a highly cross-linked set of data about self, the world, and interactions between the two. The script acts as a filtering mechanism for fresh data: nothing is accepted into a script unless it can be made to fit with what already exists. The script evolves over time as new information is incor-

porated, and socialization modifications occur as a result of its involvement in meaningful relationships. The nature of this evolution (e.g. in terms of what can or cannot be incorporated into
the script) is itself determined by, and is characteristic of, the existing script.

The concept of scripts is useful at all levels of organizational analysis. At the macro
level it is useful for understanding how an organization perceives itself within its environment. At a micro level it helps to make sense of the social learning processes between
individuals.

The collective enactment of relationship scripts is the mechanism by which the
organizational self-concept is realized, capabilities are leveraged, experiences are
formed, and learning takes place. In other words, the collective enactment of scripts is
the manifestation of the organizational being.

The Schema. The schema is the total cognitive construct which contains the collection of interconnected beliefs and perceptions about self and the universe, together
with their spatial, temporal, social, and semantic relationships. Schemata embrace self-
concept, scripts, and processes for *environmental sensemaking*, together with mechanisms for their linguistic and semiotic *articulation*.

A model of cognitive infrastructure

The cyclical representation of the cognitive infrastructure in Figure 2.4 illustrates
mutual dependence of the above defined components.

The organization's collective schema and self-concept are the perception "shapers"
for the action-perception cycle of Figure 2.1. The script is rooted in the organizational
self-concept and is the framework within which relationships are enacted. The collective scripts in an organization are instrumental in selecting (i.e. recognizing as "relevant") data and cues that shape the organization's perception of its environment.

The enactment of relationships (which corresponds to action in Figure 2.1) is the
mechanism through which environmental sensemaking takes place. Environmental
sensemaking is the process through which an organization dynamically incorporates
data and cues from the environment to develop a perception of the "here-and-now"
competitive terrain and its likely development over time. Through the enactment of
relationships, an organization generates "new information" which may modify and
refresh its schema, which in turn will inform the self-concept, scripts, and relationship
enactment mechanisms.

An organization's self-concept and its schema for environmental sensemaking are
integrally related. Uniqueness of identity derives from occupying a specific space at a
given point in time. Self-concept is a perception of identity and must of necessity
incorporate a locus of being *relative* to the space and time that surrounds it (i.e., its
environment). The salient "space" in this analysis is the competitive landscape within
which firms compete on competences (Rumelt 1994). In other words, the organizational self-concept exists relative to a perception of the environment, and the perception of the environment is in turn shaped by the self-concept.

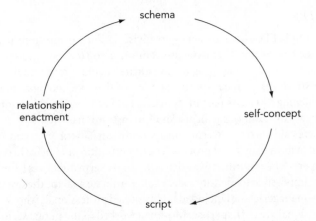

FIG. 2.4 *The cognitive infrastructure for intersubjective sensemaking and leveraging of capabilities.*

The role of this organizational cognitive structure in developing and leveraging capabilities is illustrated in the following three case studies.

CASE STUDIES

The cases discussed here all involve some form of business transformation. The first two cases concern IT-enabled business transformation, and the third concerns the restructuring and transformation of the corporate center of a multinational organization.

In the first two cases, the case methodology utilized a series of interviews with individual stakeholders, as well as workshops with stakeholder groups. The workshops were based on Checkland's Soft Systems Methodology (Checkland and Scholes 1990) and enabled the articulation of the various stakeholders' *Weltanschauung* (i.e. "world-outlook"). The methodology for the final case was comprised of a series of interviews with headquarters, business sector, and service function staff.

There is a wealth of literature on IT-enabled change, much of it normative in proposing "how it should be done." However, even organizations that do it "by the book" (often with the help of experienced consultancy firms) sometimes fail to develop and leverage new capabilities to the degree to which they aspired. Their experiences suggest that a high degree of rationalized process congruence is not enough for success. A key contention of this discussion is that the degree of underlying cognitive congruence fundamentally affects the outcome of such exercises. The framework illustrated in Figure 2.4 is used to develop this contention.

Case 1: ITED

Case 1 is about ITED, a quango[1] set up to advise national institutions in an important economic sector ("Sector X") on the use of information technology in the delivery of a national service. Its mandate was to investigate enabling technologies and to guide Sector X institutions to make appropriate use of these technologies in meeting their professional obligations. As part of its brief, ITED produced publications and educational packages for promoting the use of IT in institutions.

ITED was established by government appointment. No coherent concept of strategy was evident in its management process. The organization operated as a constellation of focused experts whose outputs were driven by short-term directives from the executive level. It was impossible to identify a clear superordinate goal for the organization.

The non-managerial staff included highly skilled professionals who were focused on their professional area of expertise. Most had worked in the public sector before joining ITED. Few managers had any commercial experience. Formally, the organization had a matrix structure, and this structure engendered confusion about lines of reporting. Politically, power resided with a small number of individuals in key senior management positions, and decision-making in the organization was carried out through a centrally dominated hierarchic structure.

Internal business systems (accounting, finance, sales, marketing, production) had developed piecemeal and created uncoordinated islands of information technology. Individual workstations, however, were connected over a local area network and had e-mail facilities. The R&D group, on the other hand, was keeping abreast of innovative technologies and was experimenting with Internet technologies for electronic publishing and dissemination of information to Sector X institutions.

The transformation concept. The possibility of a business transformation in ITED was introduced by individuals in the R&D group who had developed expertise in Web technologies. They had demonstrated (in a pilot project) that electronic publishing was technologically viable. However, a subsequent feasibility study to investigate the leveraging of this capability revealed the need to carry out a business process redesign (BPR). The main advantages of carrying out such an exercise were identified as

(1) developing a "customer" orientation and a better understanding of customer needs (using Web technologies for two-way dialogues);
(2) sharing of information and data resources between teams and functions (by introducing a shared database with networked access along with organizational changes to enable the different constituencies to work together);
(3) designing a process in which fragmented activities were combined to deliver a more customer-sensitive service product offering;
(4) enabling ITED to build specialized Web capabilities using the domain knowledge and multimedia and design expertise that already existed in the "expert ghettos" that had been created over the years.

---

[1] A *quango* is a "quasi-autonomous national government organization."

Table 2.1 summarizes the changes in the organization implied by this IT-enabled process redesign.

The feasibility study report was circulated in the organization, considered at the executive level, and shelved. Three years after the feasibility study, ITED formed a new team dedicated to the exploitation of Web technologies in the dissemination of its materials. Two years later, ITED does not yet have integrated internal IT systems. Web technologies are not used to enhance customer feedback. Most recently, an event triggered by a change of government has challenged ITED's hitherto rather insular model of existence. ITED has been asked to meet performance targets defined in terms of technology uptake and leverage in the institutions that ITED was originally set up to help.

Analysis. ITED had good knowledge-creation capability. In the example used here, the R&D group's Web technology capability and the development of the prototype were state of the art at the time. ITED failed, however, to leverage this capability.

The organization possessed the knowledge required to do a BPR exercise. ITED even had experts who advised others on "best practice" for managing this type of change process. The justification of the matrix structure of the organization and the language of the management teams reflected concepts articulated by the BPR "gurus" of the day. In other words, the organization had ample access to the conceptual framework for BPR-led change management.

Application of the cognitive congruence framework provides an insight into why ITED failed to leverage its capabilities during the time of the case.

TABLE 2.1 *The existing and the implied new organization profiles for ITED*

	Existing profile	Implied profile
Strategy	No coherent strategy	Collaborative networking with key stakeholders
Structure	Matrix organization with centralized power structure	Networked, cross-functional, and team-based
Style	Bureaucratic	Empowerment
Systems	Function-based "islands of automation"	Integrated data, open systems technology
Staff	Professionals dedicated to excellence in own "discipline"; middle managers insecure	Flexible, empowered
Skills	Experts in relevant disciplines	Creative leveraging of expertise
Super-ordinate goals	Not discernible	Promote (measurably) the effective and efficient use of IT in Sector X nationwide

Note: cf. Pascale and Athos 1981.

As illustrated in Figure 2.5, ITED suffered from an incomplete schema. The schema lacked elements of the external environment that would enable people in ITED to make sense of its announced *raison d' être*. As a result, the boundary for intersubjective sensemaking and leveraging capabilities in ITED excluded external stakeholders. In ITED's schema, the government mandate that created ITED was the only justification for ITED's continued existence. The lack of a meaningful incorporation of the mandate into ITED's schema, however, led to formation of a self-concept in which ITED was simply a center of expertise. The professionals inside ITED essentially conformed to this schema: they existed with ITED to do work that required their expertise. The relationship scripts and the enactment of the relationships were then congruent with this self-concept. Experts did "expert types of things," and managers ensured that experts worked within clear project boundaries and did not dissipate their energies by engaging in non-project activities. The schema was therefore reinforced. No process of organizational inquiry inside ITED challenged this schema, and until the change of government, there was little or no outside pressure to encourage ITED to extend its schema. This is reflected in the absence of a coherent strategy in the organizational profile in Table 2.1. Government intervention may eventually lead ITED to extend its schema to incorporate the external environment more explicitly. Early signs are a renewed attempt to develop an IT strategy, the arrival of a new CEO, and an extensive restructuring of the organization.

Case 2: A financial services company

Case 2 is about Finsoc, a financial services organization. Like many other financial institutions, in the "boom time" of the early 1980s Finsoc engaged in a program of very rapid growth through acquisition. Acquisitions included businesses like estate agents and insurance companies that were outside the traditional business area for Finsoc. The recession of the late 1980s reversed this trend. In order to survive, Finsoc rational-

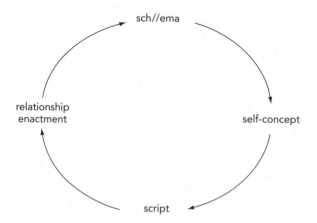

Fig. 2.5   *The gap in the cognitive infrastructure for ITED.*

ized its portfolio and divested itself of its less profitable businesses. The period was a bloody one in the organizational memory. The divestitures coincided with the appointment of a new CEO who launched a major business transformation program.

The organization had always been a hierarchical one. The strategic imperative for rationalization and the related sense of urgency reinforced a strong command-and-control culture. Staff who survived the cuts were very compliant, and management directives were never challenged. The work organization was task-based, and the skills base was narrowly focused on specific product lines. IT systems were accounts-based, rather than customer-based. IT implementations were based on outdated technologies and provided little in the way of support for customer-oriented cross-selling of products.

The transformation concept. The transformation program was designed to turn Finsoc into a customer-focused organization in every aspect. Issues of strategy, structure, technology, people, and roles were all defined and planned for. Several consultancy firms were employed to work with Finsoc personnel throughout the transformation process. Issues of change management were addressed, and resources were allocated for change management experts to run workshops with Finsoc staff to enable them to adjust to their new roles and modes of working. The then existing and the desired organizational profiles for Finsoc are summarized in Table 2.2.

The organization was restructured. Business focused teams were created with a view to developing multi-skilled personnel who could cross-sell products. A new IT and information systems infrastructure (providing facilities such as consolidated customer profiles, product databases, and workflow management) was installed to enable the teams to work effectively. The software was designed to support relationship-oriented personalized transactions, with staff being able to update customer histories with

TABLE 2.2 *The existing and the desired profiles for Finsoc*

	Existing profile	Desired profile
Strategy	Rationalization	Consolidation in catchment area, then growth
Structure	Centralized	Web, networked, cross-functional, team-based
Style	Command-and-control	Empowerment
Systems	Account-based, function-based, old technology	Integrated data, open systems technology
Staff	Insecure, compliant	Flexible, empowered (some outsourcing)
Skills	Task-based, product specialization	Cross-product marketing, service orientation
Super-ordinate goals	Survival	Be "first choice" provider

details of individual circumstances as they became apparent. A service orientation was emphasized.

The restructuring, the new technological infrastructure, and staff training in the new technology went according to plan, and Finsoc acquired the desired IT-related capabilities smoothly and rapidly. The behavioral changes required for leveraging these systems, however, did not materialize in step with the new enabling infrastructures. Deployment of the new systems by the newly formed teams did not result in improved performance. Despite the textbook-like implementation of the transformation process, Finsoc did not succeed in leveraging the capabilities it had invested in.

A study to review the early experience revealed that the teams were not effective and, despite the workshops that they had attended, staff felt unable to work in the new mode. Middle management and teams reported feeling isolated.

Analysis. Application of the cognitive congruence framework suggests why Finsoc failed to leverage its capabilities. Analysis of Finsoc's efforts to build and leverage new capabilities revealed the pattern shown in Figure 2.6. Despite the team-based restructuring, the power base of Finsoc remained with a small number of individuals who had also been responsible for the directive rationalization in the recession. The work with consultants and the change management workshops established a widely used rhetoric about the organization's self-concept along the lines of "We used to be a command-and-control organization . . ." The rhetoric usually continued, albeit less forcibly, ". . . Now we are a team-based organization."

The rhetoric served superficially as an affirmation of intended change, but the actual self-concept of the firm was never challenged. The scripts for relationship enactment did not fundamentally change. Managers and team participants continued to behave as if the command-and-control culture had survived—except that in the new structure individuals were never sure where authority lay. People were reluctant to make decisions and were afraid to experiment or act on their own initiative. There was an uneasy feeling that the organization was less effective in its new form than it had been under

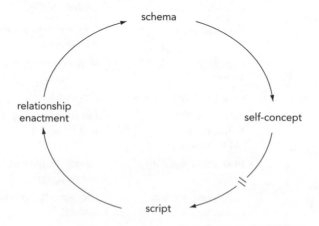

Fig. 2.6   *The gap in the cognitive infrastructure for Finsoc.*

the old regime, in which people knew what was expected of them and understood how the reward and punishment mechanisms worked.

In terms of the cognitive infrastructure model, Finsoc had a well-developed schema for the external environment. The internal schema was consistent with the self-concept of a "team-based organization." However, the self-concept was incongruent with the relationship scripts in actual use, which still conformed to command-and-control behaviors. The enactment of relationships in Finsoc therefore failed to leverage the firm's new resources, all of which could have been leveraged in a more empowering context. Moreover, the schema was not confronted with the incongruence between the rhetoric and reality of the relationship scripts. The incongruence remained unchallenged until enough data relating to the business performance indicators became available to signal the problem.

In terms of the learning cycle and the leveraging of capabilities (Figure 2.3), it would appear that initially Finsoc had an inadequate (perhaps virtually absent) process of intersubjective inquiry for developing an organizational understanding of the actions needed to actually realize the transformation rhetoric. The "codification" stage of the cycle was flawed because it resulted in mere rhetoric rather than in meaningful communication of the *actionable* knowledge required in the transformation exercise. Consequently the "diffusion" and "absorption" phases were impotent (only the rhetoric was adopted), and Finsoc failed to leverage the collective knowledge of the consultants and gurus that it had acquired.

Subsequently, in a follow-up to this analysis, Finsoc management addressed the issue of incongruence between the self-concept and the scripts. Significant changes undertaken recently include a new competence-based appraisal scheme and a comprehensive program of continuous personal development to promote new desired behaviors and attitude changes. Finsoc has received awards for the quality of its service and for its financial performance since beginning this second wave in the change process.

Case 3: A natural resources company

Case 3 is about Groupe Tulip, an international group of natural resource companies with two joint European parents. The case has been analyzed in greater detail elsewhere (see Merali and McGee 1998b), and the following account is a selective summary of some key features of the case.

The case focuses on the corporate headquarters and its relationships with the multinational business units in its corporate portfolio. Historically Groupe Tulip was vertically integrated, with extensive formal planning procedures. Its businesses range from exploration and extraction of resources ("upstream") to consumer product marketing ("downstream"). The gains realized from effectively integrating activities along the supply chain were important. In recent years some vertical disintegration resulted in upstream and downstream companies acquiring more distinct identities and benefiting from economies directly attainable within the scope of the business (as opposed to corporate) operations.

Groupe Tulip recently completed a major restructuring exercise. This was accompanied by a fundamental change in the headquarters self-concept and resulted in significant changes in the headquarters-business relationships.

The transformation concept. Restructuring of the corporation coincided with the arrival of a new CEO who was a key actor in the process by which the headquarters redefined its self-concept. In intensive facilitated workshops, headquarters managers re-evaluated their behaviors, attitudes, and fundamental beliefs relating to the center and its role in the group. This process enabled senior management to develop a coherent script for the future of the center and its relationships with its businesses. Out of this process also came a renewed self-concept for the corporate center and the idea of launching a corporate-wide "Transformation" program as a vehicle for the enactment of the new script.

The desired headquarters style was articulated as changing from being "directive" to being "influencing" and "interactive," from "telling" to "listening." The desired headquarters' role was articulated as changing from "overseeing" to "strategic leadership." The articulation of the strategic leadership role was heavily associated with the realization that the current internally focused, programmatic schema was inadequate for enabling Groupe Tulip to position itself favorably in the uncertain industry context that it faced. They concluded that corporate leadership now needed to facilitate the development of appropriate new capabilities to deliver sustainable performance in a dynamic environment. The desired strategy was articulated as changing from being planned to becoming more "emergent." The desired processes required to enact the new role were variously articulated as "coaching and learning," "advisory," and "engagement."

Table 2.3 summarizes the organizational profiles for the "pre-transformational" entity and for the "new center" that management aspired to cultivate.

The emphasis of the new business organization was on the achievement of high performance and the establishment of a socially responsible image as part of the global corporate image of Groupe Tulip. The focus of the headquarters-business relationship was intended to establish a coordinated, outward-looking performance culture. The Transformation program was the vehicle for achieving this change.

A corporate-wide framework was established for target setting and performance evaluation. The center developed a corporate scorecard template (Kaplan and Norton 1992) setting out the fundamental criteria to be used for setting performance targets and for evaluating performance. The corporate template was adopted by all the businesses, with adaptations to reflect their specific contexts. Internal and external benchmarking was introduced as the basis for developing stretch performance targets, and businesses were encouraged to make performance data visible across the entire corporation. The process was regarded as an empowering one, and businesses were "mentored" to develop target-setting and self-evaluation capabilities.

Information technology (IT) was a key element of the mechanism for disseminating "best practice" documentation. Intranet technology provided the coordination and communication infrastructure across the global businesses to support knowledge creation and the leveraging of existing knowledge across businesses.

The headquarters was strongly committed to ongoing investment in social processes

TABLE 2.3 *Characteristics for the old and the desired organizational profiles for Groupe Tulip*

	"Old" organizational profile	"Desired" profile
Strategy	Planned	Emergent
Structure	Matrix dominated; distorted by powerful "local barons"	Well-defined formal relationships and procedures, organic informal networking
Style	Closed, directive, command-and-control, reactive	Open, engaging, interactive, credible, proactive, collaborative
Systems	Implicit, organizational networks with localized information gatekeepers; somewhat prone to political obfuscation	Visible, shared systems, exploiting internal and external intelligence and sustained by formal and informal networks
Staff	Professional, technically and organizationally focused	Open and professional
Skills	Technical excellence, political alacrity	Technical excellence, positioning skills (i.e. pursuing personal development in the context of a holistic organizational perspective)
Super-ordinate goals	Return to shareholders	Sustainable value to shareholders and industry leadership with integrity

for transferring expertise. It actively invested in stimulating a high level of networking amongst individuals and in leveraging the networks to transfer expertise. To this end, cross-business conversations were engineered, and international projects were set up to establish global networking capabilities across businesses. Management believed that although knowledge management can be facilitated by the use of IT, the development of a social knowledge network was a prerequisite for successful organizational learning.

The Transformation process was used to develop organizational capabilities in self-evaluation and empowerment, maintaining a congruent corporate identity, networking capabilities, vertical and horizontal collaboration, and the intersubjective development of organizational identity. These capabilities were intended to enable Groupe Tulip to react to external changes in a coordinated fashion.

Analysis. The Groupe Tulip case illustrates the development of a congruent cognitive infrastructure. Here, the redefinition of the corporate self-concept resulted in a radically different enactment of the headquarters-business relationship.

The headquarters self-concept shaped new relationship scripts, and a congruent dynamic corporate schema was maintained through the relationship enactment. New communication channels supported new scripts for corporate headquarters and

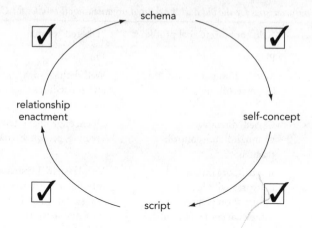

FIG. 2.7 *The congruent cognitive infrastructure for Groupe Tulip.*

the businesses, and their new relationship enactments. Communication channels emerged and developed to enable the incorporation of knowledge developed in the business units into the corporate mental map, thereby allowing the businesses to share and shape the corporate mental map. (See Figure 2.7.)

DISCUSSION

The cognitive congruence model helps us to understand the varying outcomes of capability development and leveraging processes in the three cases studied. The first case concerns an organization that failed to leverage its capabilities because it failed to commit itself fully to the organizational and systems changes that would enable it to actually realize the desired changes. The second case concerns an organization that was committed to changing its systems and structure in order to develop and leverage competences, but had difficulty in realizing the self-concept adequately to make effective use of its new systems and structure. The final case is one of an organization that perceived the need to develop a "transformational capability" to deal effectively with its dynamic competitive context. It focused its attention on adequately developing both a new organizational self-concept and an appropriate relationship infrastructure that would enable it to react to external changes in a coordinated fashion.

Congruence of cognitive infrastructure and the leveraging of capabilities

The model of cognitive infrastructure identifies the elements and interdependencies of a congruent organizational cognitive infrastructure: the four elements of schema, self-concept, scripts, and relationship enactment are in harmony, and congruence is maintained between externally and internally informed dynamic schema, self-concept, scripts, and relationship enactment. This gives rise to what I have called the wisdom of action, in which congruence between action and context is maintained, and a virtuous action-perception cycle is sustained for the leveraging of organizational capabilities.

In the ITED and Finsoc cases, when the cognitive infrastructure became incongruent so that the four components were no longer in harmony with each other and with the internal and external environments, the action-perception cycle became dysfunctional. The result of incongruence is ineffective leveraging of capabilities and wasting of resources. As the case analyses suggest, incongruence commonly arises from

(1) de-coupling of the cognitive components within the organization (as in the Finsoc case);
(2) de-coupling of the organization from the external context (as in the ITED case).

The central assertion in this discussion is that internal and external congruence of the cognitive infrastructure is necessary for the effective leveraging of organizational capabilities.

Collective versus individual perceptions and actions

In building organizational identity, a collective organizational schema will impose formal structures, systems, and job and role specifications that reinforce the schema and its associated self-concept. Relationship scripts and the enactment of relationships may be circumscribed by limitations on resources or opportunities imposed by the formal structures and processes adopted. Incremental adaptive learning may take place within formal structures that defend the *status quo*. More creative, discontinuous forms of learning, however, require open structures and processes which enable the dynamic incorporation of environmental information into an organization's schema. Processes of intersubjective inquiry that are empowered to challenge the *status quo* are essential in developing and maintaining the congruent cognitive infrastructure required for the dynamic leveraging of capabilities.[2]

The process of intersubjective inquiry plays a fundamental role in organizational learning and in the renewal of the collective organizational schema. The collective network of relationship enactment in an organization informs its collective schema. Both the processes of intersubjective inquiry and relationship enactment therefore provide mechanisms for the engagement of individuals or groups of individuals in revising personal and collective schemata. A clear organizational schema can inform the schemata of an organization's members, while the diversity of individual perceptions can augment the collective schema. Organizational double-loop learning can be

---

[2] Issues of individual versus collective perceptions and actions introduce an additional layer of complexity to this mode of analysis. Cognitive dissonance occurs when individual (or group) schemas and scripts are incompatible with their organizational counterparts. Consideration of the potentially dissonant relationship between self-concept and conformance in an organization is beyond the scope of this chapter, but is discussed elsewhere (Merali 2000).

promoted by creating contexts within which cross-boundary discourse and inter-subjective inquiry can be sustained. These processes play a vital role in generating the requisite variety (Ashby 1956) of mental models needed to spawn innovative opportunities for building and leveraging organizational competences. In the Groupe Tulip case, the corporate center focused on providing an environment suitable for nurturing this type of activity and succeeded in cultivating a dynamic, congruent cognitive infrastructure. In contrast to the other two cases, the desired transformation for Groupe Tulip was articulated in terms that included changes in cognitive infrastructure as well as changes in business processes and operations.

IMPLICATIONS OF THE COGNITIVE CONGRUENCE FRAMEWORK FOR THEORY AND PRACTICE

The importance of knowledge management and organizational learning in competence-based competition has been widely discussed in the recent literature (Hamel and Heene 1994; Hamel and Prahalad 1994; Lei, Hitt, and Bettis 1996; Merali 1997; Merali and McGee 1998a, 1998b; Nonaka and Takeuchi 1995; Sanchez and Heene 1997; Sanchez, Heene, and Thomas 1996; Teece, Pisano, and Shuen 1997). This literature stresses the importance of "learning by doing." One perspective on the cognitive congruence framework presented in this paper is that it is concerned with the organizational cognitive processes of forming mental schemata and acting out relationships that underpin and shape learning by doing. Only by achieving congruence in the cognitive infrastructure of an organization can new knowledge be created and applied in action to create new competences. By introducing structures and processes as units of analysis in the study of competence building and leveraging, this framework enables the integration of theory from multiple disciplines that can contribute to the development of insights into the creation, management, and leveraging of organizational knowledge.

The cyclical relationship between action and perception underpins much existing theory about learning by doing. From a pragmatic viewpoint, the cognitive congruence framework helps us to understand the social processes that select and legitimize the particular action-perception cycles that an organization enacts in building and leveraging competences. Congruent action-perception cycles lead to congruent intersubjective activities that enable people in an organization to be effective in leveraging capabilities. Flawed, incongruent cycles result in dysfunctional relationships and behaviors and lead to dissipation of personal and organizational energy. Organizational symptoms of cognitive incongruence are apparent in socially observable phenomena including high levels of displacement activity (staff turnover and internal transfers), low staff morale, and intrusive management control.

The cases reported here illustrate several descriptive and explanatory aspects of the model. In this regard, the framework offers practitioners a sensemaking device: it facilitates the articulation of, and discourse about, observable aspects of competence leveraging processes. The framework can therefore be used to diagnose an organization's action-perception cycle to surface "flaws" in the underlying cognitive framework. Such insights can assist in the design of better organizational processes for building and leveraging capabilities. The three organizations studied—all with a need to change, and all with new CEOs—initiated transformation processes to develop and leverage new capabilities. By applying the cognitive infrastructure model to cognitive elements in these transformation processes, it was possible to surface formerly hidden workings that shed light on the outcomes of the transformation processes in each case.

REFERENCES

ARGYRIS, C. and D. A. SCHON (1978). *Organizational Learning.* Reading, MA: Addison-Wesley.

ASHBY, W. R. (1956). "Self-regulation and requisite variety," in *Introduction to Cybernetics.* London: John Wiley.

BERNE, E. (1961). *Transactional Analysis in Psychotherapy.* New York: Grove Press.

BOISOT, M. (1987). *Information and Organizations: The Manager as Anthropologist.* London: Fontana/Collins.

CHECKLAND, P. B. and J. SCHOLES (1990). *Soft Systems Methodology in Action.* Chichester: John Wiley.

HAMEL, G. and A. HEENE (eds.) (1994). *Competence-Based Competition.* New York: John Wiley.

—— and C. K. PRAHALAD (1994). *Competing for the Future.* Boston: Harvard Business School Press.

KAPLAN, R. S. and D. P. NORTON (1992). "The balanced scorecard: Measures that drive performance," *Harvard Business Review,* Jan.–Feb., 71–9.

LEI, D., M. J. HITT, and R. BETTIS (1996). "Dynamic core competences through meta-learning and strategic context," *Journal of Management,* 22, 549–69.

MERALI, Y. (1997). "Information, systems, and *dasein*," in F. Stowell (ed.) *People, Organizations, and Environment.* New York: Plenum.

—— (1998). "Evaluating cognitive functions in competence leveraging," working paper, Warwick Business School.

—— (2000). "Conformity, rhetoric, and self-concept in organisational transformation," working paper, Warwick Business School.

—— and N. FREARSON (1995). "Information and realisation," unpublished Research Note.

—— and J. McGEE (1998a). "Information competences and knowledge creation at the corporate centre," in G. Hamel, C. K. Prahalad, H. Thomas, and D. O'Neal (eds.) *Strategic Flexibility: Managing in a Turbulent Environment.* Chichester: John Wiley, 195–218.

—— —— (1998b). "Planning the migration: Re-writing the script for the corporate centre," in M. Hitt, E. J. Ricarti i Costa, and R. D. Nixon (eds.) *New Managerial Mindsets: Organisational Transformation and Strategy Implementation.* Chichester: John Wiley, ch. 15.

NELSON, R. and S. WINTER (1982). *An Evolutionary Theory of Economic Change.* Cambridge; MA: Harvard University Press.

NONAKA, I. and H. TAKEUCHI (1995). *The Knowledge Creating Company.* New York: Oxford University Press.

PENROSE, E. (1959). *The Theory of the Growth of the Firm.* London: Blackwell.

PETERAF, M. A. (1993). "The cornerstones of competitive advantage: A resource-based view," *Strategic Management Journal,* 14, 179–91.

PORTER, M. E. and V. E. MILLAR (1985). "How information gives you competitive advantage," *Harvard Business Review*, Jul.–Aug., 149–60.

PRAHALAD, C. K. and R. A. BETTIS (1986). "The dominant logic: A new link between diversity and performance," *Strategic Management Journal*, 7, 485–501.

——— ——— (1995). "The dominant logic: Retrospective and extension," *Strategic Management Journal*, 16, 5–14.

RUMELT, R. (1994). "Forward," in G. Hamel and A. Heene (eds.) *Competence-Based Competition*. New York: John Wiley.

SANCHEZ, R. (1997). "Managing articulated knowledge in competence-based competition," in R. Sanchez and A. Heene (eds.), *Strategic Learning and Knowledge Management*. Chichester: John Wiley.

——— and A. HEENE (eds.) (1997). *Strategic Learning and Knowledge Management*. Chichester: John Wiley.

——— ——— and H. THOMAS (eds.) (1996). *Dynamics of Competence-Based Competition*. Oxford: Elsevier Pergamon.

SCOTT-MORTON, M. S. (1991). *The Corporation of the 1990s*. New York: Oxford University Press.

SENGE, P. M. (1990). *The Fifth Discipline*. New York: Doubleday/Century.

STONIER, T. (1990). *Information and the Internal Structure of the Universe*. New York: Springer-Verlag.

TEECE, D. J., G. PISANO, and A. SHUEN (1997). "Dynamic capabilities and strategic management," *Strategic Management Journal*, 18, 509–33.

WEICK, K. E. (1995). *Sensemaking in Organizations*. Thousand Oaks, CA: Sage Publications.

WERNERFELT, B. (1984). "A resource-based view of the firm," *Strategic Management Journal*, 5, 171–80.

3

Managing the Dissemination of Competences

JOHAN STEIN AND JONAS RIDDERSTRÅLE

INTRODUCTION

Systems to support competence building and leveraging within the modern firm are becoming increasingly complex. Today, most firms have to navigate a knowledge landscape that covers greater geographical and technological areas than ever before. Simultaneously, competences are becoming increasingly specialized and sophisticated, and product life cycles are rapidly decreasing in industry after industry. Human nature, however, remains essentially the same. This observation motivates the present discussion. Almost forty years ago Michael Polanyi (1962) remarked "We can know more than we can say." His principal argument was that knowledge is sometimes tacit, since it may be difficult to formalize and communicate. In this discussion, we explore the implications of this idea for competence dissemination.

As we see it, significant management problems can be linked to the fact that we often say less than we know. Further, people sometimes "can say more than they know" and "can hear things different from what is said"—both also critical aspects of competence management. All these phenomena result from the nature of people and the social contexts in which competences are created and exploited. Consequently, unless we base our management theories and practices on realistic assumptions about people and organizations, we risk ending up with management ideas based on nothing more than idealistic theoretical concepts. Though they may sometimes be appealing, simplistic concepts that disregard the realities of human nature and the social context are likely to have limited practical applicability.

A number of management scholars have investigated various aspects of organizational knowledge such as articulability, codifiability, and teachability (Kogut and Zander 1992; Winter 1987). Others have focused on describing the role of knowledge in processes through which new competencies are created, imitated, assimilated, disseminated, diffused, exploited, or destroyed (Hedberg 1981; Hedlund 1994; Nonaka and Takeuchi 1995). However, few of these contributions have specifically addressed more managerial aspects and implications of competence dissemination.

The theory of competence-based management offers a conceptual framework founded on some key assumptions that reflect "real-world" human and social characteristics. (Heene and Sanchez 1997; Sanchez, Heene, and Thomas 1996). Our discussion here extends the competence perspective's insistence on realism by focusing on the management of competence dissemination processes. This issue is critical, because improved competence dissemination potentially leads to a greater dispersion of competences throughout an organization and increases the likelihood of new competences being created through novel combinations of existing competences. Greater dispersion of competences may enhance internal competition and pressure for increased competence creation at more than one location. Increased competence dispersion can also decrease a firm's dependence on a relatively limited number of experts.

This discussion can be seen as offsetting rationalistic economic models that implicitly assume that people

(1) actively direct their attention to those who are supposed to "know more;"
(2) immediately understand (i.e. interpret correctly) what an expert is saying;
(3) assimilate objectively better knowledge without losing any of its content, either quantitatively or qualitatively;
(4) diffuse this knowledge to colleagues in a similar manner and for the benefit of the firm.

We will argue here that such simplistic models contradict many findings of cognitive psychology and sociology and overlook ways in which a social context often hampers processes of competence dissemination. Empirical studies substantiate that people often shift between states of "knowing more than they can say," "saying more than they know," and "hearing things different from what is said." To manage such practical problems, some managers are devising new strategies to improve the efficiency of competence dissemination processes. In our discussion we consider a number of such strategies.

THEORETICAL FOUNDATIONS

In order to describe and analyze the dissemination of competences, we adopt a socio-cognitive perspective on organizational processes. From this perspective, competences are seen to depend on both shared beliefs about how things are and how things should be done. An organization's social representations manifest these beliefs. Among social representations of this sort are various routines, such as routines for searching and selecting information. Several scholars have described the role of shared beliefs in organizational competencies. At the organizational level we find elements of shared beliefs in "paradigms" (Brown 1978), "theories in use" (Argyris and Schön 1978), "logics of action" (Karpik 1978), "rationalities of action" (Crozier and Friedberg 1980), and (within the competence perspective) "strategic logics" (Sanchez, Heene, and Thomas 1996). At the industry level, shared beliefs figure prominently in "industry wide conventional practices" (Cyert and March 1963), "consensual beliefs" (Porac, Thomas, and Baden-Fuller 1989), "industrial wisdoms" (Hellgren and Melin 1993), "dominant logics" (Prahalad and Bettis 1986), and "industry recipes" (Spender 1989).

In the theory of competence-based competition, scholars have argued that managerial cognition plays an important role in directing competence building processes both within and between organizations (Gorman, Thomas, and Sanchez 1996). Competition has even been described as "a contest between managerial cognitions" (Sanchez and Heene 1997). Several contributions to the theory of competence-based competition highlight ways in which cognitive processes influence the building and leveraging of competences (cf. Boisot, Griffiths, and Moles 1997; Durand 1997; Sanchez 1997; Sanchez and Heene 1996; van der Vorst 1997). Among other things, these contributions accentuate how managers' cognitive processes of detection and interpretation affect the ability of a firm to respond to environmental changes. For example, van der Vorst (1997) refers to an organization's "blind spots" as a bias in competence building and leveraging that results when managers' cognitive processes are focused on a specific set of beliefs about an organization's environment.

Our socio-cognitive perspective builds on the assumption that individuals are constrained creators of competence. This constraint is the consequence of our bounded rationality (Cyert and March 1963; March and Simon 1958). Boundedly rational individual cognitions, in turn, influence emotions, needs, values, interests, intentions, and expectations. Jointly, these factors govern action and the interpretation of action (Locke and Henne 1986). Our discussion here addresses a number of cognitive skills that managers may use to cope with bounded cognitive capacity.

Since human attention is limited in capacity, of necessity we must be selective in gathering and attempting to process information in order to avoid information overload. Even so, not all the information we attend to can be remembered fully or accurately. Limited memory, structured in terms of cognitive schemes and scripts, is used to impute meaning to stimuli (sensory inputs). Sensemaking inevitably involves processes of reduction and extrapolation (Reed 1988). In reduction, the amount of information is reduced when meaning is created because current stimuli are matched or related to prior stimuli that may not correspond fully or exactly to the current stimuli. In extrapolation, prior situations invoked in matching long-term memory to current stimuli add information to the sensory input.

Along with heuristics, long-term memory (experience) is used to process information (Anderson 1990). Cognitive processing may be automatic when it proceeds without intention and without giving rise to conscious awareness (Posner and Snyder 1975). For instance, some routines or skills are so well-rehearsed that they require very minimal active cognitive capacity (attention). Distinct signals from the social context may be needed to attract the awareness of individuals; very strong signals may be needed before they begin to question their experiences (Anderson 1990; Posner 1989).

The outcome of information processing through reduction and extrapolation is meaning (understanding). Such meaning can be referred to as belief, which implies that beliefs fundamentally exist in the minds of "individuals." The needs, values, interests, intentions, and expectations that result from individual beliefs are thus all highly personal and vary distinctly between individuals (Swanson and Hansen 1988; Lubinski, Benbow, and Ryan 1995). Therefore, what one individual believes and takes to be "knowledge" may not be knowledge for someone else.

A number of cognitive biases contribute to our bounded cognitive capacity. For instance, individuals typically first try to verify, rather than falsify, their experiences in the process of enacting beliefs (Simon 1989). Also, we commonly tend to overestimate the likelihood of events that are easy to recall or imagine from our experiences. As a consequence of these two heuristic biases, individuals often overgeneralize their experiences to contexts that differ from those in which their experiences were gained. Moreover, humans do not often think like good statisticians. Everyday beliefs or theories about "how things are or should be" are often based on a few, possibly quite dissimilar events. Such beliefs would not qualify as theories in a scientific community with strict requirements for establishing the validity and reliability of beliefs. However, because individuals need to economize in using their limited cognitive capacity to process information, we often build our "knowledge" on such logically and empirically "weak" theories.

An individual's knowledge does not need to stem from his or her own real-life experiences, because we have the capacity to undertake "internal simulation" (Gardenfors 1992), which means that we can produce "new experiences" simply by connecting and combining prior experiences. Internal simulation is often referred to as *intuition,* since we are not able to directly relate a given situation to a prior real-life situation. Moreover, individuals often think that their experiences are genuine, even though they are really the result of an internal simulation process.

Emotions and cognition also influence when and to what extent individuals question their knowledge. Potential dissatisfaction with some bit of knowledge will vary with an individual's "level of aspiration" (Cyert and March 1963), which in turn emanates from that individual's cognitive and emotional processes. Aspiration levels in a group of people may therefore vary considerably. Some individuals are very sensitive to the reliability and performance of their theories, whereas others are much more forgiving and tolerant. People who have this form of sensitivity question their theories more regularly (Anderson 1983). As a result, certain individuals are more learning oriented, and they are more likely to develop new knowledge to replace old knowledge deemed unsatisfactory.

Individuals are not just passive perceivers of their environments. We are active constructors of meaning (Weick 1979). Information that an individual receives is decoded, through reduction and extrapolation, into some kind of meaning for that receiver (Bourne *et al.* 1986; Weick 1995). As a result, the specific meaning a receiver attaches to a bit of information may be quite different from the original meaning intended by the sender.

A sender of information encodes some knowledge in the form of written, verbal, and nonverbal symbols that can be transmitted. Thus, senders transmit symbols which they themselves can decode. There are several reasons why receivers do not interpret information exactly as intended by senders, including reasons that depend on the sender, the receiver, and the social context (we discuss the social context in the next section).

As for senders, their knowledge may be tacit (Polanyi 1962) and they may be unable to find a symbol that exactly represents what they know. Individuals will vary in their abilities to create symbols which enable others to decode their knowledge, since some symbols are more ambiguous than others (Goldhaber 1993). Needs, values, and interests of senders may also come into play. For instance, people can intentionally use ambiguous symbols to make others more dependent on them (Pfeffer 1981). Further, they may strengthen a desired identity by giving others partial, but not full, access to their knowledge (Goldhaber 1993).

Receivers may also lack the ability to understand others, as a result of their limited cognitive capacity and prior experiences (Anderson 1990; Posner 1989). Their experiences and emotions may also influence them to interpret information in different ways than those intended by the sender (Ortony, Clore, and Collins 1988). It is not unusual in management, as in other areas of human activity, for people to miscommunicate because key words used in their communications have meanings not fully explained or understood in an appropriate way by the communicating parties.

LIMITING STRUCTURES: HOW THE SOCIAL CONTEXT AFFECTS COMPETENCE CREATION

Further restrictions are placed upon individuals' abilities to receive knowledge as a consequence of the structures and systems inherent in the organizations which they inhabit. In this way social context influences the nature and direction of knowledge and competence creation processes (Ridderstråle 1996; Stein 1996). Four factors in particular may support or hamper both the will and ability of individuals to disseminate and create knowledge. The discussion in this section will focus on the impact of these four factors: economic, cultural, political, and technical structures.

Schumpeter (1936) and Rosenberg (1976), among others, stress the importance of economic incentives in stimulating behavior. Thus, a certain set of incentives may stimulate one type of dissemination process whereas another set may yield different and even opposite results. What Schumpeter and Rosenberg argue is that both individuals and firms are rent-seekers. However, collectively shared beliefs, including norms and values, can also influence individuals to disseminate knowledge—even when this behavior does not bring them gains. For instance, individuals may feel they have a moral obligation to share some knowledge. Some cultures, on the other hand, foster a form of individualism that makes people less prone to say what they know (Hofstede 1980). Apart from individualism, culture can also make individuals reluctant or unwilling to disseminate their knowledge, since it may not be legitimate in that culture "to tell the whole truth" (Goldhaber 1993).

The distribution of power may also influence the dissemination of knowledge. Those who can influence others to conform to their intentions can be regarded as powerful (Bourdieu 1977; Giddens 1984; Pfeffer 1981). In addition to legal authority (Weber 1947), power can be based on the ability to provide access to scarce resources or knowledge, the ability to define norms, to control information flows, etc. (Mintzberg 1983; Pfeffer 1981). Power may create situations in which people cannot be totally frank and open, because it could be politically hazardous to do so.

Technical or functional structures in a society or an organization may also influence the dissemination of knowledge in numerous ways. Through horizontal and vertical division of labor, groups of individuals are organized into roles centered around specialized tasks and capabilities. As a consequence, individuals often come to build their identity around roles which promote the development of specialized knowledge and capabilities. Vygotsky (1962) argues that people belong to "*communities of practice*" in which they share knowledge that is both a "*signature*" of their belonging to this community and a major source of change. As the complexity of knowledge increases, it becomes more difficult for individuals to absorb new knowledge (Winter 1987). Sometimes advanced absorptive capacities may be needed to assimilate new knowledge (Cohen and Levinthal 1990). Familiarity with terminology is often required to access fields of knowledge (Simons 1989; Weick 1995). This specialization of language results from the ongoing division of labor. As a result of specialization of work and language, it often becomes difficult for individuals to take part in wider conversations beyond their own specializations.

PROBLEMS IN MANAGING PROCESSES OF KNOWLEDGE DISSEMINATION

Polanyi has suggested that "we can know more than we can say." Since knowledge may be tacit, it may sometimes be difficult to codify and transfer. The skills required to win a major contract, for example, may not be easy to communicate. Two aspects of this communication problem are worth noting. *Articulation* of knowledge itself may be difficult, i.e. we have difficulty creating any kinds of adequate symbols at all. However, it can also be that one symbol or set of symbols may not fit all groups, and this impedes transfer of competence across hierarchical levels and departmental boundaries or over institutional and geographical borders. As a consequence, problems of adaptation often occur.[1]

In addition, sometimes knowledge is, often consciously, withheld by people in an organization. Three aspects of the social reasons why people may say less than they know are worth mentioning. Sometimes people keep information confidential so that it can be used advantageously at a later date. We refer to this situation as *monopolization* of knowledge. Information, if not used now, may be regarded as a "knowledge-option" to be used at a later date—e.g. when an appropriate problem or situation comes along.

Withholding information may also result from *fear of retaliation*. Some issues in an organization are taboo, and it is not acceptable to discuss these things. For instance, it may be "forbidden" to question the current strategy or organizational structure of the firm. Moreover, in some companies it is not acceptable for subordinates to disagree with the boss, even in cases when the subordinates have knowledge that suggests the boss is wrong. People may choose silence rather than risk their jobs or future promotions.

[1] Sanchez (1997) takes exception with some scholars who seem to assume that "tacit knowledge" includes knowledge that is fundamentally incapable of articulation by individuals. In our discussion, we refer to tacit knowledge as knowledge that can in principle be articulated with the help of some symbols, even though this may be difficult.

The further aspect of organizations that limits communication of knowledge relates to *restrictions* imposed by the lack of an appropriate infrastructure for knowledge transfer and transformation in some firms. This constraint will limit the ability to spread knowledge to others when the number of people we can (or are allowed to) communicate with is limited. Restrictions may result from the physical architecture or geographical dispersion of a company, but they can also result from established reporting relationships, norms determining who gets to take part in meetings, and the nature of a firm's information systems.

It is also common that "we can say more than we know." This observation has two interpretations. As argued earlier, through *extrapolation* and *reduction* individuals often build complex theories on rather limited empirical foundations. These "theories" are then typically generalized—indeed, sometimes *overgeneralized*—across situations and time. Further, people sometimes resort to *manipulation* and *exaggeration* (i.e. lying, cheating, and boasting) to gain personal advantages, to avoid problems, or just to impress people.

Finally, it is also the case that "we can hear things different from what is said." As outlined earlier, people exercise selective attention, and we often selectively pay attention to information that is consistent with our earlier experience. Moreover, our *interpretation* of enacted information tends to be to our own advantage. Sometimes, information may have a significant emotional or political component. When information is affective, the same message can be interpreted as either criticism or praise, depending on the sender. Finally, sometimes we simply lack appropriate schema for interpreting certain kinds of information, and may invoke a familiar but inappropriate interpretive schema.

STRATEGIES FOR MANAGING KNOWLEDGE DISSEMINATION

In this section, we will draw on some results from our empirical studies within our framework to clarify some of the problems managers face when trying to promote dissemination of knowledge. We also discuss some strategies used to manage these problems (see Table 3.1.).

Several case studies provided insights into processes of knowledge dissemination in building and leveraging competences. Our studies included interviews with sixteen top-level managers at three firms: Ericsson Components, ABB Signal, and CelsiusTech Systems. Secondary sources such as internal documents provided further data. Following procedures advocated by van de Ven and Poole (1990) for studying innovation processes, a list of key events in each firm's competence building and leveraging processes was established. Our unit of analysis was processes for "dissemination of knowledge."[2] Patterns of activity initially observed in our studies were continuously compared against new observations.

---

[2] Van de Ven and Poole (1990: 320) define such processes as "major recurrent activity or a change in one of the core concepts in the research framework."

TABLE 3.1   *Problems and strategies for managing processes of knowledge dissemination*

Knowledge dissemination aspect	Problems	Strategies
"Know more than we can say"	Articulation	Socialization & Education
	Monopolization	Compensation & Documentation
	Retaliation	Toleration & Motivation
	Restriction	Communication & Rotation
"Say more than we know"	Extrapolation/Reduction	Communication & Reflection
	Manipulation/Exaggeration	Correction & Selection
"Hear things different from what is said"	Extrapolation/Reduction	Socialization & Standardization

The head offices of all three companies are situated in Stockholm, Sweden. Ericsson Components, with some 1600 employees, is a supplier of advanced microelectronic and power components. The largest single buyer is the Ericsson Group. ABB Signal AB (now called AdTranz), which is part of the ABB Group, has around 400 employees and supplies customized signaling solutions for railways. The third company, CelsiusTech Systems, employs 900 people and specializes in advanced systems technology for a wide range of defense and civil applications. The problems of knowledge dissemination evident in our case studies can be grouped into three main issues we have identified: (i) people may know more than they can readily say; (ii) people may say more than they know; and (iii) people may hear things different from what is said.

Knowing more than we can say

In managing the articulation of knowledge, the use of *socialization* and *education* stand out in our analysis. Several methods were applied in the companies we studied to promote socialization. When recruiting personnel, their "social competence" is deemed an important criterion. The telecommunications company Ericsson distinguishes and evaluates an employee's technical/professional competence, business competence, and human competence. The human competence concerns interactions with people and an individual's communicative capabilities and cultural awareness (Ericsson 1996).

Further, team work and the promotion of a strong company culture were thought to stimulate dissemination of knowledge through social interaction. Top executives of these firms say that they take great care to create emotional ties between the company and its employees. These ties help to promote increased sharing of knowledge within the firms, and to avoid leaking information to competitors. All of the companies we studied are dependent on their engineers. Even though a majority of the top executives say that nearly every engineer identifies himself/herself with the respective company, the R&D managers often told a different story. According to these executives, engineers appear to be more emotionally tied to their professional colleagues than to the people in their companies. Consequently, engineers primarily legitimize their actions by reference to a group of engineers rather than a group of employees within their firm. Since technical knowledge is organized around certain competence areas, engineers are socialized into these communities. Executives noted that while professional communities enhance intradisciplinary learning, they often inhibit interdisciplinary learning. Several managers added that engineers often do not want to be socialized into new functional roles. A reason for this tendency may be that they want to avoid "identity crisis" and a perceived lack of capability if they move to a new expertise domain.

Education may be a method for increasing socialization, as well as for giving individuals knowledge which facilitates encoding and decoding of information. Managers at Ericsson stated that it is important for individuals to have secondary capabilities, since otherwise it would be difficult to establish effective communication networks. Moreover, all companies mix people from different departments when composing groups for executive education courses. This blending of professional backgrounds is thought to form and strengthen interpersonal links between functions. Notably, educational efforts at all of the firms studied include activities to strengthen the emotional bonds among employees. "Know-who" is thus seen as critically important in ensuring an efficient process of "know-how" dissemination.

To handle the problem of monopolization of knowledge, companies use different *compensation* schemes (i.e. positive feedback). At Ericsson, people are explicitly evaluated on the basis of how well they disseminate knowledge. In fact, the Ericsson Group has an official definition of competence that recognizes the key role of knowledge sharing: "Competence is to acquire, use, develop, and share knowledge, skills, and experiences" (Ericsson 1996). Further, at all three firms, individuals are not only evaluated by their bosses, but also by their colleagues. For example, people are asked to rate the extent to which their colleagues contribute to their own competency development. Managers noted that dissatisfactions of coworkers about how well and to what extent an individual absorbs and disseminates knowledge often surface during these evaluations.

Moreover, *documentation* is widely used to enable as many employees as possible to gain access to critical information. Databases, usually with restricted access, are also used to support the dissemination of knowledge.

Managers seek to counter the fear of retaliation by instituting a climate of *toleration*— for mistakes, for questioning, and for experimentation. A few managers even argued that it is better to know why you have failed than to succeed without understanding why. At the same time, some managers noted that the organizational climate must not be too tolerant. It is acceptable to make mistakes, but not to make the same mistake twice. Individual responsibility to learn from mistakes is emphasized in all three firms studied. Some managers also stated that they encourage people to speak up when they believe that the company or department is moving in the wrong direction. People are presented with positive incentives to take action and to rely on their own judgment.

All three companies work actively to overcome many of the restrictions imposed by established channels of communication. At Ericsson, areas have been established in which information can be exchanged both formally and informally. Offices outside of Stockholm have been rebuilt to provide more meeting places, information technology is used to build international networks of communication, and the majority of engineers have mobile office phones. It is notable that all three companies seem to be moving toward a new type of *communication* infrastructure. The former "push-oriented" systems—top management providing the organization with information on a "need to know" basis—are being replaced by new processes that are more "pull-oriented." In these systems, critical information is made available to more people, and it is then the task of individuals to search for information on a "need to find out" basis. Combined with the *rotation* of personnel, these systems are thought to have relieved many of the restrictions of knowledge transfer of the past. However, no one believes that IT-based solutions can manage all the problems of knowledge sharing. Rather, IT systems must be treated as complements to increased interpersonal contacts.

Saying more than we know

Managers in the firms we studied also try to address "weak" theories that result from reduction and extrapolation by increasing communication between people with different perspectives. Some managers stressed that this process has to start with themselves—they should be role models for others. Thus, they personally take great care in trying to be as *reflective* as possible. A problem recognized by a few managers, however, is that this behavior can sometimes be interpreted as a sign of weakness and indecisiveness.

When engaged in discussions, some managers also try to encourage people to explain not only their views and opinions, but also their basic assumptions. This process helps to explore why certain measures may be necessary in certain situations, and how these actions are supposed to lead to a beneficial result. Other executives stressed the use of "stretch goals," believing they can have a positive impact. By challenging the organization, these managers hope to create instability that will trigger increased communication and reflection and force people to question the *status quo*.

Problems of manipulation and exaggeration of knowledge are handled by both *correction* of current employees, and by careful *selection* of new organization members. Several managers argued that it is important to take rapid and decisive steps in critiquing people who appear to be putting their own personal interests before those of the organization. Just as compensation may be the carrot, correction is the stick. According to some managers at the three companies, the use of negative feedback had not been a common practice for a long time in their organizations. Other managers said that they try to discuss with employees how their individual goals can be linked to those of the business—a discussion that is also critical when recruiting people. The majority of managers argued that the relationship between employer and employee has to be based on mutual trust and benefit. As suggested earlier, a number of the managers said that it is not just the technical skills of people that matter, but more generally their ability to contribute to the development of others within the organization.

Hearing things different from what is said

Finally, difficulties related to the interpretation of what others are saying often resulted from the different terminologies and vocabularies used in different fields of technology. In this regard, *socialization* was felt not only to contribute to more rapid articulation, but also to make interpretations less heterogeneous. Further, the firms studied make efforts to *standardize* the language (symbols) and frameworks of employees. By training people in a similar manner, and by exposing them to carefully chosen models and frameworks, managers hope to develop a more homogeneous interpretation of symbols. If a common, pull-oriented information system provides essential infra- and infostructure, a common language enables mutual understanding, while language differences often lead to unnecessary argumentation. For accurate knowledge creation and dissemination to take place, it is critical that sender and receiver communicate within a shared framework of meaning.

CONCLUDING REMARKS

We have argued that a framework for analyzing competence management must rest on realistic assumptions about the nature of people and the social contexts in which knowledge is created and disseminated. Bounded rationality must be recognized as limiting the ability of people in organizations to create and interpret knowledge. Moreover, the economic, cultural, political, and technical infrastructures of social contexts also influence the creation and transfer of knowledge and thus the management of competence. We have tried to explain various reasons why boundedly rational people in social contexts are likely to "know more than they can say," "say more than they know," and "hear things different from what is said."

To overcome the practical problems of managing knowledge that result from these limitations and distortions, managers must take action to improve the efficiency and coherence of knowledge dissemination processes. We have described some ways in which managers can try to influence the will and the ability of individuals to both diffuse and assimilate knowledge. We have briefly related some methods that executives at Ericsson, ABB, and CelsuisTech are using to create conditions that facilitate knowledge dissemination. The ongoing challenge to these and other organizations is to find new and better ways to help people say more fully and precisely what they know, and hear (and understand) more exactly the knowledge that others can share with them.

REFERENCES

ANDERSON, C. R. (1983). "Motivational and performance deficits in interpersonal strategies: The effects of attributional style," *Journal of Personality and Social Psychology*, 16, 53–66.

ANDERSON, J. R. (1990). *Cognitive Psychology and its Implications*. New York: Freeman.

ARGYRIS, C. and D. SCHÖN (1978). *Organizational Learning: A Theory of Action Perspective*. Reading, MA: Addison-Wesley.

BOISOT, M., D. GRIFFITHS and V. MOLES (1997). "The dilemma of competence," in R. Sanchez and A. Heene (eds.), *Strategic Learning and Knowledge Management*. Chichester: John Wiley.

BOURDIEU, P. (1977). *Outline of a Theory of Practice*. Cambridge: Cambridge University Press.

BOURNE, L. E., R. L. DOMINOWSKI, E. F. LOFTUS, and A. F. HEALY (1986). *Cognitive Processes*. Englewood Cliffs, NJ: Prentice-Hall.

BROWN, R. H. (1978). "Bureaucracy as praxis: Toward a political phenomenology of formal organizations," *Administrative Science Quarterly*, 23, 365–82.

COHEN, W. and D. LEVINTHAL (1990). "Absorptive capability: A new perspective of learning and innovation," *Administrative Science*, 35, 128–52.

CROZIER, M. and E. FRIEDBERG (1980). *Actors and Systems: The Politics of Collective Action*. Chicago: University of Chicago Press.

CYERT, R. and J. G. MARCH (1963). *A Behavioral Theory of the Firm*. Englewood Cliffs, NJ: Prentice-Hall.

DURAND, T. (1997). "Strategizing for innovation: Competence analysis in assessing strategic change," in A. Heene and R. Sanchez (eds.), *Competence-Based Strategic Management*. Chichester: John Wiley.

ERICSSON (company document) (1996). *The Ericsson Competence Model*. Stockholm: Ericsson.

GARDENFORS, P. (1992). *Blotta Tanken*. Nora: Nya Doxa.

GIDDENS, A. (1984). *The Constitution of Society: Outline of the Theory of Structuration*. Berkeley: University of California Press.

GOLDHABER, G. M. (1993). *Organizational Communication*. Madison, WI: Brown & Benchmark.

GORMAN, P., H. THOMAS, and R. SANCHEZ (1996). "Industry dynamics in competence-based competition," in R. Sanchez, A. Heene, and H. Thomas (eds.), *Dynamics of Competence-Based Competition: Theory and Practice in the New Strategic Management*. Oxford: Elsevier Pergamon.

HEDBERG, B. (1981). "How organizations learn and unlearn," in P. Nystrom and W. Starbuck (eds.), *Handbook of Organizational Design*. London: Oxford University Press, 3–27.

HEDLUND, G. (1994). "A model of knowledge management and the N-form corporation," *Strategic Management Journal*, 15 (Summer Special Issue).

HEENE, A. and R. SANCHEZ (eds.) (1997). *Competence-Based Strategic Management*. Chichester: John Wiley.

HELLGREN, B. and L. MELIN (1993). "The role of strategists' way-of-thinking in strategic change processes," in J. Hendry, G. Johnson, and J. Newton (eds.), *Strategic Thinking: Leadership and the Management of Change*. New York: John Wiley.

HOFSTEDE, G. (1980). "Culture and organizations," *International Studies of Management*, 10 (4), 15–42.

KAHNEMAN, D. and A. TVERSKY (1982). "The simulation heuristic," in D. Kahneman, P. Slovic, and A. Tversky (eds.), *Judgment under Uncertainty: Heuristics and Biases*. New York: Cambridge University Press, 201–8.

KARPIK, L. (1978). *Organizations and Environment: Theory, Issues, and Reality*. London: Sage.

KOGUT, B. and U. ZANDER (1992). "Knowledge of the firm: Combinative capabilities and the replication of technology," *Organization Science*, 3, 383–97.

LOCKE, E. A. and D. HENNE (1986). "Work motivation theories," in C. Cooper and I. Robertson (eds.), *International Review of Industrial and Organizational Psychology*. Chichester: John Wiley, 1–35.

LUBINSKI, D., C. P. BENBOW, and J. RYAN (1995). "Stability of vocational interest among intellectually gifted from adolescence to adulthood: A 15-year longitudinal study," *Journal of Applied Psychology*, 80, 139–61.

MARCH, J. G. and H. SIMON (1958). *Organizations*. New York: John Wiley.

MINTZBERG, H. (1983). *Power in and around Organizations*. Englewood Cliffs, NJ: Prentice-Hall.

NONAKA, I. and H. TAKEUCHI (1995). *The Knowledge-Creating Company*. Oxford: Oxford University Press.

ORTONY, A., G. CLORE, and A. COLLINS (1988). *The Cognitive Structure of Emotions*. Cambridge: Cambridge University Press.

PFEFFER, J. (1981). *Power in Organizations*. Marshfield, MA: Pitman.

POLANYI, M. (1962). *Personal Knowledge: Towards a Post-Critical Philosophy*. Garden City, NJ: Doubleday.

PORAC, J. F., H. THOMAS, and C. BADEN-FULLER (1989). "Competitive groups as cognitive communities: The case of Scottish knitwear manufacturers," *The Journal of Management Studies*, 26 (4), 397–417.

POSNER, M. I. (1989). *Foundations of Cognitive Science*. Cambridge, MA: MIT Press.

—— and C. R. SNYDER (1975). "Attention and cognitive control," in R. Solso (ed.), *Information Processing and Cognition*. Hillsdale, NJ: Erlbaum.

PRAHALAD, C. K. and R. A. BETTIS (1986). "The dominant logic: A new strategic linkage between diversity and performance," *Strategic Management Journal*, 7 (6), 485–501.

REED, S. K. (1988). *Cognition: Theory and Applications*. Pacific Grove, CA: Brooks/Cole.

RIDDERSTRÅLE, J. (1996). *Global Innovation: Managing International Innovation Projects at ABB and Electrolux*. Stockholm: Institute of International Business, Stockholm School of Economics.

ROSENBERG, N. (1976). *Perspectives on Technology*. Cambridge: Cambridge University Press.

SANCHEZ, R. (1997). "Managing articulated knowledge in competence-based competition," in R. Sanchez and A. Heene (eds.), *Strategic Learning and Knowledge Management*. Chichester: John Wiley.

—— and A. HEENE (1996). "A systems view of the firm in competence-based competition," in R. Sanchez, A. Heene, and H. Thomas (eds.), *Dynamics of Competence-Based Competition: Theory and Practice in the New Strategic Management*. Oxford: Elsevier Pergamon.

—— —— (1997). "Competence-based strategic management: Concepts, issues for theory, research, and practice," in A. Heene and R. Sanchez (eds.), *Competence-Based Strategic Management*. Chichester: John Wiley.

—— —— and H. THOMAS (eds.) (1996). *Dynamics of Competence-Based Competition: Theory and Practice in the New Strategic Management*. Oxford: Elsevier Pergamon.

SCHUMPETER, J. A. (1936). *The Theory of Economic Development*. Cambridge, MA: Harvard University Press.

SIMON, H. A. (1989). *Models of Thought, volume 2*. New Haven: Yale University Press.

SIMONS, H. W. (ed.) (1989). *Rhetoric in the Human Science*. London: Sage.

SPENDER, J.-C. (1989). *Industry Recipes: The Nature and Sources of Managerial Judgement*. Oxford: Basil Blackwell.

STEIN, J. (1996). *Lärande inom och mellan Organizations* (Learning within and between Organizations). Lund: Studentlitteratur.

SWANSON, J. L. and J. C. HANSEN (1988). "Stability and vocational interests over 4-year, 8-year, and 12-year intervals," *Journal of Vocational Behavior*, 33, 185–202.

VAN DE VEN, A. H. and M. S. POOLE (1990). "Methods for studying innovation development in the Minnesota innovation research program," *Organization Science*, 1, 313–34.

VAN DER VORST, R. (1997). "The blind spots of competence identification: A system-theoretic perspective," in A. Heene and R. Sanchez (eds.), *Competence-Based Strategic Management*. Chichester: John Wiley.

VYGOTSKY, L. S. (1962). *Thought and Language*. Cambridge, MA: MIT Press.

WEBER, M. (1947). *The Theory of Social and Economic Organization*. New York: Oxford University Press.

WEICK, K. (1979). *The Social Psychology of Organizing*. Belmont: Addison-Wesley.

—— (1995). *Sensemaking in Organizations*. Thousand Oaks, CA: Sage.

WINTER, S. (1987). "Knowledge and competence as strategic assets," in D. Teece (ed.), *The Competitive Strategy: Strategies for Industrial Innovation and Renewal*. Cambridge, MA: Ballinger.

4

Competence-Based Competition: Gaining Knowledge from Client Relationships[1]

PETTERI SIVULA, FRANS A. J. VAN DEN BOSCH, AND TOM ELFRING

INTRODUCTION

Knowledge creation and organizational learning have become central concerns in strategic management. Theory and research in strategic management have generally focused on firms' internal processes for knowledge creation, integration, and sharing (Grant 1996; Kogut and Zander 1992). Less attention has been paid to *how* firms acquire and absorb knowledge from various external sources. Recent contributions to the competence-based approach to management, however, have pointed to strategic alliances and collaborative partnerships with clients as potential sources of firm-addressable knowledge (Quelin 1997; Sivula, van den Bosch, and Elfring 1997; Stein 1997). Innovation studies (e.g. von Hippel 1988) showed that users and clients often create new knowledge and innovations that can be commercialized by upstream firms. These studies suggest that a firm's interactions with its customers may be an important source of new knowledge. In the discussion below, we analyze customer relationships as a source of new organizational knowledge.

We define organizational knowledge in broad terms to include tacit or uncodified knowledge as well as explicit and codified knowledge. Knowledge absorption from customer relationships involves two key processes of organizational learning: (1) creating new knowledge within the firm from client relationships, and (2) leveraging this new knowledge within the firm and in client relationships. The management of such learning and knowledge leveraging processes is critical to a firm's ability to build new organizational competences (Sanchez and Heene 1997). We study these processes in the context of knowledge intensive business service firms (abbreviated as "BSF"),

[1] A previous version of this paper was presented at the Fourth International Conference on Competence-Based Management, June 20–8, 1998, Oslo, Norway. The authors gratefully acknowledge the valuable comments of Ron Sanchez. Moreover, they would like to thank the management of both case companies for providing the opportunity to do in-depth case research. This research was funded by Erasmus Research Institute of Advanced Studies in Management (ERASM).

including both specialist and general management consulting firms, to gain insights into processes of strategic organizational learning.

Several kinds of interactions with BSF clients create important forms of knowledge that often remain tacit in BSFs (Sivula, van den Bosch, and Elfring 1997). These important forms of knowledge include experience and skills (Penrose 1959), understanding the particular circumstances of a client's business context (Hayek 1945), and knowledge about how to develop client contacts (Mills and Moberg 1990). In our discussion, we consider how in knowledge-intensive BSFs the processes of knowledge absorption (Cohen and Levinthal 1990), development, and deployment depend on certain characteristics of the client's context in which these knowledge processes take place. We also analyze the processes of knowledge absorption, development, and deployment, and their impact on the content of knowledge acquired, to gain insights into processes of organizational competence building. The potential for client relationships to generate strategically important knowledge depends on the extent to which knowledge derived from one client relationship may be re-used in other client relationships. We argue that the potential to derive strategically useful knowledge depends on interaction intensity and duration. The more interactive the client–BSF relationship, the more knowledge creation and absorption processes may take place, and the longer-term the client relationship, the better the opportunity for the absorption and the utilization of useful knowledge.

The *research questions* we address are: (1) What type of knowledge is absorbed from clients; and (2) How does a client context influence knowledge absorption? We present two conceptual frameworks and a typology of client relationships to answer these questions. The first framework describes the transfer and transformation of knowledge in a BSF–client relationship. The second framework describes the type of knowledge absorbed in four different types of client relationships. These frameworks will be illustrated by case studies of KPMG in the Netherlands and Tieto Group in Finland.

KPMG and Tieto Group are management consulting firms that typify knowledge intensive BSFs (for more extensive descriptions of these firms, see Sivula 1997). BSFs offer a useful context for studying knowledge absorption from customers. Effective service delivery often requires close interactions between service provider and the customer (Fuchs 1968), because service production and service consumption are typically intrinsically overlapping (Mills and Moberg 1990). The inseparability of a firm's and its customer's activities in knowledge-intensive service delivery requires interactive encounters with customers, which are essential to achieve the transfer of tacit knowledge from the client to the BSF. After presenting two brief case studies of knowledge absorption from clients, we discuss some implications for management of knowledge in various kinds of client relationships.

KNOWLEDGE EXCHANGE IN CLIENT INTERACTIONS

In this section we develop a conceptual framework for describing and analyzing the transfer and transformation of knowledge in a BSF's customer relationships. To this end, we first discuss some important properties of knowledge, such as distinctions between tacit and uncodified knowledge and explicit and codified knowledge. Second, we elaborate on the important interplay between tacit and explicit knowledge. Third, knowledge exchange in client relationships is described and a conceptual framework for classifying forms of knowledge exchange is proposed.

On the nature of knowledge in client relationships

The degrees of *explicitness* and of *codification* are fundamental characteristics of knowledge (Boisot 1983, 1998; Nonaka 1994; Sanchez 1997). The explicitness of knowledge is the extent to which an individual has articulated some (previously tacit) knowledge in a form that can be understood by at least some other people (Sanchez 1997). Explicit knowledge may take the form of oral or written statements, diagrams, drawings, or other representations. Explicit knowledge can be codified—i.e. placed in some ordering framework or hierarchical structure that identifies forms of knowledge and their relationships. The degree of codification influences the transferability of knowledge and the mechanisms of knowledge transfer. Codified knowledge may be stored in tangible sources such as databanks, manuals, directives, professional journals, etc., and transferred by various technical means of transmission or transportation.

Nonaka (1994: 16) has suggested that "knowledge that can be expressed in words and numbers only represents the tip of the iceberg of the entire body of possible knowledge." Knowledge may remain tacit and uncodified because it is difficult to articulate (Polanyi 1966). Some forms of tacit knowledge include *experiential knowledge* that is often transferred by active participation (Penrose 1959) and *circumstantial knowledge* that is highly context dependent (Hayek 1945). Uncodified knowledge is "unorganized knowledge" (Hayek 1945: 521): "There is beyond question a body of very important but unorganized knowledge which cannot possibly be called scientific in the sense of knowledge of general rules: the knowledge of particular circumstances of time and place."

Important forms of uncodified or tacit knowledge in BSFs may be associated with (1) the skills and capabilities (coordinated set of activities) of employees and teams and (2) experiential and circumstantial knowledge, such as knowledge about the values and unwritten rules of conduct specific to a given context (e.g. a client's organization). Knowledge may commonly remain (i) tacit because it is difficult to articulate and transfer (Polanyi 1966) and/or (ii) uncodified because it changes with rapidly changing circumstances (Hayek 1945). As Nonaka noted: "Tacit knowledge is deeply rooted in action, commitment, and involvement in a specific context" (1994: 16). The transfer of tacit knowledge is usually slow and may often be transferred only to a limited audience (Boisot, Griffiths, and Moles 1997).

Tacit knowledge may be based in skills that are realized and improved through action. Uncodified circumstantial knowledge, because it is context- or time-specific knowledge, may be realized and improved through interaction with the environment. High context-specificity may also limit the usefulness of articulating and codifying tacit knowledge. For these forms of knowledge, it may be easier and faster to learn by trying to articulate, codify, and transfer explicit knowledge. Rather, the transfer of tacit knowledge is often accomplished through participation and interaction.

Interplay between uncodified and codified knowledge

The literature suggests a number of classifications of knowledge. For example, Norman and Ramirez (1994) classified knowledge as generative, productive, and representative. In their classification scheme, generative knowledge is associated with the creation and absorption of new knowledge that provides the basis for a knowledge-intensive BSF's service production (based on productive knowledge) and service delivery (based on representative knowledge). In a service context, knowledge transfer and transformation are overlapping. Service production and delivery are often simultaneous, and it may be difficult to make a distinction between the use of productive and representative knowledge.

In Nonaka's (1994) analysis of knowledge creation in organizations, knowledge may be created by:

(1) socialization: tacit knowledge of one person becomes tacit knowledge of another person;
(2) combination: explicit knowledge is combined with other explicit knowledge;
(3) externalization: tacit knowledge is articulated to become explicit knowledge;
(4) internalization: explicit knowledge becomes tacit knowledge.

In our framework we emphasize the process of *knowledge transfer* in these processes.

The degree of codification of knowledge influences the transferability of knowledge between the knowledge-intensive BSF and its business environment. Boisot (1983) has suggested that organizational knowledge undergoes a transformation from uncodified to codified to uncodified (externalization followed by internalization in the Nonaka framework). The diffusion of knowledge in the cycle is determined by the degree of codification: more codified knowledge is more easily diffused. The codification process transforms unorganized personal knowledge into classified and documented forms of knowledge through processes of abstraction, structuring, and classification. Abstraction transforms knowledge into forms that can be applied to a more extensive and varied range of phenomena, thereby improving individual knowledge processing capacities and creating mental economies (Boisot 1983). Structuring and classifying knowledge, on the other hand, improve the transferability of knowledge (Sanchez 1997). However, the abstraction process inherent in codification reduces the "richness" of tacit knowledge. As Boisot pointed out: "Codification always involves a data sacrifice . . . Science and technology both progress by eliminating complexity, by giving structure to what was hitherto ineffable, by simplifying what was intractable" (1995: 493). This leads, however, to a value paradox: "Codified knowledge is inherently more diffusable than uncodified knowledge. That is to say, as it gains in utility it loses in scarcity" (Boisot 1995: 493).

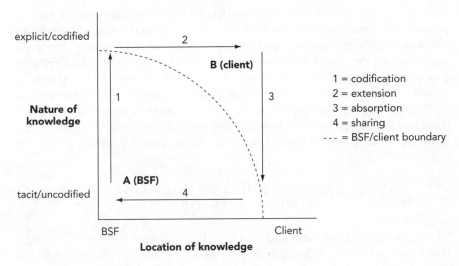

FIG. 4.1 *A framework for describing the transfer and transformation of knowledge in a BSF's customer relationships.*

A conceptual framework: knowledge transfer and transformation in BSF–client relationships

Figure 4.1 describes processes of knowledge codification, extension, absorption, and sharing in a BSF's interactions with its clients. In the codification process represented by Arrow 1, tacit knowledge is classified and explanations of causalities are articulated and generalized, making the knowledge more abstract and improving the transferability of knowledge. In the context of BSFs, knowledge codification facilitates service delivery either by enabling knowledge to be transferred directly to the client or by using codified knowledge like problem solving tools to facilitate service delivery, as represented by Arrow 2. The application of codified knowledge by the BSF in the client's context leads to learning and the creation of new knowledge, usually in tacit form. Arrow 3 represents the processes of creating new tacit knowledge about the client (unwritten rules in the client's organization, informal power structures, the client's preferences, etc.) and about ways to deliver the service (task-oriented skills). New tacit knowledge is created by individuals—including employees of the BSF—who share this knowledge internally with other BSF employees, as represented by Arrow 4.[2]

The framework summarized in Figure 4.1 suggests that the need to commercially utilize and extend its knowledge base creates incentives for a BSF to engage in a continuous knowledge exchange with its clients. Figure 4.1 may also be used as a tool for

[2] Boisot and Griffiths (2001) point out that sustaining processes for sharing internal knowledge requires an appropriate incentive structure. Van den Bosch, Volberda, and de Boer (1999) discuss how a firm's organization form and combinative capabilities influence a firm's ability to identify, assimilate, and exploit new external knowledge.

analyzing the dynamics of knowledge transfer and transformation from the point of view of a BSF. Codification and knowledge absorption (Arrows 1 and 3) *transform* the nature of knowledge. Extension and sharing (Arrows 2 and 4) *transfer* knowledge. Depending on the degree of codification of transferred knowledge, the transfer of knowledge may require different processes. Codification of knowledge in one domain (Arrow 1) facilitates its extension to another domain (Arrow 2) and decreases the need for intensive interpersonal interactions to achieve a transfer of knowledge. The transfer of tacit knowledge, however, requires more participation, interaction, face to face communication, and involvement than the transfer of codified knowledge.

CLIENT RELATIONSHIPS AS THE CONTEXT OF KNOWLEDGE ABSORPTION

To analyze knowledge absorption in a BSF's client relationships, we next develop a typology of BSF–client relationships. Our typology is based on two important *dimensions* affecting knowledge absorption: the *duration* of client relationships and the *interaction intensity* of client relationships. Longer duration and greater intensity of interactions in client relationships increase the opportunity for the absorption of tacit knowledge, because of increased opportunities to observe a client's context and organization and to interact with the client. Juxtaposing these two dimensions suggests *four different types of client relationships* (see Figure 4.2): the client partnership, the loyal client relationship, co-makership, and the market exchange relationship. We use this typology of client relationships to frame propositions about knowledge absorption opportunities in different types of client relationships. These propositions then form the basis for the analyses of our case studies.

Two dimensions of BSF–client relationships

As suggested in Table 4.1, the *interaction intensity* between the BSF and client may be either transactional or cooperative. In a transactional relationship, a client adopts an arm's length market transaction approach in interacting with the BSF. Often there is a standardized solution to a client's problem, and the client wants simply to purchase an existing, well-understood service or product. Organizational boundaries between the BSF and the client are clearly recognized and maintained. The client's concern for cost and efficiency encourage competition between suppliers, and selection of a BSF is based on the price of a desired service. Teams are not utilized or have only a limited role in service delivery.

In a cooperative relationship, close cooperation between BSF and client in service delivery is essential to solving the client's problem. The client usually does not know the nature of the solution to its problem and needs to establish a close working partner relationship with a BSF to define and solve its problem. In these processes, there may be an existing service of the BSF that solves the problem that the client is not aware of. Alternatively, there may not be any pre-existing BSF service product for the client's

TABLE 4.1   *Two dimensions of business service firm–client relationships*

Dimensions	Attributes	Characteristics
Interaction intensity in client relationships	transaction	• client typically knows solution for his or her problem • arm's length approach to suppliers • no utilization of cooperative teams • clear and high organizational boundaries between the BSF and the client organization • market driven exchange of goods/services and money • the market efficiency and the price of services dominates the relationship • competition among suppliers • one-way flow of knowledge
	cooperation	• client does not know a solution for his or her problem • cooperation in service delivery • exchange of resources (ideas, knowledge, employees) • utilization of teams • blurred organizational boundaries • two-way flow of knowledge
Duration of client relationships	short-term	• single client assignments • no bonds developed between the BSF and the client • project is in the middle of the activities • task orientation • identifiable and practical goals
	long-term	• repeat engagements • strong bonds between the BSF and the client • relationship is in the middle of the activities • long-term benefits for both parties

problem, and the client must be willing to cooperate with the BSF to create new ways of solving its problem. The utilization of BSF–client teams, in which ideas and knowledge are freely exchanged, is then required, and in this sense organizational boundaries between the BSF and the client become blurred in the team members' interactions.

The *duration* of the client relationship may be either long-term or short-term. Long-term client relationships may consist of a number of repeat engagements or a single long-term engagement. Occasional client assignments or a first-time client assignment may be categorized as short-term assignments. In short-term assignments, the current project dominates the client relationship, and the activities of the BSF are focused and task-oriented.

Figure 4.2 identifies four types of BSF–client relationships based on four combinations of interaction intensity and duration of client relationships as shown in Table 4.1: the loyal client relationship, the client partnership, co-makership, and the market exchange relationship.

The *loyal relationship* indicates a long-term relationship in which the client takes a transactional approach to the BSF. The client may need a particular service regularly, but prefers to maintain an arm's length relationship with the BSF. Typically, the client

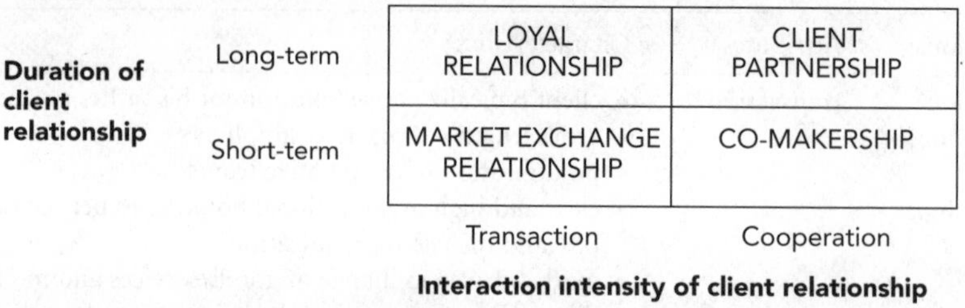

P. Sivula, F. van den Bosch, T. Elfring

Duration of client relationship	Long-term	LOYAL RELATIONSHIP	CLIENT PARTNERSHIP
	Short-term	MARKET EXCHANGE RELATIONSHIP	CO-MAKERSHIP
		Transaction	Cooperation

Interaction intensity of client relationship

Fig. 4.2 *Two dimensions of knowledge absorption opportunity: duration and interaction intensity suggest typology of four client relationships.*

is fully aware of existing solutions for fulfilling a need and prefers to use a pre-existing service product. In this case, the client knows with whom and how to solve its problem and where to get this service. The BSF has a service product that is a solution to the client's problem and is able to deliver and to a limited extent customize the service because of the BSF's experience from the repeat engagements with the client.

The *co-makership* relationship is common in the business service sector and is characterized by close interaction with the client in service delivery. Both identification of a client's problem and service delivery may require considerable interaction with the client and lead to long-term, intense interactions. Although co-makership may also occur in short-term but repeated engagements, normally the goal of co-makership is solving a client's problem on a non-recurring basis. Thus, a BSF cannot use only its earlier knowledge about a client to solve the client's problem, but must draw on other knowledge and experience about related clients, industries, and problems. To be successful in co-makership relationships, a BSF must be able to absorb specific knowledge from other client relationships and "generic" knowledge from other sources to create problem solving methods and procedures that are useful in solving problems in specific client contexts. Management consulting is often based on this kind of client relationship.

Client partnerships are cooperative client relationships that explicitly aim at achieving competitive advantage and benefit for both firms by developing and using new knowledge with the partner. In such partnerships, it is not unusual that neither the client nor the BSF have in mind a solution for the problem that they agree to work on together. A client partnership may be undertaken as a formal joint venture with the client or it may take the form of a client relationship in which the client's and the BSF's processes become closely intermingled or integrated. A loyal client relationship may develop into a client partnership, especially when there are multiple organizational points of involvement with the BSF and the BSF is interested in developing additional services of interest to the client.

A *market exchange relationship* is a "faceless" relationship in which there is no interactive or long-term cooperation between the BSF and the client. In such relationships, clients already have in mind solving their problem by using an existing standard service product of the BSF. Examples include providing non-customized software services like "off-the-shelf" programs or information services like stock market data typically provided to a large number of "faceless" clients. Services provided through market exchange relationships may be important businesses for a BSF or a means for initiating other types of client relationships, depending on the BSF's strategy.

Client relationships as contexts for knowledge absorption: an integrative framework

We now consider how the various types of client relationships we have identified may serve as platforms for organizational learning. Knowledge processes take place within each type of client relationship, but the opportunities for the creation and transfer of tacit knowledge differ in the four types of client relationships. Von Hippel (1988) emphasized the importance of distinguishing different types of new knowledge (innovations) that can be obtained from various kinds of customers. Von Hippel made a useful distinction between the "solution content" and the "need content" of new knowledge that may be derived when, for example, users developed their own prototypes of scientific instruments. We develop a classification of the *content* of transferred knowledge (solution content vs. need content) in terms of the degree of specificity of transferred knowledge (non-specific knowledge vs. client-specific knowledge).

Non-specific knowledge refers to knowledge and skills that may be leveraged from one client relationship to other client relationships without breaking commitments of confidentiality to the first client. Non-specific knowledge often takes the form of solution content, but may include client knowledge that can be used as benchmarking data in further assignments in the same industry or development of professional skills that may be used in an industry context. *Client-specific knowledge* is knowledge about the client and its internal and external environment, in either codified or tacit form, that improves a BSF's understanding of its client's goals, sensitivities, and processes. Client-specific knowledge improves a BSF's ability to suggest and offer additional services that support a client's processes or to customize its services to specific client needs. Client-specific knowledge thus often takes the form of need content. Because client-specific knowledge is idiosyncratic to a specific client, it often remains tacit within the BSF.

Figure 4.3 summarizes our *integrative framework*. In Figure 4.3, we propose that increasing duration of client relationships tends to increase the specificity of knowledge absorbed by the BSF. The longer-term the client relationship, the more opportunity for the absorption of client-specific knowledge, especially with respect to client needs. When there is opportunity for repeat engagements, BSFs have greater incentives to absorb client-specific knowledge. The less opportunity for repeat engagements, the higher the motivation for a BSF to identify and absorb non-specific (solution content) knowledge during the engagement. Interaction intensity is asserted to improve the opportunity to absorb tacit knowledge. The more intense the interaction and cooperation with the client, the more opportunity for the absorption of a client's tacit knowledge, especially "need-content" knowledge. In general, low-intensity interactions will favor absorbing "solution-content" knowledge, while higher-intensity interactions will invite absorption of "need-content" knowledge.

The integrative framework suggests several propositions, but we focus here on two propositions, each investigated through a case study in the next section. The propositions and the case studies deal with two of the four types of client relationships—the client partnership and the market exchange. In terms of the dimensions of knowledge absorption opportunities presented in Figure 4.3, these client relationships represent *polar cases*.

The extensive exchange of knowledge characteristic of client partnerships results from the intermingling and intensive interactions of the client's and the BSF's processes during a long-term cooperative engagement. We therefore propose that such processes offer good opportunities for the absorption of tacit client-specific knowledge. Market exchange relationships are characterized by low interaction intensity and short-term duration. Accordingly, we propose that the low interaction intensity of market exchange relationships generally does not favor the transfer of client-specific tacit knowledge to the BSF. We also propose that the short-term duration of the client relationship limits the opportunity for the absorption of non-specific knowledge.

TWO CASE STUDIES

In the KPMG case, the client relationship investigated was a long-term auditing relationship in the Netherlands. The research analyzed documents and interviews with employees of the BSF, including the engagement partner and a senior manager (Sivula

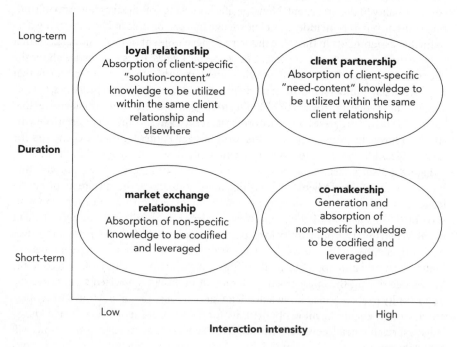

FIG. 4.3 *Key integrative framework–client relationships as contexts for knowledge absorption.*

1997). Case analyses were reviewed by the interviewed persons to validate the material. The client in the case is a large real estate fund for whom KPMG has audited the financial statements since the establishment of the fund. Cooperation between the client and KPMG has increased substantially over the years of the relationship as the client relationship became more open and the scope of contacts became broader. Opportunities developed to provide management advisory activities which went beyond auditing services. Figure 4.4 represents the knowledge absorption and transfer processes in this client relationship. The positioning of the knowledge processes (Arrows 1, 2, 3, and 4) implies that the absorption and transfer of knowledge occurs often in tacit form and primarily in the locus of the client's processes.

The case analyses established that this client relationship led to joint development of knowledge useful in solving the client's problems and for which neither the client nor the BSF had pre-existing answers. New knowledge was created through continuous, sustained cycles of knowledge creation, absorption, and transfer processes. In such processes, a client may push its BSF beyond its current limits of knowledge by asking questions that are beyond the current expertise of the BSF. There are unlikely to be disputes as to the appropriability of jointly created knowledge, and a client is likely to be willing to share highly client-specific and confidential knowledge with the BSF, when such knowledge could or will be only utilized within that client relationship. This partnership type of client relationship allowed KPMG to increase its advisory role in the client relationship and to take on new challenges and opportunities for learning. The KPMG engagement partner described the outcome of the cooperation in this client relationship:

Having these non-structured discussions, we are contributing to their process of defining issues that have strategic importance. We are not involved with the formal process of finding

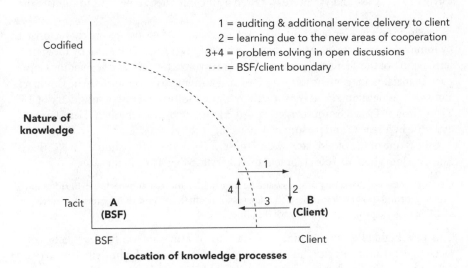

FIG. 4.4 *Knowledge processes in client relationship.*

the strategy, but we do contribute by having these discussions. It is also an advisory function, but it is not structured necessarily.

Non-specific knowledge absorbed in this client relationship was rather general in nature. The KPMG engagement partner gave an example of non-specific knowledge from this client relationship that could be applied in other contexts:

One of the things that the client has told me is that they basically want to distance themselves from certain things that the other companies in the same type of industry have been doing in terms of how they value the properties they have, how they determine income, and what the strategic things are.

Through intense interactions with the client, much tacit knowledge about client needs was absorbed. Non-specific knowledge about possible solutions was acquired from external sources. The KPMG engagement partner commented on the role of tacit knowledge in the client relationship:

Most of the knowledge that I get from the client is tacit knowledge. What are the issues that the client is dealing with, what the client perceives to be the problem, how does the client deal with these problems—that is something that is not qualified to be put in writing. You have to have interaction to get that kind of knowledge. I think my interaction with the client is probably more a mix of the two [tacit and codified knowledge].

Due to the nature of the client relationship, KPMG was able to intermingle the client's processes and KPMG's processes of knowledge creation and transfer and develop new ways of cooperating with the client.

A Tieto Group case illustrates knowledge absorption and learning transfer in the other polar case: market exchange client relationships. This case study was conducted in Finland and consisted of document analysis and interviews with Tieto Group staff (Sivula 1997). Case analyses were reviewed by the interviewed persons to validate the results.

As illustrated in Figure 4.2, market exchange client relationships are characterized by minimal customer involvement and contacts in service delivery and by the short-term nature of the client relationship. The case involves the service of providing Compact financial management software for small and middle-sized firms. The Compact software was developed and is provided by Unic, a software services subsidiary of TT Tieto Group. Tieto Group merged with Unic in 1995 to strengthen Tieto Group's expertise in financial and personnel management software systems.

Unic is one of the oldest, largest, and most innovative software houses in Northern Europe. Unic's business development manager described Unic in this way:

Openness, new ways of doing business, and an urge to look for new approaches in business have been important at Unic. We believe that to sustain profitability and to improve it requires, in addition to good products, new ways of thinking.

This case highlights the learning implications of arm's length, faceless client contacts in a business services market that typically rewards highly efficient service delivery. The Compact software was developed in the beginning of 1994 after scanning the market to identify promising software products for small and middle-sized firms. Compact's team leader describes how the Finnish version of Compact was developed:

Making such market potential profitable requires high volume and new ways of providing services to these customers. How to do this? Should we build the system ourselves or is it possible to find such a system elsewhere in the world so that we can build a Finnish version out of it? Pretty quickly it became obvious for us that we should not try to reinvent the wheel. Typically, in our industry every firm builds its own version from the beginning and there are very few real partnerships in this field. Well, we tried to find one and came up with the Swedish firm XOR in Malmö that had a suitable program for us. The program was called Compact and the Swedish firm had developed it since 1991. We negotiated about developing a Finnish version of Compact in 1994 and ended up with a deal in which XOR develops the technological solutions and Unic brings its expertise in business management. This was a very successful division of labor. Technically Compact was ready, but we needed to adjust it to the Finnish context. For instance, bank connections differ in Finland and Sweden.

Three versions of Compact software (versions 2.0, 3.0, 3.1) and a new salary module for Compact were subsequently developed, as well as a new financial management software, Wintime, on the basis of experience with Compact. Experience in providing Compact software to users enabled development of new and improved services. These new services were based on knowledge absorbed in original client engagements. This knowledge was subsequently leveraged to develop new products and services for new clients.

Figure 4.5 describes the knowledge processes in the Compact case. The nature of the initial Compact service (Arrow 1) can be characterized as the transfer of codified knowledge (embedded in the Compact software) through market transactions. Service delivery of the software, however, demands other knowledge processes. Arrow 2 represents learning about specific client operations and adjusting the software to suit

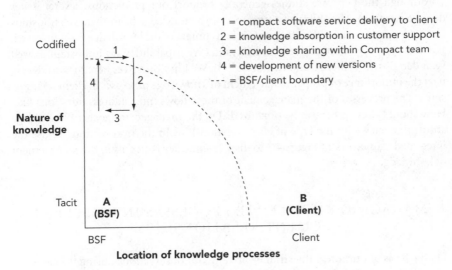

FIG. 4.5 *Knowledge processes in market exchange relationship.*

the client context. Arrow 3 represents knowledge absorption by the Compact team. Arrow 4 represents the codification (in the form of new Compact versions) of new knowledge gained from adapting the Compact software to various client contexts. Knowledge sharing within Tieto Group was facilitated by a strong emphasis on team-work in acquiring knowledge about its customers by conducting market research and by analyzing customer feedback to the customer support desk.

The primary locus of knowledge processes in this case is internal to the service provider. For example, one of the key skills in creating new knowledge is the ability to ask critical questions during customer support in order to acquire better knowledge about the effectiveness of the solutions to customer problems provided by Compact. This knowledge absorption process focuses on identifying and capturing non-specific knowledge that may be leveraged and utilized widely. The later versions of the Compact software incorporated non-specific knowledge and leveraged that knowledge by codifying and packaging it into new software versions sold to users.

Comparison of cases

The KPMG–client relationship was characterized by long duration and high inter-action intensity. It appears to have offered a good opportunity for the absorption of significant tacit, client-specific knowledge, as suggested in Figure 4.3. The Tieto Group case concerns a client relationship characterized by a short-term duration and an arm's length transaction orientation. Our typology (Figure 4.2) and framework (Figure 4.3) suggest that such a market exchange context provides less opportunity and incentive for the absorption and transfer of client-specific knowledge. However, opportunities for absorbing non-specific knowledge will arise. The Tieto Group case study provides evidence of the second proposition.

Although the two case studies generally support our predictions, several issues deserve attention. The ability of a firm to absorb knowledge from client relationships clearly depends on more than the content and context of the knowledge flows involved. For example, organization form and combinative capabilities are important as well (van den Bosch, Volberda, and de Boer 1999). We limit ourselves here to considering next the importance of proper management of knowledge processes in client relation-ships. The processes of the management of these flows must address questions like: How should these processes be organized? Do the management goals of knowledge absorption vary with the type of client relationship? In the next section, we use the integrated framework of Figure 4.3 to discuss some key concerns in the management of knowledge processes.

MANAGING KNOWLEDGE PROCESSES IN DIFFERENT CLIENT RELATIONSHIPS

On the basis of our integrative framework and our observations during the cases, we identified some additional general patterns in the management of knowledge in different types of client relationships. The management of knowledge in different client relationships must be based on identification of the type of knowledge to be absorbed and the transfer of the knowledge in an appropriate way. To make strategic choices, a knowledge intensive BSF must answer several strategic questions before starting to manage knowledge processes in customer relationships (Storbacka, Sivula, and Kaario 1999). For example:

(1) What kind of client relationships does the firm want to develop?
(2) Are existing client relationships consistent with the firm's strategic logic? Are there some aspects of the firm's strategic logic that suggest the firm should seek out particular types of customer relationships?
(3) Is it possible to change the nature of the firm's current client relationships?
(4) What kind of interactions are there currently between client processes and the firm's processes? Are these interactions captured in the Client Relationship Management (CRM) systems in use?
(5) Is the strategy of the BSF being led by competences that arise from deliberately chosen client relationships?

The proposed typology of four client relationships may be used to judge the knowledge potential of the firm's current client relationships and whether the firm's client relationships are being managed consistently and deliberately to build desired competences.[3]

Different client relationships impose different *adaptation requirements* on BSFs (see figure 4.6).[4] In market exchange relationships, the firm dominates the service delivery, and clients essentially have to adapt themselves to the service being offered by the BSF. In the client partnership, however, the client and the firm mutually adapt in the service delivery process to identify and exploit new value creation opportunities. These polar differences in adaptation requirements suggest that the more a BSF needs to adapt its service delivery to a client's requirements, the more the BSF may benefit from proactive preparation of client-specific knowledge or ready-made solutions that may be applied in quickly solving a customer's problems. Two processes of managing knowledge in client relationships are therefore of critical importance: First, managing alignment of BSF and client processes in client partnerships to promote knowledge development and exchange. Second, managing the codification and packaging of knowledge for efficient service delivery in market exchange relationships. We next elaborate these processes.

The management of knowledge in client partnerships should be focused on achieving alignment of BSF and client processes in knowledge development and exchange. To find new ways of creating value in the BSF–client relationship, there must be trust between the firm and the client and adequate mutual incentives to find new ways of

---

[3] Analyzing the management of knowledge in client relationships, as in other relationships of a firm, should also consider the content of the managerial knowledge (van den Bosch and van Wijk, Ch. 8, in this volume) required to manage knowledge absorption by the firm. See Dijksterhuis, van den Bosch, and Volberda (1999) for an analysis of the context on shared managerial schemas.

[4] Adaptation requirements regarding organizational form and combinative capabilities appropriate for gaining knowledge are discussed in van den Bosch, Volberda, and de Boer (1999). For a coevolutionary perspective on adaptation requirements, see Lewin and Volberda (1999).

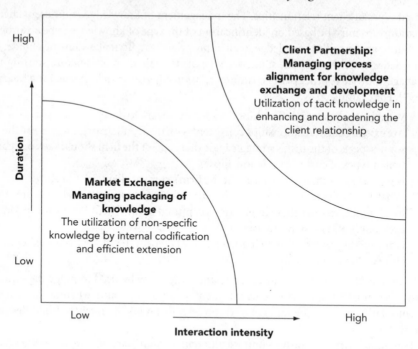

FIG. 4.6   *Challenges to management of knowledge in two different client relationships.*

cooperating and aligning the client's and the BSF's processes. If clients are willing to share their knowledge about the essence of their value creation processes, BSF partners may be able to identify new value creation opportunities. Since much of the interaction between the client and the BSF in this context requires sharing tacit knowledge, it is essential that the BSF's process of managing knowledge recognizes and gives "credit" for tacit knowledge absorbed. In terms of Boisot's (1998) three-dimensional I-space concept, the knowledge assets acquired in this type of client relationship may be difficult to abstract and codify. Moreover, "knowledge that is hard to articulate and to structure does not travel far" (Boisot 1998: 77). The challenge for the management of knowledge processes in this context is therefore to increase the value of these tacit knowledge assets by trying to abstract, codify, and transfer client-specific knowledge. New forms of organizing in client partnerships require explicit processes for meeting this challenge (Hedlund 1994; van Wijk and van den Bosch 2000).

In market exchange relationships the efficient absorption, codification, and "packaging" of knowledge in readily transferable forms seems to be critical to effective knowledge management. In effect, the solution to one client's problem must be codified and transferred directly to other clients. The codification process should lead to standard service products or even physical products like software that enable efficient leveraging of knowledge in a client environment in which customer contacts are minimal and short-term. In terms of Boisot's (1998) three-dimensional I-space concept, the knowledge processes required in this type of client relationship must excel in both the abstraction and codification dimensions to support ready diffusion.

CONCLUSION

In the competence-based view of competition, a competence is defined as "the *ability to sustain the coordinated deployment of assets* in a way that helps a firm *achieve its goals*" (Sanchez and Heene 1996: 8, original emphasis). Our research contributes to the competence-based view in three ways. First, we develop a typology of client relationships and an integrative framework that helps to clarify several important types of knowledge absorption opportunities. Second, we investigated two types of client relationships—the client partnership and the market exchange relationship—to test propositions derived from our framework. Third, we highlight client relationships as a key source of valuable new organizational knowledge. Our framework, supported by the analyses of the two case studies, suggested basic implications for the management of knowledge in two types of client relationships. In market exchange relationships, the managerial challenge in building new competences is the capture and leveraging of non-specific knowledge through codification, internal transfer, and efficient leveraging to other client contexts—i.e. managing the "packaging of knowledge." In client partnerships, however, managing the absorption and use of tacit knowledge to enhance and broaden a given client relationship is the key challenge.

REFERENCES

BOISOT, M. H. (1983). "Convergence revisited: The codification and diffusion of knowledge in a British and a Japanese firm," *Journal of Management Studies*, 1, 159–90.

—— (1995). "Is your firm a creative destroyer? Competitive learning and knowledge flows in the technological strategies of firms," *Research Policy*, 24, 489–506.

—— (1998). *Knowledge Assets*. Oxford: Oxford University Press.

—— and D. GRIFFITHS (2001). "Possession is nine-tenths of the law: Managing a firm's competence base in a regime of weak appropriability," in R. Sanchez (ed.), *Knowledge Management and Organizational Competence*.

—— —— and V. MOLES (1997). "The dilemma of competence: Differentiation versus integration in the pursuit of learning," in R. Sanchez and A. Heene (eds.), *Strategic Learning and Knowledge Management*. Chichester: John Wiley.

COHEN, W. M. and D. A. LEVINTHAL (1990). "Absorptive capacity: A new perspective on learning and innovation," *Administrative Science Quarterly*, 35, 128–52.

DIJKSTERHUIS, M. S., F. A. J. VAN DEN BOSCH, and H. W. VOLBERDA (1999). "Where do new organizational forms come from? Management logics as a source of coevolution," *Organizational Science*, 10 (5), 569–82.

FUCHS, V. R. (1968). *The Service Economy*. New York: Columbia University Press.

GRANT, R. M. (1996). "Prospering in dynamically competitive environments: Organizational capability as knowledge integration," *Organization Science*, 7 (4), 375–87.

HAYEK, F. A. (1945). "The use of knowledge in society," *American Economic Review*, 35, 519–30.

HEDLUND, G. (1994). "A model of knowledge management and the n-form corporation," *Strategic Management Journal*, 15, 73–90.

KOGUT, B. and U. ZANDER (1992). "Knowledge of the firm: Combinative capabilities and the replication of technology," *Organization Science*, 3, 383–97.

LEWIN, A. Y. and H. W. VOLBERDA (1999). "Prolegomena on evolution: A framework of research on strategy and new organizational forms," *Organization Science*, 10 (5), 519–34.

MILLS, P. K. and D. J. MOBERG (1990). "Strategic implications of service technologies," in D. E. Bowen, R. B. Chase, and T. G. Cummings (eds.), *Service Management Effectiveness*. San Francisco: Jossey-Bass.

NONAKA, I. (1994). "A dynamic theory of organizational knowledge creation," *Organization Science*, 5 (1), 14–37.

NORMAN, R. and R. RAMIREZ (1994). *Designing Interactive Strategy: From Value Chain to Value Constellation*. Chichester: John Wiley.

PENROSE, E. T. (1959). *The Theory of the Growth of the Firm*. Oxford: Basil Blackwell.

POLANYI, M. (1966). *The Tacit Dimension*. London: Routledge & Kegan Paul.

QUELIN, B. (1997). "Appropriability and the creation of new capabilities through strategic alliances," in R. Sanchez and A. Heene (eds.), *Strategic Learning and Knowledge Management*. Chichester: John Wiley.

SANCHEZ, R. (1997). "Managing articulated knowledge in competence-based competition," in R. Sanchez and A. Heene (eds.), *Strategic Learning and Knowledge Management*. Chichester: John Wiley.

—— and A. HEENE (1996). "A systems view of the firm in competence-based competition," in R. Sanchez, A. Heene, and H. Thomas (eds.), *Dynamics of Competence-Based Competition: Theory and Practice in the New Strategic Management*. Oxford: Elsevier Pergamon.

—— —— (1997). *Strategic Learning and Knowledge Management*. Chichester: John Wiley.

SIVULA, P. (1997). "Competing on knowledge from customers," Ph.D. series in General Management, 29, Rotterdam School of Management.

—— F. A. J. VAN DEN BOSCH, and T. ELFRING (1997). "Competence building by incorporating clients into the development of a business service firm's knowledge base," in R. Sanchez and A. Heene (eds.), *Strategic Learning and Knowledge Management*. Chichester: John Wiley.

STEIN, J. (1997). "On building and leveraging competences across organizational borders: A sociocognitive framework," in A. Heene and R. Sanchez (eds.), *Competence-Based Strategic Management*. Chichester: John Wiley.

STORBACKA, K., P. SIVULA, and K. KAARIO (1999). *Create Value with Strategic Accounts*. Helsinki: Kauppakaari Oyj.

VAN DEN BOSCH, F. A. J., H. W. VOLBERDA, and M. DE BOER (1999). "Coevolution of firm absorptive capacity and knowledge environment: Organizational forms and combinative capabilities," *Organization Science*, 10 (5), 551–68.

VAN WIJK, R. A. and F. A. J. VAN DEN BOSCH (2000). "Creating the N-form corporation as a managerial competence," in R. Sanchez and A. Heene (eds.), *Advances in Applied Business Strategy, Volume B: Implementing Competence-Based Strategy*. Greenwich, CT: JAI Press.

VON HIPPEL, E. (1988). *The Sources of Innovation*. New York: Oxford University Press.

PART III

GROUP KNOWLEDGE AND GROUP/ORGANIZATION LEARNING INTERACTIONS

5

TOWARDS A KNOWLEDGE-BASED FRAMEWORK OF COMPETENCE DEVELOPMENT

STEFFEN P. RAUB

INTRODUCTION

Managing organizational competences in order to achieve strategic change and gain competitive advantage is one of the central tasks of strategic management. For most scholars and practitioners in the field of strategy, this statement has become conventional wisdom. However, the debate about the theoretical foundations of competence-based management and what the concept really means for management practice is still a very lively one.

The resource-based view of the firm (Barney 1991; Conner 1991; Mahoney and Pandian 1992; Peteraf 1993; Wernerfelt 1984) may be regarded as an intellectual predecessor of the competence-based view. Essentially, the resource-based view regards firms' idiosyncratic resource endowments as their main source of sustainable competitive advantage. The better organizational resources fulfill the criteria of value, rareness, and limited imitability and substitutability, the more likely they are to be significant generators of economic rents (Barney 1991). Among the various competence-based approaches, the "core competence" concept (Hamel and Prahalad 1994; Prahalad and Hamel 1990) is most directly related to the resource-based view.[1] Core competences are defined as complex organizational properties that result from organizational learning and, as such, are hard to imitate and substitute. Therefore, extending the conceptualization of the resource-based view, "core competences" make a significant contribution to a firm's competitive strength.

A broad stream of literature on the related concepts of "organizational capability" (Collis 1991, 1994; Grant 1991, 1996; Zander and Kogut 1995), "core capability" (Leonard-Barton 1992, 1995) and "dynamic capability" (Nelson 1991; Teece, Pisano, and Shuen 1997) provides useful extensions to the core competence perspective. These

---

[1] The close connection between both approaches is confirmed by proponents of core competence approaches and resource-based theorists alike. Indeed, commenting on Prahalad and Hamel's work, Wernerfelt (1995: 171) concedes that "these authors were single-handedly responsible for diffusion of the resource-based view into practice."

approaches stress above all the socially complex, multi-level nature of capabilities and analyze their role as organizational coordination mechanisms.

The theory of competence-based competition (Hamel and Heene 1994; Sanchez, Heene, and Thomas 1996; Heene and Sanchez 1997) takes yet another approach. Its proponents analyze the way strategic goals are identified and attained through a cycle of identification, creation, and leveraging of organizational competencies. More recently, the theory of competence-based competition has put additional emphasis on the importance of strategic learning and knowledge management for the development of organizational competence (Sanchez and Heene 1997). This approach presents an opportunity for linking the literature on competence-based competition with the existing body of research on learning and knowledge management—an opportunity which the present chapter attempts to seize.

In the following sections, elements of a *knowledge-based framework* of competence development will be outlined. Based on an in-depth case study of various ecology-related projects in a large Swiss retailing company, competence development is described as a sequence of *imagination, implementation,* and *integration* activities. The knowledge-related processes in each stage are analyzed by observing the role of *know-what, know-why,* and *know-how,* as well as the links between these different levels of knowledge. The conclusion suggests implications of this framework for further research on competence-based competition.

LEARNING, KNOWLEDGE, AND ORGANIZATIONAL COMPETENCE

There are several important precursors to the theoretical links between competence-based theory and concepts of organizational learning. For instance, Selznick's (1957/1997: 23) seminal description of "distinctive competence" focuses on processes of institutionalization, which define the purpose as well as the structures and decision-making processes of organizations. He observes that due to ongoing organizational learning, "the enterprise takes on a special character, and this means that it becomes peculiarly competent (or incompetent) to do a particular kind of work."

Prahalad and Hamel (1990: 82) are even more explicit in defining core competence as "the collective learning in the organization." Despite these early insights, research on organizational competence largely ignored the role of organizational knowledge. At the very least, it failed to provide sufficiently detailed accounts of "strategic learning" processes involved in the development of competence. With its explicit focus on learning and knowledge management in the context of competence-based competition, however, the Sanchez and Heene (1997) edited volume represents a notable exception.

Recent developments of organizational learning theory are characterized by a strong focus on organizational knowledge. Nonaka and Takeuchi's (1995) analysis of organizational knowledge creation is a case in point. Their contribution focuses on the interplay of "tacit" and "explicit" knowledge and describes a "spiral of organizational knowledge creation" resulting from conversion processes between both types of knowledge. The tacit–explicit dichotomy in organizational learning theory has had a significant influence on strategic management research. Tacit knowledge has often been mentioned as an important source of sustainable competitive advantage, whereas advantages based on explicit knowledge are regarded as more unstable, due to the fact that they can be more easily understood and reproduced (Dierickx and Cool 1989).

Sanchez (1997) points out that such an exclusive focus on tacit knowledge may be overly restrictive. As a result, he calls for a better understanding of how explicit, articulated knowledge can become a source of advantage in competence-based competition. As a starting point for an analytical framework, Sanchez suggests a distinction between know-how (focused on the understanding of the current state of a process), know-why (regarding the theoretical principles governing the process) and know-what (concerned with the purpose to which know-how and know-why are applied). Based on this distinction, he develops a number of propositions regarding the effective leveraging of different kinds of knowledge depending on the dynamics of the competitive environment the firm faces.

While this framework focuses on competence leveraging, it may also hold some promise for analyzing earlier stages in the competence building cycle. Viewed from the perspective of how new competences are imagined and developed, a number of interesting new research questions emerge. For instance: Are certain kinds of knowledge more important than others in the various stages of organizational competence development? How do different kinds of knowledge interact? How are changes in one type of knowledge influenced by developments at another level? Are there any particularly critical links between different knowledge levels which define the firm's ability to effectively and efficiently imagine, build, and leverage organizational competencies? To address these issues, the framework has been applied to the imagination, implementation, and integration stages of organizational competence development in a Swiss retail company.

COMPETENCE DEVELOPMENT: THE CASE OF "SWISSCO"

The observation of competence development processes which forms the core of this chapter is based on an in-depth case study of a large Swiss retail grocery company, which for confidentiality reasons, will be referred to as "Swissco." The study focuses on the development of Swissco's competence in the area of ecology-related retailing.

Swissco and the Swiss retail grocery industry

The Swiss retail grocery market is dominated by four major competitors, the combined market share of which exceeds 60 percent. Swissco is one of these leading firms and operates on a national basis with more than 1500 sales outlets. It employs more than 45,000 people, and its turnover of more than 12 billion Swiss Francs (for fiscal year 1998) represents approximately 15 percent of the Swiss retail grocery market.

The origins of the company in the consumer cooperative movement of the late nineteenth century are still reflected in its present organization structure. The operation of retail outlets falls within the responsibility of regional cooperatives. These are separate legal entities with their own management and full profit and loss responsibility. Swissco's corporate headquarters is responsible for central marketing and most purchasing activities. It also serves as an administrative service provider to regional cooperatives.

Ecology has traditionally been a very important issue in Switzerland. In the 1970s and 1980s, "technical ecology"—such as recycling, energy reduction, logistics and packaging issues—dominated consumers' perceptions of ecology. The 1990s witnessed a shift towards "product-related ecology," which resulted in an increasing demand for food and non-food products grown and manufactured according to stricter ecological standards. In the past two decades, the ecological awareness of Swiss consumers has constantly increased. In 1990, a study by the Swiss Marketing Society classified 57 percent of the Swiss population as "concerned by environmental issues," of which more than half were considered "highly concerned by environmental issues."

As of 1997, "green products" still accounted for less than 5 percent of the total turnover of big retail companies. However, selected segments displayed annual growth rates of nearly 50 percent. In addition, a firm's ecological activities had an increasingly important influence on customers' image of a company. Today, consumers make a clear distinction between two environmentally active retailers—Swissco, and one of its major competitors—and the other firms in the industry, which are much less involved in ecology-related issues. As a result, the two leaders enjoy a significant competitive advantage in terms of ecology image.

The study

This study was carried out during April 1996 to April 1997. An initial unstructured interview with a member of Swissco's top management—who was also, at the time, responsible for environmental issues—provided an overview of ecology-related activities within the company. Altogether, three project teams and a staff unit concerned with environmental issues (known internally as the "environmental staff") were identified and investigated. Interviews focused on a closer analysis of the various ecology-related activities within these units. The three projects observed were headed by so-called "decision teams," each comprising four to five managers, who were also interviewed. In addition, interviews with several managers from the environmental staff as well as from a variety of functional departments were conducted. The investigation also yielded a large amount of internal documents (such as memos, strategy papers, meeting minutes, consultants' reports, and studies commissioned from market research firms) to substantiate accounts of project development. In combination with information from the public domain (annual reports, environmental reports, consumer information leaflets etc.), these documents provided a basis for data triangulation.

The study initially focused on reconstructing the history of the projects, identifying significant incidents and exploring the nature of each project's interaction with other projects and organizational units. Following an inductive approach, the framework of competence development pursued by Swissco was successively constructed (Glaser and Strauss 1967; Eisenhardt 1989), and different stages of competence development were identified.

Ecological projects at Swissco

Swissco started dealing with environmental issues in the mid-1970s. The company's involvement began with a number of small-scale, isolated initiatives. About a decade later, environmental initiatives were regrouped into formally defined projects, which helped them gain focus. The first "environmental" project recognized as such attempted to link environmental issues with marketing aspects. It was named "EcoOne," and one of its major achievements was the introduction of an "eco-label" to be used on environmentally friendly products sold by Swissco. EcoOne concentrated on environmentally improved packaging solutions, in terms of reducing both environmentally harmful substances and packaging volume. During the late 1980s, the project slowly expanded to include a range of "green" offerings in the non-food sector, such as recycled paper and recycled plastic products, as well as personal hygiene and cleaning products. Eventually, a range of fresh food products grown according to an externally certified ecological standard was introduced.

In parallel to this product-oriented expansion, a number of technical initiatives were launched. Projects at the regional cooperative level led to reduced energy consumption through improved heating and lighting systems, reduced dust emissions, improved water use, and extensive recycling programs. Corporate headquarters amplified this trend by introducing a formal "eco-organization" in 1991. It appointed a small working group—the so-called "environmental staff"—to deal with issues of technical ecology and to coordinate ecological activities throughout the organization.

In the early 1990s, ecological projects began to develop at a faster pace. A new project, named "EcoFood," started to promote a range of ecological food products. It included ecological fruits and vegetables developed by EcoOne, extended the range of fresh produce and expanded into milk products and meat. Today, EcoFood has developed into a flagship project within Swissco's ecological product range.

At about the same time, another project, named "EcoTex," started operations. EcoTex encompassed a line of ecological textiles developed in cooperation with two partners in the Swiss yarn and textile industries. Products were made of cotton grown according to an externally certified eco-standard. Moreover, EcoTex banned the use of chemicals such as chlorine, heavy metals, or formaldehyde in the bleaching, dying, and finishing stages of the production process. Figure 5.1 provides an overview of how ecological projects at Swissco developed over time.

In 1996, a fundamental reorganization of Swissco's ecological activities occurred. A coordination team was created to promote exchange between projects and to serve as an interface with top management. Existing redundancies between the different projects and between projects and the ecology-staff were removed. At the beginning of 1997, the success story of Swissco's environmental activities became a central feature of

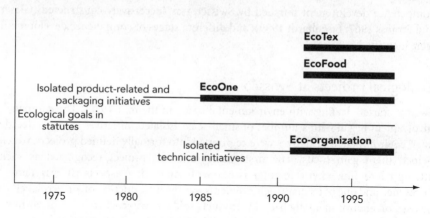

FIG. 5.1 *Development of ecological projects at Swissco.*

its annual report. At this time, Swissco's top management referred to the four projects as its "competence brands."

DEVELOPMENT OF "ECOLOGICAL COMPETENCE"

The development of "ecological competence" at Swissco illustrates the importance of various processes of interaction between the firm's know-what, know-why, and know-how. These processes will be analyzed by highlighting the role of each form of knowledge and the relationship between the different forms in three stages of competence development: imagination, implementation, and integration. Table 5.1 provides an overview of knowledge-related processes in the different stages.

Imagination—the idea of "ecological retailing"

The idea of exploiting ecology-related aspects of the retail business and elevating them into an important part of the firm's strategy was the result of a long development process within Swissco. As early as the mid-1970s, consumers' increasing ecological awareness began to affect the Swiss retail sector. Swissco monitored these developments closely. By the early 1980s, it became clear that ecology was becoming a strategic issue and that Swissco's isolated, small-scale activities would no longer suffice. The firm needed a strategy for its ecological activities in order to exploit the developing opportunities in this segment and to successfully respond to its competitors' initiatives.

Outlining a new strategic logic. In the mid-1980s, Swissco's top management formulated a strategic intent to exploit the opportunity of "ecology-oriented retailing." While this new "strategic logic" (Sanchez, Heene, and Thomas 1996) indicated a shift in priorities and a general strategic direction to follow, it by no means represented a full-fledged strategic plan. Instead, the imagination stage of Swissco's ecological com-

TABLE 5.1 *Stages of competence development and knowledge-related processes*

	Imagination	Implementation	Integration
Know-what	*diagnosing* identifying relevant strategic issues; outlining a new strategic logic;	*defining* evaluating and selecting new initiatives; defining the new strategic logic;	*deploying* aligning organizational and knowledge structures;
Know-why	*innovating* translating the strategic logic; exploring innovative theories;	*implementing* defining standards and procedures; establishing an appropriate knowledge architecture;	*integrating* transferring knowledge between projects;
Know-how	*identifying* localizing individual and functional know-how; identifying external knowledge sources.	*interrelating* building and maintaining links to other know-how carriers.	*improving* adopting new standards and procedures; codifying know-how.

petence was characterized by an interplay of top management's emerging strategic intent and various bottom-up initiatives originating in different organizational units. Far from pursuing a top-down approach to strategy development, Swissco's top management explicitly sought middle managers' advice on how to translate its strategic intent into more detailed projects and action plans. In this process, top management directly relied upon middle management to identify specific *strategic options* for competence building (Sanchez 1993) within the broad strategic objective initiated and led by top management.

Starting in the 1970s, isolated ecology-related initiatives had led to an accumulation of certain ecological expertise in Swissco. Through their involvement in ecological activities, some managers had developed their own private theories of consumer attitudes towards ecology and of the ways retail companies could benefit from this trend. However, these managers were dispersed throughout the organization and lacked the resources and authority to pursue their ideas on a larger scale. Top management's proposal of a new strategic logic that attributed significantly more importance to ecological issues allowed these "centers of expertise" to emerge and to be expressed in the form of new organization-wide projects. Thus, the initial members of new project teams played a crucial role in the imagination stage by suggesting how Swissco's emerging strategic logic could be translated to the operational level. Essentially, they defined strategic issues in more detail, offered their theories on how to deal with these issues, and identified relevant knowledge that could be accessed inside and outside the organization.

Exploring innovative theories. The main challenge for new projects was to transform Swissco's strategic intent into activities which responded appropriately to current

customer needs and competitive challenges. As a first step, this required a clear definition of the strategic issues to be tackled. Due to the general increase in ecological awareness at the customer level, various issues related to ecological retailing emerged. One
example concerned garbage bag disposal fees, which many municipal administrations
had recently introduced. These fees added a new economic dimension that reinforced
consumers' existing ecological concerns. As a result, packaging was perceived as an
important issue, and the development of innovative solutions for reducing and recycling packaging was seen as a significant strategic opportunity. The EcoOne project
team identified packaging as a potential strategic issue and developed a range of proposals for addressing customer concerns for ecologically improved packaging.

   At a later stage, public attention focused on the dangers of ecologically questionable
food and non-food products. Due to a succession of scandals and related media coverage, toxic substances in textiles appeared on the agenda. In addition, a general trend
towards healthier food prompted a debate about the ecological standards of conventional food production. This shift of consumer attention to ecologically improved food
products was identified by two other project teams. The EcoFood and EcoTex projects
were proposed to develop new products in the food and non-food sectors, respectively.
Each new project developed a detailed strategic action plan for implementing an "ecological retailing" strategy in its area of activity.

   Identifying relevant knowledge. The project teams' ability to develop innovative
strategic plans depended to a significant degree on the creativity and insight of a few
key players. However, implementing these projects necessarily required support from
a large number of individuals in various departments and at various levels of the firm.
It was therefore necessary to identify individual and functional knowledge inside the
organization, as well as external sources of knowledge, which would be instrumental in
implementing the strategy. Project teams soon found out that they exercised an
"attractive power" on existing ecological knowledge at Swissco. As soon as the start of
a new project was announced, individuals with a personal interest in ecological issues
and relevant expertise made themselves known to the team members and often
declared their interest in participating.

   The resulting increasing diversity in the composition of the project teams also facilitated knowledge identification, as new members provided access to their own specific
knowledge networks. Participants with a marketing background, for instance, would
provide access to various market research and advertising resources. Purchasing managers provided knowledge about ecological initiatives at the supplier level and contacts
with ecologically interested producers. Finally, specialists in ecological matters were
usually linked to various external networks, including environmental organizations,
pressure groups, and political parties.

   Organizational knowledge in the imagination stage. When analyzed from a
knowledge-based perspective, the imagination stage of competence development is
characterized by a dominance of processes at the know-what and know-why levels. At
Swissco, strategic issue diagnosis triggered the process that led to the development of
organizational competence and identified the main elements in a new strategic logic,
leading to a period of change in the organization's "purpose theory" (Sanchez 1997). As

a result, possible new strategic logics were examined in the light of existing know-why related to ecological issues in retailing. From this interplay of know-what and know-why forms of knowledge, strategic plans for innovative projects emerged. Note that the organization's know-how remained unmodified in this stage. However, identification of existing know-how, both inside and outside the organization, served as a basis for know-how evaluation and acquisition in the subsequent implementation processes.

Implementation—the development of ecology-focused projects

As a result of the imagination stage, several new ecological projects emerged, each exploring the opportunity of ecology-oriented retailing in a different way. The implementation stage was characterized by two critical challenges. First, the specific projects to be implemented had to be decided. Second, strategic plans developed at the project level had to be transformed into coordinated activities at the organizational level.

Defining the strategic logic. The projects' strategic plans served as a starting point for a more detailed definition and elaboration of Swissco's strategic logic. A major task for top management in the implementation stage consisted of evaluating the compatibility of new projects with Swissco's overall strategic intent. This involved assessing the projects' ability to take advantage of current developments in the competitive environment and their potential for contributing to Swissco's ecological product range. By evaluating new projects and deciding whether or not and in which order they should be implemented, top management eventually arrived at a more comprehensive and detailed definition of Swissco's ecology strategy.

While strategic plans for each of the projects were developed by a small core of team members, implementation required deployments of significant amounts of resources to overcome organizational inertia and resistance and to secure the commitment of organization members on whom implementation would depend. Projects that were positively evaluated received top management support in the form of management communication and resource allocation. Communication of management support for selected projects was particularly important for gaining support from each cooperative retail location, which was critical for the implementation of new projects at the point of sale. Resources were used for various purposes ranging from internal price subsidies to advertising and promotional activities as well as training and development.

Implementing new theories. From a strategic point of view, the evaluation and selection of identified ecological projects strongly shaped the definition of Swissco's strategic logic in the area of ecology-related retailing. From an operational perspective, however, selecting and supporting a new project required implementation at the organizational level. Due to Swissco's largely decentralized organization structure, this was not an easy task. The most critical issue in terms of implementation involved gaining support from the regional cooperatives, on the one hand, and from the central Purchasing department, on the other hand. Without appropriate implementation at the point of sale, new projects initiated at corporate headquarters were bound to fail. Likewise, without support from Purchasing, appropriate ecological products could not be found and sourced in sufficient quantities. Thus, while the decision teams provided the general strategic direction for each project, implementation depended very much on the commitment of both Purchasing and Sales managers.

Each of Swissco's ecological projects pursued a unique strategy. In the field of packaging, EcoOne focused on the introduction of an "eco-label" for products with environmentally friendly packaging. The range of products was streamlined and products with excessive packaging were eliminated. At the same time, improved packaging solutions for Swissco's own brands were planned and various initiatives for packaging recycling were tested in retail outlets. In the food sector, EcoFood aimed at developing an entire range of ecological food products in close collaboration with an environmental organization. It focused on providing information and support to agricultural producers who participated in this project and who, in return, were granted exclusive use of the label awarded by the organization. Finally, in the textile area, EcoTex started to collaborate with yarn and textile producers and various ecological organizations, such as the World Wildlife Fund, with the goal of establishing an integrated and closely monitored chain of ecological textile production.

Over time, projects received increasing amounts of support from within the organization. Purchasing managers became active in identifying and introducing extensions to the ecological product ranges. Sales management in the cooperatives put additional effort into the presentation of ecological products at the point of sale. In some areas, such as fresh produce, they even established their own networks of regional suppliers. As a larger number of participants started to work together across functional and hierarchical boundaries, coordination became a critical issue. Decision teams played an important role in establishing coordination mechanisms for the various contributions. They achieved this in two ways: first, by defining standards and procedures, and second, by highlighting and reinforcing links between the different carriers of know-how involved in the new product development process.

Defining standards and procedures. Smooth collaboration between the different project participants—decision teams, Purchasing managers, suppliers, environmental organizations, Marketing and Sales managers—required a set of standards and guidelines to be followed for each new product introduction. These referred to product characteristics, such as tolerated raw materials and ingredients, production methods, packaging, pricing, and promotional activities. Decision teams were responsible for defining and monitoring these standards. In addition to this, decision teams also defined a standard process to be followed for new ecological product introductions.

In an early stage, decision teams put significant efforts into guiding each new product proposal and providing consulting to individual managers involved in the process. Typically, proposals from Purchasing or Sales would be forwarded to the decision team, who decided whether it was suitable as a complement to the existing product range. If the response was favorable, the team obtained external certification for the product and authorized a nationwide introduction of the product, which in turn was implemented by Purchasing and Sales. As the number of new product introductions increased and more and more people became involved in the project, this mode of central coordination had to be modified. To achieve this, decision teams delegated a large amount of their tasks to staff members and focused instead on defining and establishing appropriate links between the various partners involved in the introduction process.

Establishing links between carriers of knowledge. Decision teams clarified the role of individuals in the process by communicating the strategic focus of the project and defining the inputs and outputs individual participants were supposed to receive and produce. As direct involvement of the decision team in the process was reduced through increasing delegation, the character of coordination changed. Devolution of responsibility led to intensified interaction between various partners, who began to rely to an increasing degree on collective knowledge of the projects' goals and procedures. With growing numbers of successful new product introductions, participants developed a good understanding of their own role in the process and of the expectations of their partners. As their interaction became increasingly routinized, decision teams focused exclusively on updating and communicating standards as well as reinforcing from time to time the projects' general goals and philosophy.

Organizational knowledge in the implementation stage. Whereas change in know-what knowledge provided the major impetus in the imagination stage, the driving force of the implementation stage is in the form of know-why knowledge. At Swissco, new projects implemented various managers' theories by transforming strategic plans into real management processes. This required enlarging the circle of participants and achieving coordination between the different individuals and functions involved. Based on their know-why knowledge, decision teams defined standards and procedures for the deployment of individual and functional know-how. By communicating these standards and by defining and reinforcing appropriate links between the various carriers of know-how, decision teams established a "knowledge architecture" (Sanchez 1997) to support and coordinate the projects' activities. Thus, know-why became a driving force for the deployment and coordination of know-how.

At the know-how level, the challenge was to apply existing organizational knowledge in the context of the new project and to establish and maintain working relationships with other sources of know-how as defined by the project team. The role of know-what in this stage is limited to a selecting function. By determining whether or not a new project "fits" the strategic logic, top management achieved two outcomes. At the operational level, selected projects were provided with sufficient resources and support for implementation. At the strategic level, every positive selection decision added the "content" of that new project to the emerging strategic logic and, hence, reshaped its scope.

Integration—towards organizational "ecological competence"

Following the definition of a new strategic logic achieved in the implementation stage, the last stage of competence development focused on integration. The components of ecological competence developed in various new projects had to be aligned in order to form a true organizational competence in ecology-related retailing. This stage encompassed establishing an organizational structure which allowed the organization-wide deployment of the newly defined strategic logic. It also concerned the transfer of specific knowledge between different projects.

Adapting the organization to the new strategic logic. As a result of the essentially autonomous development of several different projects, very little integration had been achieved across various areas of activity. Instead, the parallel development of packaging, food, and non-food initiatives, combined with separate activities initiated by the ecology staff, had led to some evident redundancies and inconsistencies in both project content and organization structure. As a result, product development became a source of conflict. Overlaps in content and unclear boundaries of responsibilities existed between the eco-organization and various ecological projects, as well as between the different projects themselves. Moreover, reporting lines were confusing. As projects had emerged in different parts of the organization, specific reporting lines for each project had been established. As a result, EcoOne reported to the VP Marketing, EcoFood reported to the VP Food Purchasing and the VP Marketing, and EcoTex reported to the VP Non-Food Purchasing. The ecology staff was organizationally disconnected from the project teams and reported directly to the President and CEO.

Swissco's inappropriately designed organization structure clearly represented an obstacle for the development of organizational competence, having the effect of isolating projects from each other and preventing coordinated decision-making at the top management level. Once the dissonance between the new strategic logic and the current organization structure had been diagnosed, Swissco's top management carried out a fundamental reorganization of the company's ecological activities. As a first step, product development and ecological "support" tasks—including ecological accounting and reporting, technical ecology, and packaging issues—were clearly separated. Support tasks were assigned to the ecology staff, whereas project teams retained sole responsibility for product development activities. In this way, the ecology staff was refocused on "basic research," whereas project teams were focused on transforming ecological knowledge into marketable solutions. In addition, improved structural alignment between projects was achieved by removing overlaps in their respective scopes. The food component of EcoOne was formally eliminated and food products remained the exclusive domain of EcoFood. EcoOne also transferred its packaging knowledge to the ecology staff and, as a result, remained exclusively focused on non-food products. Thus, after the reorganization, each organizational unit involved in ecological issues was clearly targeted towards one specific area of responsibility and capability.

In addition to the redistribution of responsibility, two new integrative teams were established. A coordination team, to which all projects reported directly, had the explicit purpose of promoting exchange between projects. Moreover, an ecology-focused strategy team, which included the Vice Presidents for Purchasing and Marketing, secured continuing attention for ecological issues at the top management level. As a result of this reorganization, coordination between projects—as well as coordination between the project teams and top management—improved significantly.

Fostering knowledge transfer between projects. Improved transfers of knowledge between different projects followed these structural improvements. As decision team members recognized the increasing interdependence of the various ecology-related activities, interaction at the project level intensified. A decisive step for fostering inter-project learning was the exchange of decision team members. This development was driven by two key members of EcoFood, who offered support to the remaining projects. They took additional positions in the EcoTex and EcoOne decision teams and provided channels for a continuous transfer of knowledge. In a similar vein, EcoTex and EcoOne exchanged decision team members. As a result of this system of interlocking team membership, coordination of activities improved greatly.

Inter-project learning essentially focused on procedures and standards. EcoFood members successfully pushed towards the universal adaptation of a very severe external bio standard (BS). Cotton production for EcoTex and the near-food parts of EcoOne (plants, flowers etc.), however, had used different, less stringent ecological standards. Within two years, all ecological projects at Swissco adhered to the stricter BS, which eventually became symbolic of the high level of the company's ecological commitment. As EcoFood was the most successful and advanced project, its working mechanisms were used as an internal benchmark for project procedures. EcoTex and EcoOne modeled their management processes for decision teams and for outside relations on EcoFood's successful example.

Inter-project learning and structural alignment provided significant cohesion to Swissco's ecology-focused projects. Relevant management processes and ecological standards were harmonized. Moreover, the new organization structure enabled an easier linking of the various skills and capabilities which had been accumulated at the project level. Multiple memberships in decision teams facilitated bottom-up coordination, and the coordination and strategy teams provided a consistent strategic vision while serving as an arbiter in situations of conflict.

Codifying new knowledge. Aligning different initiatives also required adopting the new common standards and procedures at the know-how level. At the outset, project teams relied on informal coordination and communication for diffusing these types of knowledge. However, increased organizational complexity of Swissco's "ecological competence" called for a more formal approach. Formalization began with written guidelines on ecological standards to be observed for each area of ecological activity. Subsequent efforts focused on the development of process handbooks, which described and standardized the entire new product introduction process, including the various steps to follow for external certification.

Organizational knowledge in the integration stage. Knowledge processes in the final stage focused above all on the integration of different competency components at the organizational level. In Swissco's context, know-what guided the aligning of organizational structures with the requirements of the new strategic logic. Thus, structure followed strategy, as the structural organizational arrangements were brought into line with the knowledge architecture defined by the emerging organizational competence. At the know-why level, transfer of knowledge was the dominant process. Alignment of initiatives occurred when theories developed in one project proved to be applicable to and beneficial for others. Mutual alignment across projects led to common standards and procedures, which reinforced the integration of competence at the organizational level. Closer integration was reflected in the adoption of new standards and procedures at the know-how level and increased codification of knowledge.

CONCLUSIONS AND IMPLICATIONS FOR FURTHER RESEARCH

Some researchers have claimed that the dominant focus on the firm level of analysis in strategic management research should be complemented by a closer examination of projects (Burgelman 1983*a*, *b*), initiatives (Birkinshaw 1997; Cohen and Machalek 1988; Kanter 1982), or activities (Løwendahl and Haanes 1997). With its focus on the project level, the present case study develops insights into the role of project-based processes in competence building and leveraging. As a result, it provides a close-up view of how mechanisms responsible for "the coordinated deployment of assets" (Sanchez, Heene, and Thomas 1996) unfold at the subunit level.

The case study identifies new projects as important drivers of organizational competence development. Project teams explored new theories of ecology-related retailing, identifying specific strategic options for competence building and leveraging, and thereby shaping Swissco's strategic logic and providing focus to its ecological activities. Project teams served as "attractors" (Doz *et al.* 1997) for individual know-how from various functional backgrounds and in so doing helped to define the knowledge architecture of Swissco's emerging ecological competence. Finally, they were a driving force for the alignment of the organization's ecological activities, which eventually led to ecological competence at the organizational level.

The case study illustrates the importance of different levels of organizational knowledge for the competence development process. It generally supports the knowledge management framework proposed by Sanchez (1997) and adds some additional insights regarding the interdependencies of *know-what, know-why,* and *know-how* in the competence development process. The case study suggests relatively strong links between certain forms of knowledge and various levels of management. At Swissco, modifying know-what appeared to be the domain of top management, with some assistance from innovative activities at the middle management level in defining more precisely the strategic options the firm could pursue. On the other hand, project teams, which were largely composed of middle managers, emerged as the most important carriers of know-why. They were the essential drivers of competence development as they defined detailed strategic plans for new projects and masterminded their implementation. Finally, the know-how required to implement new activities was mostly found at lower management levels and to some extent even resided outside the organization.

The division of labor between top and middle management at Swissco is very much in line with Nonaka's (1988, 1991) description of "middle-up-down" management in a knowledge-creating company. In Nonaka's concept, top management creates a vision or dream. Middle management then implements this vision and resolves any contradictions which might arise between the daily experience of lower management levels and "grand theory" defined by top management. The case study of Swissco illustrates this process in the formation and use of organizational knowledge. Middle managers emerged as the predominant carriers of know-why in the organization. They possessed a deep understanding of both the fundamental working mechanisms of the retail market as well as the strategic implications of ecological trends on retailing. This enabled them to develop innovative projects compatible with top management's emerging know-what knowledge. Moreover, middle managers were in a privileged position to assess the know-how available within the organization for implementing the required strategic change. Due to this information, they were able to define an appropriate knowledge architecture for new projects and to establish the required links between projects at the know-how level. In sum, middle management used its know-why to embody top management know-what in workable strategic projects, while at the same time assembling and linking the know-how involved in the implementation of these new endeavors.

The analysis of competence development at Swissco suggests that, depending on the stage of the development process, specific links between specific forms of knowledge become critical. The imagination stage, for instance, appears to depend to a large degree on effective linking of know-what and know-why. Modifications of know-what provide the necessary momentum for strategic change. Without support from the level of know-why, however, such change might result in a strategic reorientation that would be inconsistent with the organization's base of resources and competencies. Conversely, while know-why-induced change may ensure compatibility with existing competences, without direction-setting know-what, it could become myopic and lead the firm into a "competency trap" (Leonard-Barton 1992; Levitt and March 1988).

Effective linking of know-what and know-why may also contribute to improved strategic flexibility (Sanchez 1993, 1995). In the long run, the autonomous development of know-why-induced strategic projects provides a source of innovation within more conservative "induced" strategy processes (Burgelman 1983*b*). The case study of Swissco basically illustrates a "modular" process of project-based competence development. Strategic change occurred in incremental steps as new projects were integrated into the strategic logic, and older projects phased out as they slowly lost relevance. This gradual step-by-step modification of know-what allowed increased flexibility in adapting Swissco's ecological competence to environmental demands, while at the same time conserving the fundamental strategic logic of "ecological retailing."

Whereas the imagination stage is focused on the interplay of know-what and know-why, this study suggests that the implementation stage depends more on the effective linking of know-why and know-how. At Swissco, middle management's know-why provided the insights needed to define and design new projects. The critical requirement for the implementation stage was the identification and coordination of different know-how carriers required to carry a project to completion. In this context, the "combinative" capability (Kogut and Zander 1992, 1993) of project teams played an important role. The integration stage is characterized by a similar focus. The new know-what being firmly defined at this stage, the essential challenge here was to align various conflicting elements of know-why and to create a structure conducive to the efficient coordinated deployment of the organization's know-how.

REFERENCES

BARNEY, J. B. (1991). "Firm resources and sustained competitive advantage," *Journal of Management,* 17 (1), 99–120.

BIRKINSHAW, J. (1997). "Entrepreneurship in multinational corporations: The characteristics of subsidiary initiatives," *Strategic Management Journal,* 18 (3), 207–29.

BURGELMAN, R. A. (1983a). "A process model of internal corporate venturing in the diversified firm," *Administrative Science Quarterly,* 28 (2), 223–44.

—— (1983b). "Corporate entrepreneurship and strategic management: Insights from a process study," *Management Science,* 29 (12), 1349–64.

COHEN, L. E. and R. MACHALEK (1988). "A general theory of expropriative crime: An evolutionary ecological model," *American Journal of Sociology,* 94, 465–501.

COLLIS, D. J. (1991). "A resource-based analysis of global competition: The case of the bearings industry," *Strategic Management Journal,* 12 (Summer Special Issue), 49–68.

—— (1994). "Research note: How valuable are organizational capabilities?", *Strategic Management Journal,* 15 (Special Issue), 143–52.

CONNER, K. R. (1991). "A historical comparison of resource-based theory and five schools of thought within industrial organization economics: Do we have a new theory of the firm?" *Journal of Management,* 17 (1), 121–54.

DIERICKX, I. and K. COOL (1989). "Asset stock accumulation and sustainability of competitive advantage," *Management Science,* 35 (12), 1504–11.

DOZ, Y. L., K. ASAKAWA, J. F. P. SANTOS, and P. J. WILLIAMSON (1997). "The metanational corporation" working paper, draft version, May.

EISENHARDT, K. M. (1989). "Building theories from case study research," *Academy of Management Review,* 14 (4), 532–50.

GLASER, B. G. and A. L. STRAUSS (1967). *The Discovery of Grounded Theory.* Chicago: Aldine.

GRANT, R. M. (1991). "The resource-based theory of competitive advantage: Implications for strategy formulation," *California Management Review,* 33 (3), 114–35.

—— (1996). "Prospering in dynamically-competitive environments: Organizational capability as knowledge integration," *Organization Science,* 7 (4), 375–87.

HAMEL, G. and A. HEENE (eds.) (1994). *Competence-based Competition.* New York: John Wiley.

—— and C. K. PRAHALAD (1994). *Competing for the Future.* Boston, MA: Harvard Business School Press.

HEENE, A. and R. SANCHEZ (eds.) (1997). *Competence-based Strategic Management.* Chichester: John Wiley.

KANTER, R. M. (1982). "The middle manager as innovator," *Harvard Business Review,* 60(4), 95–105.

KOGUT, B. and U. ZANDER (1992). "Knowledge of the firm, combinative capabilities, and the replication of technology," *Organization Science,* 3(3), 383–97.

—— —— (1993). "Knowledge of the firm and the evolutionary theory of the multinational corporation," *Journal of International Business Studies,* 24 (4), 625–45.

LEONARD-BARTON, D. (1992). "Core capabilities and core rigidities: A paradox in managing new product development," *Strategic Management Journal,* 13 (Special Issue), 111–25.

—— (1995). *Wellsprings of Knowledge: Building and Sustaining the Sources of Innovation.* Boston: Harvard Business School Press.

LEVITT, B. and J. B. MARCH (1988). "Organizational learning," *Annual Review of Sociology*, 14, 319–40.

LØWENDAHL, B. R. and K. HAANES (1997). "The unit of activity: A new way to understand competence building and leveraging, " in R. Sanchez and A. Heene, (eds.), *Strategic Learning and Knowledge Management.* Chichester: John Wiley, 19–38.

MAHONEY, J. T. and J. R. PANDIAN (1992). "The resource-based view within the conversation of strategic management," *Strategic Management Journal*, 15 (5), 363–80.

NELSON, R. R. (1991). "Why do firms differ, and how does it matter?" *Strategic Management Journal*, 12 (Winter Special Issue), 61–74.

NONAKA, I. (1988). "Toward middle-up-down management: Accelerating information creation," *Sloan Management Review*, 29 (3), 9–18.

—— (1991). "The knowledge-creating company," *Harvard Business Review*, 69 (6), 96–104.

—— and H. TAKEUCHI (1995). *The Knowledge-Creating Company: How Japanese Companies Create the Dynamics of Innovation.* New York: Oxford University Press.

PETERAF, M. A. (1993). "The cornerstones of competitive advantage: A resource-based view," *Strategic Management Journal*, 14 (3), 179–91.

PRAHALAD, C. K. and G. HAMEL (1990). "The core competence of the corporation," *Harvard Business Review*, 68 (3), 79–91.

SANCHEZ, R. (1993). "Strategic flexibility, firm organization, and managerial work in dynamic markets: A strategic options perspective," *Advances in Strategic Management*, 9, 251–91.

—— (1995). "Strategic flexibility in product competition," *Strategic Management Journal*, 16, 135–59.

—— (1997). "Managing articulated knowledge in competence-based competition," in R. Sanchez, and A. Heene (eds.), *Strategic Learning and Knowledge Management*, Chichester: John Wiley.

SANCHEZ, R. and A. HEENE (eds.) (1997). *Strategic Learning and Knowledge Management.* Chichester: John Wiley.

—— —— and H. THOMAS (1996). "Towards the theory and practice of competence-based competition" In R. Sanchez, A. Heene, and H. Thomas (eds.), *Dynamics of Competence-Based Competition*, Oxford: Elsevier Pergamon.

SELZNICK, P. (1957/1997). *Leadership in Administration.* New York: Harper & Row. Reprinted in N. J. Foss (ed.), (1997), *Resources, Firms, and Strategies.* Oxford: Oxford University Press.

TEECE, D. J., G. PISANO, and A. SHUEN (1997). "Dynamic capabilities and strategic management," *Strategic Management Journal*, 18 (7), 509–33.

WERNERFELT, B. (1984). "A resource-based view of the firm," *Strategic Management Journal*, 5 (2), 171–80.

—— (1995). "The resource-based view of the firm: Ten years after," *Strategic Management Journal*, 16 (3), 171–4.

ZANDER, U. and B. KOGUT (1995). "Knowledge and the speed of the transfer and imitation of organizational capabilities: An empirical test," *Organization Science*, 6 (1), 76–92.

6

Dormant Capabilities, Complex Organizations, and Renewal

CHARLES BADEN-FULLER AND HENK W. VOLBERDA*

INTRODUCTION

The competence-based perspective suggests that firms exist because they are mechanisms that are capable of building and exploiting unique knowledge and competences. A central issue within this perspective is the question of how firms change and adjust their knowledge and competences in responding to new competitive circumstances. On the one hand, in its normative mode, the competence perspective emphasizes the need to create new capabilities and build learning organizations. In this mode, managers are often represented as having considerable freedom. On the other hand, in researching competence building and leveraging processes, the competence view observes various traps, rigidities, and inertia in organizations, and from this perspective it appears that managerial choice is severely constrained. The importance of integrating both perspectives to provide theoretically sound and pragmatic guidelines for managers has been stressed by many (Sanchez and Heene 1997; Volberda 1996, 1998).

In this chapter, we use case studies carried out over significant time periods to explore the process of competence building capable of supporting major change in large, complex, diversified organizations. By examining multiple units, multiple levels, and historic patterns within four firms, we show that change and renewal in large corporations is possible and that managers often have considerable—though sometimes unrecognized—latitude for choice. We introduce the concept of *dormant capabilities* that are available to business managers to regenerate old competences, to build new ones, and to overcome existing core rigidities. Temporally dormant capabilities are the result of competences that were created previously but were rejected or "retired" by the

* We gratefully acknowledge funding for the research from Anglian Water, KLM, Novotel, PTT Post, and Shell UK, and for the time freely given by many executives in helping us with our work. We also thank Aimé Heene, Ron Sanchez, our colleagues at our departments, and members of the 4th International Conference on Competence-Based Competition for their helpful comments. We also thank Roland Calori, ESC Lyon; John Howell and Brian Hunt, University of Bath; Ysanne Carlisle, Open University; and Jeroen Menting, Ronald Boers, and Gerda Joppe, formerly at the Rotterdam School of Management, all of whom helped collect the data and write the original cases, and in many cases assisted in writing this draft. We also thank Robert Grant, Marc Huygens, and three referees from the American Academy of Management for helpful comments on an earlier draft. All errors are our own.

organization at some time in the past. We also use the concept of organizationally separated capabilities that can be "imported" (at least in part) from other units in a large firm. We explain why dormant and organizationally separated capabilities have particular cognitive importance in organizations, and why they bring the possibility of improving latitude for managerial choice.

CORE COMPETENCES, CORE RIGIDITIES, AND CHANGE

The newly emerging competence literature embraces elements of the resource-based (e.g. Barney 1991; Grant 1991) and evolutionary (Nelson and Winter 1982) views of firms and challenges assumptions in previous management theory that organizations can change at will. In their evolutionary theory, Nelson and Winter (1982) present firms as repositories of routines which endow them with the ability to search for new knowledge, yet at the same time embody mechanisms which limit attention spans and the capacity to absorb new information. This routinization of activity simultaneously constitutes both a source of potential competitive advantage and a barrier to change. In a similar manner, in the resource-based view, the firm is seen as a bundle of assets, routines, and knowledge that must be identified, selected, developed, and deployed to generate superior performance (Learned *et al.* 1969; Penrose 1959; Sanchez, Heene, and Thomas 1996; Wernerfelt 1984). Firm-specific assets, routines, and knowledge create organizational competence with a limited capacity to change.

The view that both successful and unsuccessful firms may be "stuck with what they have, and have to live with what they lack" (Teece, Pisano, and Shuen 1997) has been explored by several researchers. Leonard-Barton (1992) and Barnett, Greve, and Park (1994) argue that firms may be unable to learn new ways and that over time, as new competitive forces emerge, core competences may become core rigidities. In a similar vein, despite the importance of achieving flexibility in responding to diverse market conditions (e.g. Pine 1993), Utterback and Abernathy (1975) make the point that in some industries high productivity may only be achievable at a cost of decreased operational flexibility. In this regard, it is important to understand that the source of core rigidity need not be just technical; it can also be cognitive. The potential for falling into this cognitive "competence trap" has been noted by Levitt and March (1988) and Levinthal and March (1993), and the sources of such cognitive limitations have been explored by a growing number of authors (Huff, Huff, and Thomas 1992; Porac, Thomas, and Baden-Fuller 1989).

The notion of core rigidities or competence traps recalls the notion of organizational *inertia* in theories of population ecology. Inertia is the property of organizations that results in a failure of organizations to achieve an effective alignment with their environments. Inertia is the opposite of *fitness*, which refers to correspondence between the behavioral characteristics or capabilities of a class of organizations and their particular environments (Hannan and Freeman 1984: 152). Although population ecology recognizes that variations and change can occur (Aldrich and Pfeffer 1976), it is usually represented as unplanned and limited (Mintzberg and Waters 1985).

Inertia is the result of the structures and procedures that organizations accumulate through time and that prevents them from responding promptly to environmental shifts. This structural and procedural baggage can consist of specialized facilities and personnel, the deeply held ideas and beliefs of organizational participants, the mind-sets of top managers, and a preoccupation with rivalrous game playing (Baden-Fuller 1989; Ghemawhat and Nalebuff 1985; Morgan 1986). The existence and consequences of such inertia have been explored by several authors (see for example Lomi 1995).

A major challenge to the pessimism inherent in the inertia concept is the longevity of some large complex organizations. Royal Dutch Shell and General Electric are two companies that were ranked in the top ten of all industrial companies in the world in 1912, and were still ranked in the top ten in 1997. Clearly, these two firms have shown a capacity for adaptation and survival. Of course, there are many other companies that have drifted from being leaders into obscurity. Whilst some may argue that survival of firms such as GE and Shell are "quirks," we argue that age or complexity—or both—may give rise to an unusual capacity for adjustment that managers may be able to exploit. Our discussion sets out to answer two related questions:

1. Does a long history give a firm any special features that enable renewal?
2. Does complexity (usually in the form of diversification) give a firm an advantage in renewal?

In undertaking our work we have built on the work of those who have studied renewal before us. For instance, there are studies of renewal in single business firms or single divisions of large complex organizations by Slatter (1984), Grinyer, Mayes, and McKiernan (1988), and Stopford and Baden-Fuller (1994). The last study is particularly relevant, because it documents changes in routines and perspectives that went against an organization's established cognitive and organizational rigidities and that altered the competitive positions of firms and the industry as a whole. In the firms studied, the possibility of managerial discretion was explored and emphasized (Baden-Fuller and Stopford 1994).

The studies cited above focused on single business units, usually within large organizations. Burgelman's study (1994: 50) of strategic business realignment within Intel Corporation dealt with change that reached across a complex organization, resulting in the decline of one unit and the emergence of a new one. Burgelman showed how the actions of front-line managers facilitated the shift in Intel from memory chips to micro-processors. In this case, managerial action was able to counter organizational rigidity, in the process revolutionizing the firm and its industry.

Burgelman's study is one of the few that takes a multi-unit perspective on inertia and renewal, and it is highly relevant for our discussion. Given the increasing importance of large multi-divisional businesses, the findings from the studies of single business units must be put into a broader corporate perspective in which a business unit is part of a large firm. Many strategists have emphasized the need to take multiple perspectives in examining how actions take place at differing organizational levels and in differing organizational parts (Ansoff 1965; Chandler 1962; Bower 1970; Goold and Campbell 1987; Bartlett and Ghoshal 1993).

In this discussion, we examine changes which take place within a selected group of large complex organizations. We show that by taking advantage of competences that existed previously in an organization, or that currently exist in other divisions, managers may be able to counter the cognitive rigidities in a given business unit. To understand how these managers managed to accomplish this, we need first to develop the concept of a dormant capability.

DORMANT CAPABILITIES AND RENEWAL

According to the competence-based view, successful businesses have developed an effective set of coordinated capabilities—often by a process of refinement over some period of time. For established businesses, these capabilities may converge over time to constitute a narrow repertoire. In short, in the evolution of successful organizations, we often see a process of adjusting the "stocks" of an organization's capabilities and the discarding of unwanted capabilities.

A change in circumstances, however, may pose a challenge to an organization's success, and organizations may then respond in one of three ways. The response typically advocated in the normative management literature is to choose and create any required new capabilities from scratch, perhaps using outsiders such as consultants to bring in routines and knowledge bases from other sources. But for large complex organizations with a significant history, there are other options. One option is to look to the past repertoires for capabilities which could be revived, and another option is to look to other divisions for capabilities which can be replicated. Our study explores these two options.

An organization's history represents possible routes for renewal. During an organization's evolution, capabilities have often been discarded that subsequently can be revived. The discarding process is sometimes called *unlearning* (Hedberg 1981). But as Imai, Nonaka, and Takeuchi (1985) and Huber (1991) point out, unlearning is hard, and people rarely forget completely established ways of doing things. The capabilities that were the foundations for old competences may persist for a long time, and the arrival of new people may not completely replace the knowledge of prior routines.

The literature on "unlearning" typically presents "past capabilities" as a liability, because forgetting them is a costly activity. Indeed, population ecologists argue that incumbent firms face disadvantages in adjusting to change because the expense of "forgetting" makes "learning" more costly for established firms than for new entrants. In contrast, our exploration asks whether "forgotten" capabilities might be remembered and put to use more quickly and easily than acquiring new capabilities. If they can, then there arises the possibility that organizational "unlearning" is an activity which creates a reservoir of hidden knowledge which can be retrieved in the future. From this perspective unlearning is not merely a frictional cost of organizational adjustment, but rather may be an investment with potential strategic benefits. Put in the language of finance, "unlearning" may create a set of call options on past capabilities that are currently dormant, but that can be exercised in changing competitive circumstances.[1]

Dormant capabilities do not fit into the normal classification schemes of capabilities and resources set out in the literature (e.g. Hamel 1994; Heene and Sanchez 1997). Our discussion demonstrates their existence and value. However, our concept is not wholly new, for the notion of dormant capabilities is related to the notion of *rediscovery* explored by Miles, Coleman, and Creed (1995), who explained how GE and Chrysler were able to overcome current rigidities and inertia in renewing their organization by appealing to the past and by rediscovering old competences.

We define a dormant capability as one that is not currently being used by an organization, but which existed in the organization in the past and is capable of being reactivated. A dormant capability is based on an "unlearned" set of routines that has been discarded but can be re-created. Our first formal research question therefore asks under what conditions a dormant capability can be a resource upon which organizations can draw in the process of renewal.

A business unit in a large organization often has other options for achieving renewal by "borrowing" or replicating capabilities from sister units. The diversification literature (for example, Rumelt 1974) suggests that diversification adds value in part because units can share skills and resources across the organization, especially when they have related markets or production systems.

Considerable work has been done to elaborate the precise nature of resource sharing across businesses. Markides and Williamson (1994), for example, explain ways in which such sharing is linked to competences across business units. They stress the importance of going beyond relatedness to identify strategic assets which must satisfy the dual condition of (1) being more efficient to transfer internally between businesses than via some external market and (2) being capable of acting as a catalyst to the creation of a market-specific asset which is the source of competitive advantage to the recipient. Christensen and Foss (1997) follow up this discussion with development of the concept of *corporate coherence,* which in the context of growth explains new combinations and diffusion of competence in large firms. Drawing on these ideas:

We define an "organizationally separated" dormant capability as one that is absent from a given organizational unit, but is present elsewhere in the organization and could be leveraged to another unit. Our second research question asks under what conditions an organizationally separated capability can be used in a renewal process, by being leveraged from one unit to another.

We are not the first to investigate cross-divisional renewal from a process perspective (cf. Lewin and Volberda 1999). Burgelman's (1994) study of Intel illustrates how middle managers renewed a dormant capability (micro-processor design) in one division by diverting funds generated in another area (memory processor production) when the competence of memory processor production was rapidly becoming a rigidity that failed to create competitive advantage against newly emerging competition.

---

[1] For a discussion of ways in which organizational capabilities create managerial options for action, see Sanchez (1993).

However, our study is among the first to make a specific analysis of capability transfer between divisions using a process perspective. In our exploration, our definition of an organizationally dormant capability is sensitive to changes in internal boundaries, since realigning internal organizational boundaries could be a mechanism for leveraging capabilities. Galunic and Eisenhardt (1996) studied new charter formations (between divisions of diversified firms) and suggested that redrawing internal boundaries was often a response to a need to overcome perceived core rigidities in a business unit.

In thinking about the internal boundaries of a complex firm, it is often necessary to recognize strategic alliance partners. The knowledge-based perspective on firms emphasizes that a firm's boundaries are not defined so much by its legal context as by the limits of knowledge creating and exploiting processes (Grant 1996; Kogut and Zander 1992; Sanchez 1999). Where the close alliances have cross-organizational "routines" or team-like behavior and the use of common "directions," then these alliances may be thought of as extensions of the firm (Grant and Baden-Fuller 1995).

RESEARCH DESIGN

Our research set out to establish the existence of dormant capabilities and to examine their role in renewal processes in five units in four large complex European organizations. The organizations participating in the study were KLM Royal Dutch Airlines (a diversified transportation group), the former KPN (which was recently split up into the Dutch KPN Telecom and the TNT Post Group), the Groupe Accor (the French restaurant and hotel group, which includes Novotel), and "Oil Company" (an anonymous name for a major, highly profitable European based multinational oil company). In each case, not only was the parent company a well established complex firm, but the unit which underwent a renewal process also had either many locations or several subunits.

Organizational units studied

In KLM, the unit studied was KLM Cargo, one of the world's leading cargo carriers with several locations and units. The focus of the change program was to begin to provide specialist services and value-added logistic services.

In the former KPN, we focused on the changes in the postal division, which is a multi-location and multi-unit business employing more than 40,000 people. Besides the change objective of increasing the efficiency of the physical transportation and distribution of mail within the Netherlands, the renewal process also included increasing activities in the distribution of data and other logistical information activities.

In Groupe Accor, the focus was on change in the core business unit Novotel (Europe) to make it more efficient and more flexible. Novotel was founded in 1967 and by 1992 owned and controlled more than 280 hotels in 46 countries, employing more than 10,000 people in Europe alone.

In Oil Company, the focus was on changes in two UK down-stream businesses: a major refinery which had many subunits, and the distribution operations that included many depots. Together these two operations represent nearly a billion dollars in assets.

Method

We adopted a *semi-grounded* approach to our research (Isabella 1990), an approach that is appropriate when new ideas are being explored to fill gaps in existing theory. Our exploration attempted to capture both the time dimension of the change processes and their intraorganizational dynamics. In each firm, interviews focusing on both histori-cal and contemporaneous events were carried out at multiple levels over a period of years.[2] Our interviews were semi-structured and aimed at surfacing important events, eliciting managers' perceptions, and documenting actions. Most interviews were tape-recorded, and interviews with more senior managers were usually transcribed in full.

Table 6.1 summarizes the five change programs we studied, indicating the relevant business units and how many people were interviewed. We typically conducted more than forty interviews over more than one year in each organization. Our interviews covered many levels and locations: top level managers (defined from the perspective of the parent), middle level managers (located in the business unit which was changing), and front line managers and operatives. (In making these hierarchical distinctions we followed the guidelines proposed in Burgelman 1983 and Kanter 1984). It should be noted that in all our cases the interviews took place during the change programs, so that we could undertake real time observations and control for retrospective bias.

Establishing that change was successful

Our five cases were not the only cases of change we studied. However, these cases stood out as examples of units where change initiatives had been successful. We defined success along two dimensions. The first was competitive success, meaning that the economic position of the business improved as measured by profitability and prod-uctivity. The data gathered for these measures cannot be revealed here for confiden-tiality reasons. The second measure, and the one most relevant to us here, is the adoption of new routines and capabilities. This is dealt with in some detail below.

IDENTIFYING CORE COMPETENCIES, CORE RIGIDITIES, AND DORMANT CAPABILITIES

We found that top managers in the businesses studied were fairly clear about the back-ground and objectives of the change programs. Whilst they did not use our terminol-

---

[2] In our study, we followed procedures used by Burgelman (1994) and Isabella (1990), who have further applied ideas from Eisenhardt (1989) and Yin (1989).

TABLE 6.1 *Details of sample and data collection*

Parent company	KLM	KPN	Oil Co.	Oil Co.	Accor
Unit which changed	KLM Cargo	PTT Post	UK Refinery	UK Distrib.	Novotel (Europe)
Number of employees in the unit (approx.)	2 500	40 000	2 500	1 000	80 000
Number of persons interviewed: from top management of group*	6	5	10	10	3
from middle management	33	10	10	10	12
from operatives	10	5	25	25	40
Time table of renewal	1994–5	1994–5	1992–3	1992	1992–4
Dates of interviews	1995	1994–5	1992–3	1992–3	1993–4

* Top management includes the CEO of the business unit where he is also represented at group level.

Notes: The middle managers include front line managers. The numbers in the categories may not be precise because of difficulties of classification.

ogy, they essentially indicated that the motives for the changes undertaken were to create new competences and to overcome existing rigidities. Using information from our interviews, we set out to identify the needed competences and the core rigidities in a given business unit prior to beginning the change process. A summary of this information is shown in Table 6.2. This table identifies and classifies core rigidities along four dimensions: missing knowledge bases, rigidities in technical routines, rigidities in managerial routines, and missing embodied values. In this regard, our classification parallels that of Leonard-Barton (1992). However, we extend Leonard-Barton's framework by also identifying whether the missing competences could be based on dormant capabilities which existed in the past or on organizationally separated capabilities elsewhere in the wider organization.

The five business units studied differed quite sharply in their missing knowledge bases and technical skills, but this was to be expected because we had chosen businesses in different industries. However, there were two dimensions common to all five businesses: all the businesses appeared to suffer from difficulties caused by too many hierarchical levels of management, and all managers spoke of the need to introduce new values supporting corporate entrepreneurship.

We use the case of Novotel to illustrate how we approached our studies. Novotel is the founding division of Groupe Accor, and until recently was one of the largest and most successful hotel chains in Europe. Following an open-forum among managers of Novotel in the spring of 1992, senior managers in Accor decided that a change program should be initiated, with the dual objectives of the reduction of costs and improved flexibility to increase differentiation. From many interviews, the General Managers of the hotels, along with all the other senior managers of Novotel, agreed that the business

TABLE 6.2 *Core rigidities, dormant capabilities, and corporate perspectives*

Parent company	KLM	KPN	Oil Co.	Oil Co.	Accor
Unit which changed	KLM Cargo	PTT Post	UK Refinery	UK Distrib.	Novotel (Europe)
Missing skills and knowledge	Value-added logistic services	Data warehousing/ distribution	Reliability; root cause analysis	Multi-skilling	Marketing; multi-skilling at all levels
Rigidities of technical systems	Focus on commodity cargo information	Focus on physical transport/ distribution	Union rules preventing new ways of working	Union rules preventing new ways of working	TQM and other technical systems
Rigidity of managerial systems	Hierarchy; passenger plane mentality	Hierarchy	Hierarchy; inappropriate measures	Hierarchy; focus on wrong measures	Hierarchy; authority
Missing values (CE = corporate entrepreneurship)	CE and leadership by lower management	CE	CE, especially by junior managers/ operatives	CE, especially by junior managers/ operatives	CE at all levels of the unit
Was capability present historically?	Yes, in isolated units	No	No	No	Yes, in Novotel's recent past
Location of dormant capability where spatially separated	—	In partner organizations and in PTT Telecom division	Other refineries in group outside the UK	UK Lubricants division	Formula One division
Mechanism for renewal	Self-generated which revealed past capability	Exploiting dormant capability from other units and partners	Largely imported from other parts of group	Self-generated; spatial possibilities largely ignored	Appeal to past; spatial possibilities largely ignored

had become too inward looking and too inflexible. The organization had developed serious rigidities, and the business lacked adequate marketing knowledge as well as operational and strategic flexibility (see the first row in Table 6.2). The point was summarized by a junior manager:

When a client comes in at ten o-clock in the evening and he asks for the room rate, what do you do when you tell him the rack rate and he says "that is too expensive for me, could you not do it for a lower price?" Well, before, I would have said "No, I'm sorry, sir. I'm not allowed to deal with prices for you."

Managers also pointed to existing technical systems as obstacles to change. One technical system was singled out as symbolically important. This was a ninety-five-item check list for quality management, which in fact greatly limited flexibility (see second row of Table 6.2). As one manager reported:

There was a sentence that everyone (had to) say at the end of a telephone conversation: "Thank you for choosing Novotel." After a while this became a pain in the neck. There was a lot of resentment by the staff at being forced to say precise words.

In addition, the organization faced managerial rigidities. It had become very hierarchical, with many levels inside and above each hotel (third row of Table 6.2).

There was a Food and Beverages Manager, there was a Rooms Division Manager, there was a Deputy General Manager, there was a General Manager, and then an assistant and too many other people who were responsible. They all worked in the same hotel, but said "This is my department" and they did not help out each other.

All these factors inhibited the development of a desired set of values promoting corporate entrepreneurship (Guth and Ginsberg 1990; Stopford and Baden-Fuller 1994). By corporate entrepreneurship, we mean the ability of employees at all levels to undertake experimental activity to improve the overall position of the hotel within a framework set by top management (fourth row of Table 6.2).

In discussing these deficiencies, senior managers were acutely aware of several paradoxes. Although widespread, the core rigidity was not universal. Messrs. Debrule and Pelison, the two co-presidents of Accor, had founded the hotel chain twenty-five years earlier on the principles of entrepreneurship. Many of those who were hired by the two founders were still present and talked about the old ways of operating. Interviews made it clear that the desired set of values supporting entrepreneurship had existed in the business in the recent past, and were still buried deep in the minds of some employees in the organization. Moreover, in a few hotels some employees still held some of the desired values, but none had been permitted to put these values into practice extensively. In addition, top managers pointed out that entrepreneurship and flexibility (the now desired organizational values and capabilities) currently existed in another fast-growing division, Formula One, which was recently set up to exploit the budget segment of the market. Our observations made it clear that in Novotel, some dormant capabilities still existed from the past, and such capabilities were also currently available in other divisions in Groupe Accor.

DORMANT CAPABILITIES, RENEWAL, AND MANAGERIAL CHOICE

All of our five cases followed different paths for change, and we review them all in turn. We begin by examining the two cases of Novotel and KLM Cargo, which demonstrate the possibility of remembering "unlearned" capabilities and routines. These will provide evidence for our first finding:

Organizations can remember past capabilities which have been "unlearned." The re-adoption of these unlearned capabilities can assist the renewal process.

Novotel

In Novotel, the appreciation of the desired capabilities and values that existed in another part of Groupe Accor was evident from the start of our study, but the realization that there was a historical dormant capability in the Novotel division only emerged after the decision to start the change program. The Groupe Accor organization, which founded Novotel in 1967, also acquired or started up other hotel and restaurant chains including: Ibis (a two-star hotel chain) in 1973; Mercure (a three-star hotel chain) in 1974; Sofitel (a luxury hotel chain) in 1980, and Formula One (an original concept of a one-star budget hotel) in 1985. The top management of Accor perceived that the Novotel recipe had become stale and that it should be revitalized. In coming to this view, management was influenced by the success of Formula One. In November 1992, group management appointed two co-presidents of Novotel: M. Brizon, former head of Ibis hotels, and M. Pelison from their New York restaurant chain. Both of the co-presidents had been working in Novotel for a year at the beginning of our study.

Although the co-presidents appointed a new top management team and reorganized all the hierarchical levels of the organization over the next two years, almost all the new appointments were made from within the Novotel group. The option of directly transferring knowledge from other parts of the organization by transferring personnel was deliberately not taken. In addition, most of the planning and executing of the renewal process was done inside Novotel, although some use was made of the training center of the Accor group. Where consultants were used, there appeared to be a bias against involving other parts of the group, even though the co-presidents were well aware of the Formula One capabilities, and its resulting vitality and flexibility.

Early in the change process in December 1992, the two co-presidents of Novotel hired some anthropologists as management consultants to advise on cultural issues. These consultants wrote a short report, which unearthed and highlighted the importance of the buried values of entrepreneurship and the hidden routine of flexibility in Novotel's past (something the consultants called the *genes* of the organization). These values and routines had been subsequently suppressed by new routines emphasizing hierarchy and procedure, such as the quality management program we mentioned earlier. That the old values and routines had been deliberately unlearned was explained:

Novotel had people joining from other hotel groups and needed to make sure that they didn't manage Novotel in the same way that they managed their former hotel. The introduction of the [quality management program] gave the GM's and their staff a quality program with references and standards.

The consultants' discovery was critical, and as time progressed management increasingly relied on it. At a conference in the spring of 1993, the Novotel top management team reflected on the changes which needed to be made and the findings of the anthropologists. The team suggested the slogan *Retour vers le Futur* ("Back to the Future"), which was felt to reinforce the idea of exploiting Novotel's historically dormant culture and capability. (In contrast, there was no evidence that anyone was concerned with the organizationally separated capability which existed in the Formula One division, and no signs that there were attempts to learn across this boundary.) Interviews with front line managers and operatives (waiters, cooks, cleaners) reinforced the cultural significance of the slogan, and how it contributed to rapid acceptance of new ways of operating. The speed and progress of the transformation were monitored by top management, and in our interviews at six different hotels in three countries we were able to corroborate those perceptions. In the judgment of Novotel management, a major transformation eventually took place in an organization employing more than 80,000 people in more than 200 locations.

It is impossible to say definitively how much change would have happened in Novotel if there had been no explicit invocation of Novotel's dormant "unlearned" capabilities and routines. However, we suggest that the scale and scope of the transformation which took place in only two years in a globally dispersed organization, was helped by the ability to refer to the organization's past. The new procedures adopted, although intended to promote the common objective of flexibility, were not technically identical to those which existed in the past. Thus, we see that dormant values were important even when not all detailed knowledge from the past was re-adopted. The re-adopted values provided a framework for combining reawakened capabilities with new learning.

KLM

KLM Cargo aims to be among the leading cargo carriers in the world. In 1994, KLM Cargo launched the "Division in Transition" change program which included not only changes in strategy and structure, but also the goal of effecting behavioral change throughout the organization. KLM Cargo's new strategy was based on serving customers that are prepared to pay for value-added air cargo and related services, the exact nature of which differs from client to client (Volberda 1998). This move required a shift in focus from managing an air network based on a central hub to providing air logistics services or even full logistics services. Providers of shipping services commodities (airlines, truckers, shipping lanes) find that the further they move downstream towards the customer, the more their strategic perspectives and operations need to shift from mono-modal to multi-modal, and from basic transport to complete logistics services.

In their efforts to develop full logistics services, managers of KLM Cargo faced some major problems (see Table 6.2). First, existing information systems had limited ability to support the targeted new services, and the skill repertoires of the employees were incomplete. New skills and new expertise were required. Second, the new strategy demanded a new organization with new values and new managerial systems. The existing organization was hierarchical and had a strongly entrenched passenger service mind set reinforced by the fact that KLM was being operated as a one system company, with all divisions sharing the same airplanes. A decision was made to reorganize into passenger and cargo divisions, but splitting the airline into two divisions resulted in a number of interdependencies and disagreements about which division owned which customers. From the perspective of top management, the renewal path did not appear to offer the potential for exploiting any obvious dormant capability. This is aptly summarized by the Executive Vice President of KLM Cargo:

Our greatest challenge is to let go; there is no place for a command and control culture (KLM's past). We have to be prepared for mistakes and to learn from them. This requires an entirely different mind set from the one we had; it demands nothing short of fundamental change.

From a top management perspective, the new business had to build a different mind set, new perspectives on competitive forces, and a new focus on competitors such as FedEx, UPS, and Nedlloyd rather than other airlines. However, the perspective of middle managers was quite different. For them, the new program was not really radical because they remembered a dormant capability of hidden values and routines from the past that was important and significant to them.

In most of our interviews, front line managers and operatives pointed out that many of the capabilities and services which were now to be provided on a large scale had existed in KLM before on a small scale. In the past, the Commercial Department had arranged special valued-added services such as the transportation of horses, art works, and dangerous goods. These special cargo activities, with their high profit margins, were developed informally without explicit reference to business plans and profit potential. These activities required the development of the appropriate capabilities and values. The new strategy to provide full logistics services eventually exploited such capabilities, which were hitherto marginal and thus largely dormant in KLM.

The KLM Cargo experience provides an interesting contrast to the Novotel case in that the existence of the dormant capabilities (in this case marginal activities relative to the old core business) was not initially considered important by top management, many of whom were only vaguely aware of those activities. However, in implementing its new strategy, middle and front line managers found the existence of the dormant capabilities very significant in supporting effective implementation.

Oil and Post

In reviewing our other three cases, a second proposition emerges:

Senior managers often *perceive relevant capabilities in other divisions, but these capabilities are not directly utilized, and no attempts are made to undertake a process of replication of the values and routines by direct transfer.*

The refinery

In the Oil Company refinery, a new manager arrived in late 1990, the third since 1983. He was told by his local management team that the refinery's serious reliability difficulties and its high costs of operations were a consequence of local operating conditions (such as poor site infrastructure and local union practices) and poor design of a new cracking tower. The poor performance had cost the Oil Company nearly one hundred million dollars over the last two years. Over the previous five years, former site managers and their management team had tried to change routines and behaviors by introducing Total Quality Management (which was a group wide initiative), new equipment, and industrial relations initiatives. However, these had demonstrably failed to deliver significant results. Blockages to change and to adopting new routines were so serious that top managers at the worldwide headquarters had openly discussed the possibility of closing the refinery, although local managers were not aware that complete closure was a serious possibility.

The new refinery manager had considerable experience operating other group refineries elsewhere in the world and had worked in a senior position at the group level monitoring refineries worldwide. From interviews with him and those he had worked with previously, it was clear that he did not believe that local conditions were exceptional. He identified "root cause analysis"[3] as a key missing skill in the refinery, and characterized both the behavior of the local unions and the working practices of the front line managers as obstacles to progress. The refinery manager appointed a new engineering manager who played a crucial role in spite of a relative lack of experience. The rest of the refinery team was unchanged during the rejuvenation process.

Following a series of discussions, first with his management team (in early 1991) and then with front line workers (in late 1991), the refinery manager persuaded his workers to adopt root cause analysis and related best practices in a systematic manner. A crisis occurred when the refinery initially appeared to go out of control technically, but in due process the new procedures proved reliable. Key personnel were "astounded" and were persuaded that the refinery manager's insistence on adopting the new procedures was a sound course of action. Interviews with front line managers and operatives revealed that they recognized that they previously underestimated the importance of these work practices.

In 1992, the refinery manager embarked on another change process to reduce staffing levels by 20 percent by integrating maintenance with operations and thereby making front line workers multi-skilled. The elimination of a traditional separation of work practices brought the refinery into line with best practice elsewhere in the group.

In these episodes of change, the refinery manager's belief that local conditions at the refinery were not exceptional was critical to the renewal process. He refused to accept the statements of technical experts who claimed that the refinery was different, and insisted that standard routines applied elsewhere in the group (organizationally separated dormant capabilities, in our terminology) were relevant.

The manager did not resort to hiring new staff from elsewhere in the group to force these routines onto the local work force. Nor did the manager resort to using other parts of the group to supply needed capabilities, even though Salomon, a benchmarking institute, had ranked several of the group's more than 100 refineries as "class of best in the world in the industry." Several group refineries could therefore have been used to provide knowledge and training for the change program, but the manager and his team deliberately avoided these options.

In one instance, the worldwide headquarters did send an audit team to investigate

---

[3] Root cause analysis is a technical procedure which is often used in continuous processes to improve quality and efficiency.

the site, but their recommendations were only partially enforced, and the audit team (which consisted of experts) did not undertake any training for local managers. In contrast, in the change processes we studied, the process of learning new routines occurred by the manager personally directing attention to critical points and critical behaviors—and by getting the workers to "learn and discover themselves," in the manager's words.

Oil distribution

The Oil Company distribution business suffered from too many hierarchical levels in both the delivery and maintenance departments. Under existing work practices, drivers did not participate in the routing systems, a task performed by another department. Maintenance tasks were also compartmentalized. Communication systems were largely absent between lower and higher tiers of the company. Moreover, the culture of the middle and front line managers was "reactive" rather than entrepreneurial.

A new managing director, who was senior to the business unit manager, arrived in late 1991 to take charge of this and other divisions. Although he was a very senior manager, he was unusually active on the front line. He was told by local distribution management that efficiency gains could be achieved, but that the pace would necessarily have to be slow because of the need to negotiate with unions and because of difficulties in managing the truck drivers. The new senior manager, however, had had some success in managing radical change, especially in the lubricants business unit. Although the lubricant's division had a much smaller, separate distribution business transporting only a small amount in bulk, it had made considerable productivity gains in the recent past. In the manager's view, these changes "showed the way," and the manager refused to believe that progress in improving distribution had to be slow. By referring to other parts of his business units, he could "see" what was possible, and he encouraged his local management team to plan a more radical course of action. Unlike the refinery manager, however, he did not give specific guidance to new routines and knowledge bases, and he did not suggest exemplars of best practice elsewhere in the group.

In response to this challenge, the local distribution management team came up with their own radical solution, which involved eliminating restrictive practices, removing several layers of management, and requiring drivers to take on some junior management tasks. The new ways of working also implicitly de-recognized the union as a bargaining organization, something that ran counter to the culture of the group, but that coincidentally had been tried successfully in the lubricants business unit.

Even though the managers made no attempt to learn directly from the experience of the lubricants group, the extent of change they effected went even further than anticipated or experienced in the lubricants group. The new ways of working were put to the work force, who overwhelmingly voted to accept the package, even though they initially included a small cut in pay, but the possibility of a more flexible schedule and more time off. The new practices were successfully implemented with very substantial technical and economic consequences. As one of the managers explained:

There have been structural changes in all the terminals. Shift managers and supervisors have been taken out of the system. Drivers do a lot more for themselves, and we have reduced the administrative support. Terminals now have only one plant manager and transport manager, and at the small terminals there is not always a plant manager. There is no longer a separate managerial and supervisory structure to look after vehicle maintenance. The garage guys are all very experienced and are now taking a lot more responsibility for the work that they do and making more of the decisions themselves.

The financial outcome was dramatic, as total costs fell by nearly 30 percent. Quality measures improved, and our interviews with more than twenty drivers revealed that "things are better now." One said:

I've just volunteered for [the changes]. Well, it's the way ahead, isn't it. I think if you're going to work all these long hours, you might as well have a few clear days off. You can go and spend a couple of days fishing or playing golf or whatever.

Another said:

It's better now without the unions, although I can't say I thought it would be at the time. Now you're in touch with your manager.

The achievements were sufficiently important to cause a member of the group's main board to describe the actions as "highly significant for the group as a whole." In the perceptions of top management, the change was even more successful than those achieved by the lubricants group.

In this case, the new UK manager's initial belief that rapid progress was possible was deeply influenced by his prior observing of many of the desired shared values (a more proactive, entrepreneurial process) and routines (flexible work arrangements) which occurred in the lubricants division. However, he rejected the idea of directly importing these capabilities, and encouraged a self-developed plan, which was subsequently developed in discussions with various departments. Although in the area of industrial relations and human resource management other staff members from inside the group were consulted, interviews with front line managers and operatives confirmed that the change plan was perceived to have been locally developed in the business unit and "owned" by them. This local ownership of the change process was also perceived to have facilitated quick and effective implementation.

PTT Post

PTT Post is one of the largest divisions of the TNT Post Group (formerly a state-owned enterprise, KPN Post, in the Netherlands) and is made up of several business units (letters, parcel service, media service, international, EMS, logistics, and philately) and joint ventures (Post Offices, GD Express Worldwide, and Interpost). Moving from a highly regulated environment, PTT Post has been preparing itself for competition, and this requires creating new competences at all levels (individual skills, technical systems, managerial procedures, and cultural values). To develop new competences and overcome inertia, top management instituted several change projects (see Volberda 1998), of which we examine three: Mail 2000, New Formulas Post Offices, and Tele Present.

In the Mail 2000 project, management worked with an outside consultant, A.T. Kearney, to improve technical competences in physical transport and distribution of mail. By automation of sorting and reducing the number of sorting hubs, they increased the efficiency of primary processes. In the Post Office project, the management went "outside" to find a role model, adopting a McDonald's management formula to drive the changes.

In the Tele Present renewal process, however, the organization relied heavily on alliance partners to transfer in missing routines. PTT Post realized that the volume of mail was falling because of competition from other forms of communication. In response to this, top management started the Tele Present project. The concept was simple: Customers could shop by telephone for presents to send through the mail system. Outside partners VNU (a Dutch publishing firm) and RTL (a European broadcasting media service company) were involved in the project which was located in a new business unit called media service. The project required the development of new values and new routines in operating a call center, an information system, a warehouse, and a distribution system. In addition, the call center relied on technology from the Telecoms division of KPN (a sister organization), the warehousing system relied on technology from sister division PTT logistics, and the distribution service used technology which already existed in the parcel post division.

To help overcome the rigidities caused by the previous values of PTT Post, the Tele Present project was set up in a special unit. Top management perceived that the absorptive capacity of the existing units would be too low, and so creation of a separate unit was deemed necessary (van den Bosch, Volberda, and de Boer 1999).

In reflecting on the case, it is clear that the existence of dormant capabilities in other divisions (Telecoms and PTT logistics) and in alliance partners (such as VNU and RTL) influenced top management's perceptions and choices in overcoming perceived rigidities in the organization.

DISCUSSION

Our findings suggest that large organizations can access capabilities that are both temporally dormant and organizationally separate, but we found that this access need not be in the form of a direct transfer. What we observed being transferred in our study often began with the accessing of a dominant logic (Bettis and Prahalad 1995), management logic (Dijksterhuis, van den Bosch, and Volberda 1999), or strategic logic (Sanchez, Heene, and Thomas 1996). For the managers we studied, dormant organizationally separate capabilities suggested a new set of possibilities for what could be done to turn around an unsatisfactory situation.

In some cases, managers were able to revive dormant values of a business unit. New capabilities could then be built on this base of revived values by reviving some dormant routines or importing some organizationally separated routines, and combining these pre-existing routines with new routines invented to suit the current situation of the organizational unit. In such situations, reviving dormant values laid a foundation for new combinations of pre-existing and new routines to form new organizational capabilities.

In other cases, managers were aware of dormant or organizationally separated routines that could be revived or "imported" to serve as a basic framework for developing new values in organizations. These routines were then supplemented with new routines developed within the organization—often in a process that was used to reinforce and solidify the new values being developed within the unit. In a basic sense, the revived or imported routines provided a form of credibility on which to build a new set of values.

In none of the cases we studied did managers believe it would be possible or desirable to try to import a set of organizationally separated values.

Let us consider some reasons why direct transfer of capabilities is difficult, and why the transfer of a strategic logic may be a more feasible approach to creating new capabilities. Grant (1996) suggested that the various forms of an organization's knowledge exist at different levels and in different degrees of codification within the organization. Mobilizing tacit forms of knowledge assets is difficult, even within the unit where they exist. Nonaka (1994) proposed that tacit forms of knowledge are not transferred directly within or between teams. Rather, some aspects of knowledge become explicit and codified, and this process transmits only a part of what is tacitly known. However, parts of knowledge that are made explicit and codified are often enough to *recreate* important knowledge in a new context. In his example of the design of a bread making machine (Nonaka 1991), the detailed knowledge of bread making utilized by the chef was not directly incorporated into the machine by the design team. Rather, certain essential features of what he did were adopted by the design team as the basis for the design concept for the machine. Grant and Baden-Fuller (1996) call this process *accessing knowledge*, emphasizing that direct wholesale transfer of knowledge is often not necessary. Lillrank (1995) explores this point further in the context of knowledge transfer from Japan to Europe. His study suggests that attempts to transfer knowledge in detail were often less effective than attempting to capture the essential features of a process and then utilizing this as a basis for improvement and renewal.

The difficulties that may be inherent in the direct transfer of knowledge are much discussed in the management literature. Hamel (1991) and Bleeke and Ernst (1991) point to some of the difficulties of direct learning across external organizational boundaries. Haspeslagh and Jemison (1991) discuss the difficulties of direct internal transfers following mergers, a theme further developed by Baden-Fuller and Boschetti (1996). Boone (1997) studied intra-corporate learning in three multinationals (Unilever, ITT, and Canon) and suggested that direct learning rarely takes place across internal boundaries, but that activities in one organizational unit can be inspirational to another unit's activities.

In their study of effective organizational learning, Cohen and Levinthal (1990) highlight the role of the absorptive capacity of the recipient. Szulanski (1996) investigated the impacts of a recipient's capacity to capture knowledge in its learning process, an issue explored in the context of interorganizational learning in biotechnology firms by Lane and Lubatkin (1997). When an organization needs renewal, the capacity to assimilate new knowledge will be limited if certain cultural and organizational values are lacking in the recipient unit. In our cases, the role of dormant values and routines appears to have been inspirational in facilitating the creation of new capabilities. As we suggest, the critical stimulus to renewal of organizational capabilities is the revival of values underlying a new strategic logic, often supported by revival or importation of routines, rather than the direct importation of new capabilities.

The concept of temporally dormant capabilities deserves more study. Essential elements of the dormant capabilities of an organization may be accessible by large numbers of people by invoking the myths and stories of past successes. Our cases suggest that the specific details of what was done in the past (i.e. past routines) may or may not be relevant to an organization's current context, because of intervening changes in technology and market requirements.

CONCLUSIONS

Our work is only an exploration. Despite the large number of interviews we conducted, the size and complexity of the organizations we studied suggest that we only touched the surface of some issues. The complex nature of large companies makes interpretation difficult and hazardous. In evaluating our conclusions, it is important to remember that ours was not a random sample. The companies studied represented five successful change programs selected from numerous studies of organizations, many of which had not been successful in achieving renewal. All five organizations that we studied allowed us to investigate them because they were proud of the success of their corporate entrepreneurship.

In the most basic sense, our evidence suggests that organizations may sometimes be able to look to the past to help them achieve renewal in the present. Our study of dormant capabilities suggests that although the path dependence of organizations may indeed be a constraint to action and thus an obstacle to change, an organization's past experience may also provide a reservoir of change possibilities. Values and routines once discarded may still be remembered. Values and routines that once created a history of success can be revived and reinterpreted, to bring an organization new advantage.

Our study suggests that in learning from the past or from other organizational units, transfer of detailed knowledge often does not need to take place. Rather, seeing what can be done, what it is possible for an organization to do, can provide the critical stimulus to change. Senior managers, especially, were deeply influenced by their perceptions of activities in other divisions; the cognitive notion that a given kind of change is possible was very influential in decisions to launch change processes. Many of our managers were eloquent on this point. A more careful test is needed before we can draw strong conclusions. For example, it would be useful to examine whether managers in smaller, less diversified companies have a more limited cognitive view of possibilities for change. Even so, our evidence to date is suggestive: Large, complex organizations may have hidden advantages of a broad base of values and routines to draw on, even though direct linkages and transfer may not be exploited.

This brings us to our final point. It appears that managers, particularly those in large complex organizations, may have considerable latitude for choice. Many of the experienced managers we interviewed did not share the pessimism of much of the academic literature about the difficulty of overcoming core rigidities. In the selected sample we studied, their actions proved them to be correct. The managers we studied perceived that they could move forward in a variety of ways, and the existence of elements of dormant capabilities gave them several degrees of freedom in designing new approaches to building new capabilities and achieving renewal of organizational competences.

REFERENCES

ALDRICH, H. E. and J. PFEFFER (1976). "Environments of organizations," *Annual Review of Sociology*, 2, 121–40.

ANSOFF, I. (1965). *Corporate Strategy.* New York: McGraw-Hill.

BADEN-FULLER, C. (1989). "Exit from declining industries and the case of steel castings," *The Economic Journal*, 99 (398), 949–62.

——— and C. BOSCHETTI (1996). "Creating competitive advantage through mergers," in H. Thomas and D. O'Neal (eds.), *Strategic Management Society Proceedings.* Chichester: John Wiley.

——— and J. M. STOPFORD (1994). *Rejuvenating the Mature Business.* Boston: Harvard Business School Press.

BARNETT, W. P., H. R. GREVE, and D. Y. PARK (1994). "An evolutionary model of organizational performance," *Strategic Management Journal*, 15 (Winter Special Issue), 11–28.

BARNEY, J. (1991). "Firm resources and sustained competitive advantage," *Journal of Management*, 17 (1), 99–120.

BARTLETT, C. A. and S. GHOSHAL (1993). "Beyond the M-form: Toward a managerial theory of the firm," *Strategic Management Journal*, 14 (Winter Special Issue), 23–46.

BETTIS, R. A. and C. K. PRAHALAD (1995). "The dominant logic: Retrospective and extension," *Strategic Management Journal*, 17 (1), 88–120.

BLEEKE, J. and D. ERNST (1991). "The way to win in cross border alliances," *Harvard Business Review*, Mar.–Apr., 78–86.

BOONE, P. F. (1997). *Managing Intra-Corporate Knowledge Sharing.* Rotterdam: Erasmus University Ph.D. dissertation.

BOWER, J. L. (1970). *Managing the Resource Allocation Process.* Boston: Harvard Business School Press.

BURGELMAN, R. A. (1983). "A process model of internal corporate venturing in the diversified major firm," *Administrative Science Quarterly*, 28, 223–44.

——— (1994). "Fading memories: A process theory of strategic business exit in dynamic environments," *Administrative Science Quarterly*, 39, 24–56.

CHANDLER, A. D. (1962). *Strategy and Structure.* Cambridge, MA: MIT Press.

CHRISTENSEN, J. F. and N. J. FOSS (1997). "Dynamic corporate coherence and competence-based competition: Theoretical foundations and strategic implications," in A. Heene and R. Sanchez (eds.), *Competence-Based Strategic Management.* Chichester: John Wiley.

COHEN, W. and D. LEVINTHAL (1990). "Absorptive capacity: New perspectives on learning and innovation," *Administrative Science Quarterly*, 35, 128–52.

DIJKSTERHUIS, M., F. A. J. VAN DEN BOSCH, and H. W. VOLBERDA (1999). "Where do new organizational forms come from? Management logics as a source of co-evolution," *Organization Science*, 10 (5), 569–82.

EISENHARDT, K. M. (1989). "Building theories from case study research," *Academy of Management Review*, 14, 488–511.

GALUNIC, D. C. and K. M. EISENHARDT (1996). "The evolution of intra-corporate domains: Divisional charter losses in high-technology, multi-divisional corporations," *Organizational Science*, 7 (3), 255–83.

GHEMAWAT, P. and B. NALEBUFF (1985). "Exit," *Rand Journal of Economics*, 16 (1), 184–94.

GOOLD, M. and A. CAMPBELL (1987). *Strategies and Styles*. Oxford: Basil Blackwell.

GRANT, R. M. (1991). "The resource-based theory of competitive advantage: Implications for strategy formulation," *California Management Review*, 33 (3) 114–35.

—— (1996). "Prospering in dynamically competitive environments: Organizational capability as knowledge integration," *Organization Science*, 7 (4), 375–87.

—— and C. BADEN-FULLER (1995). "A knowledge-based theory of inter-firm collaboration," *Best Papers of the Academy of Management*. Vancouver: Academy of Management.

GRINYER, P. H., D. G. MAYES, and P. MCKIERNAN (1988). *Sharpbenders: The Secrets of Unleashing Corporate Potential*. Oxford: Blackwell.

GUTH, W. D. and A. GINSBERG (1990). "Corporate entrepreneurship," *Strategic Management Journal*, 11 (Special Issue), 5–15.

HAMEL, G. (1991). "Learning in international alliances," *Strategic Management Journal*, 12, 83–103.

—— (1994). "The concept of core competence," in G. Hamel and A. Heene (eds.), *Competence-Based Competition*. Chichester: John Wiley.

HANNAN, M. T. and J. H. FREEMAN (1984). "Structural inertia and organizational change," *American Sociological Review*, 49, 149–64.

HASPESLAUGH, P. C. and D. B. JEMISON (1991). *Managing Acquisitions*. New York: Free Press.

HEDBERG, B. (1981). "How organisations learn and unlearn," in P. Nystrom and W. Starbuck (eds.), *Handbook of Organizational Design, Volume 1*. New York: Oxford University Press.

HEENE, A. and R. SANCHEZ (eds.) (1997). *Competence-Based Strategic Management*. Chichester: John Wiley.

HUBER, G. (1991). "Organizational learning," *Organization Science*, 2 (1), 88–115.

HUFF, J. O., A. S. HUFF, and H. THOMAS (1992). "Strategic renewal and the interaction of cumulative stress and inertia," *Strategic Management Journal*, 13, 55–75.

IMAI, K., I. NONAKA, and H. TAKEUCHI (1985). "Managing the new product development process: How companies learn and unlearn," in K. Clark, R. Hayes, and C. Lorenz (eds.), *The Uneasy Alliance*. Cambridge, MA: Harvard Business School Press.

ISABELLA, L. (1990). "Evolving interpretations as change unfolds," *Academy of Management Journal*, 33, 7–41.

KANTER, R. M. (1984). *The Change Masters*. London: Unwin.

KOGUT, B. and U. ZANDER (1992). "Knowledge of the firm, combinative capabilities, and the replication of technology," *Organizational Science*, 3, 383–97.

LANE, P. J. and M. LUBATKIN (1997). "Relative absorptive capacity," paper presented at the EGOS conference, Budapest.

LEARNED, E., C. CHRISTENSEN, K. ANDREWS, and W. GUTH (1969). *Business Policy: Text and Cases*. Homewood, IL: R. Irwin.

LEONARD-BARTON, D. (1992). "Core capabilities and core rigidities: A paradox in managing new product development," *Strategic Management Journal*, 13 (Summer Special Issue), 111–25.

LEVINTHAL, D. A. and J. G. MARCH (1993). "The myopia of learning," *Strategic Management Journal*, 14 (Winter Special issue), 95–112.

LEVITT, B. and J. G. MARCH (1988). "Organisational learning," in W. R. Scott (ed.), *Annual Review of Sociology, Volume 14*. Palo Alto, CA: Annual Reviews.

LEWIN, A. Y. and H. W. VOLBERDA (1999). "A prolegomena on co-evolution: A framework for research on strategy and new organizational forms," *Organization Science*, 10 (5), 519–34.

LILLRANK, P. (1995). "The transfer of management innovations from Japan," *Organization Studies*, 16, 971–89.

LOMI, A. (1995). "The population ecology of organizational founding," *Administrative Science Quarterly*, 40, 111–44.

MARKIDES, C. and P. WILLIAMSON (1994). "Related diversification, core competences, and corporate performance," *Strategic Management Journal*, 15, 149–65.

MILES, R. E., H. J. COLEMAN, Jr., and W. E. DOUGLAS CREED (1995). "Keys to success in corporate redesign," *California Management Review*, 37 (3), 128–45.

MINTZBERG, H. and J. A. WATERS (1985). "Of strategies deliberate and emergent," *Strategic Management Journal*, 6 (3), 257–72.

MORGAN, G. (1986). *Images of Organization*. Beverly Hills: Sage Publications.

NELSON, R. R. and S. G. WINTER (1982). *An Evolutionary Theory of Economic Change*. Cambridge, Mass.: Harvard University Press.

NONAKA, I. (1991). "The knowledge creating company," *Harvard Business Review*, Nov.–Dec., 96–104.

—— (1994). "A dynamic theory of organizational knowledge creation," *Organization Science*, 5, 14–37.

PENROSE, E. (1959). *The Theory of the Growth of the Firm*. Oxford: Basil Blackwell.

PINE, J. B. (1993). *Mass Customization: The New Frontier in Business Competition*. Boston: Harvard Business School Press.

PORAC, J., H. THOMAS and C. BADEN-FULLER (1989). "Competitive groups as cognitive communities," *Journal of Management Studies*, 26 (4), 397–417.

RUMELT, R. (1974). *Strategy, Structure, and Economic Performance*. Boston: Harvard Business School Press.

SANCHEZ, R. (1993). "Strategic flexibility, firm organization, and managerial work in dynamic markets: A strategic options perspective," *Advances in Strategic Management*, 9, 251–91.

—— (1999). "Modular architectures in the marketing process," *Journal of Marketing*, 63 (Special Issue), 92–111.

—— and A. HEENE (1997). "Competence-based strategic management: Concepts and issues for theory, research, and practice," in A. Heene and R. Sanchez (eds.), *Competence-Based Strategic Management*. Chichester: John Wiley.

—— —— (eds.) (1997). *Strategic Learning and Knowledge Management*. Chichester: John Wiley.

—— —— and H. THOMAS (eds.) (1996). *Dynamics of Competence-Based Competition*. Oxford: Elsevier Pergamon.

SLATTER, S. (1984). *Corporate Recovery*. London: Penguin.

STOPFORD, J. M. and C. BADEN-FULLER (1994). "Creating corporate entrepreneurship," *Strategic Management Journal*, 15 (7), 521–36.

SZULANSKI, G. (1996). "Exploring internal stickiness: Impediments to the transfer of best practice within the firm," *Strategic Management Journal*, 17 (Winter Special issue), 27–44.

TEECE, D. J., G. PISANO, and A. SHUEN (1997). "Dynamic capabilities and strategic management," *Strategic Management Journal*, 18 (7), 509–33.

UTTERBACK, J. M. and W. J. ABERNATHY (1975). "A dynamic model of process and product innovation," *Omega*, 3 (6), 639–56.

VAN DEN BOSCH, F. A. J., H. W. VOLBERDA, and M. DE BOER (1999). "Co-evolution of firm absorptive capacity and knowledge environment: Organizational forms and combinative capabilities," *Organization Science*, 10 (5), 551–68.

VOLBERDA, H. W. (1996). "Towards the flexible firm: How to remain vital in hypercompetitive environments," *Organization Science*, 7 (4), 359–87.

—— (1998). *Building the Flexible Firm: How to Remain Competitive.* Oxford: Oxford University Press.

WERNERFELT, B. (1984). "A resource-based view of the firm," *Strategic Management Journal*, 5, 171–80.

YIN, R. K. (1989). *Case Study Research: Design and Methods.* Newbury Park, CA: Sage Publications.

7

Why Less Knowledge Can Lead to More Learning: Innovation Processes in Small vs. Large Firms

FIONA MURRAY AND NICOLAY WORREN

INTRODUCTION

Since Schumpeter's analysis of the role of small firms in the process of "creative destruction" in *The Theory of Development* (1934), a growing body of work has sought to understand the influence of firm size on the processes of technological innovation. In the face of financial constraints and a limited knowledge base, small firms may nonetheless possess a superior ability to innovate. In contrast, sizable, mature firms often encounter systemic problems in transforming their extensive knowledge base to stimulate new innovations, despite the advantages of large research and development budgets, economies of scale and scope in production, and established links to customers. Compared to small firms, large mature firms' core competences tend to become core rigidities and, as a result, they are often late to introduce or adapt to innovations that radically reshape technologies or markets.

In this chapter we try to shed light on the nature of small firm advantages in building knowledge assets and organizational competence. Traditional economic explanations have focused largely on the differing incentives to innovate, rather than the different *capabilities* of large versus small firms. Contrary to the assumption in economic reasoning that a large knowledge base is always an advantage, we propose that the *limited* knowledge base possessed by small entrepreneurial firms may be one of their key advantages. This advantage may be particularly significant when considered in the context of four other factors that are commonly observed in small firms:

(1) product development processes that more readily accommodate change and uncertainty;
(2) problem-solving heuristics that facilitate creative re-combination of knowledge;
(3) close network ties between individuals that support transfers of non-codified knowledge;
(4) an internal organizational climate conducive to innovation.

We explain how a limited knowledge base—when combined with these specific organizational characteristics—enables knowledge and competence-building processes in small firms that differ significantly from the processes commonly encountered in mature firms. We illustrate our propositions with examples from three small companies and three large companies that we have been studying.

The study of small versus large firms from a competence perspective suggests differences between large and small firms along several key dimensions. By comparing innovation processes in small versus large firms, we can improve our understanding of competence development processes that are central to the evolution of all organizations.

INNOVATION AND FIRM SIZE: EMPIRICAL EVIDENCE

Innovation success of large firms

Large firms are often characterized as having great advantages over small firms in the generation and application of new knowledge. The work of Alfred Chandler presents some compelling evidence. In numerous detailed studies he documented the role of large, multinational corporations in innovation. He suggested that large firms can spread the cost of research and development over a large output, can afford to devote significant resources to R&D, and can derive substantial economies of scale and scope in manufacturing and distribution (Chandler 1990). Chandler pointed to the importance of large-scale investment in R&D to the survival and growth of large firms in the oil, chemicals, and electrical equipment industries. The streams of new products that emerged from the R&D laboratories of firms such as Du Pont, General Electric, and (most famously) Bell Laboratories served to underline the role of large scale R&D in innovation (Hounshell 1996). The longevity of the pharmaceutical industry also illustrates this effect, with mergers and acquisitions continuing to strengthen the efficacy of large firms in innovation (Henderson 1995). From this perspective, the large and multi-specialized knowledge base of the large firm is viewed as a crucial advantage in innovation.

A range of studies has confirmed the dominant position of large firms as innovators in some industries. Acs and Audretsch (1988) showed that large firms introduce a disproportionate number of innovations, relative to their market share, in industries as diverse as textiles, apparel, paper, and fabricated metal products. Other studies based on patent data show that large, established firms dominate innovation in chemicals, drugs, power plants, telecommunications, and semiconductors (Malerba and Orsenigo 1995).

Innovation failure in large firms

Despite a compelling logic and some significant evidence for the locus of innovation resting with large firms, evidence of the failure of some large established firms to innovate suggests that large firms do not always dominate innovation. A recent study of the disk drive industry in the United States highlighted the success of new entrant firms in each wave of architectural innovation (which shifted disk diameters from 14 to 8, 5.25, and 3.5 inches). Incumbent firms failed to innovate, and small firms entered the market and captured significant market share (Christensen and Bower 1996). Across a number of industries there is a growing body of evidence that the lead of large firms in innovation has been wrested from them by small start-ups who, despite an apparently small knowledge base, enter a market and quickly take the market share away from large firms. Henderson and Clark (1990) in their study of the photolithography sector showed that incumbent firms failed in creating architectural innovations. In a cross-sectional study of the pharmaceutical industry between 1969–87, Graves and Langowitz (1993) argued that although larger firms produced a greater number of new chemical entities (NCEs), the level of innovation productivity (as measured by NCEs per sales dollar or R&D dollar) did not increase with firm size. In other words, this study failed to find evidence for economies of scale in pharmaceutical R&D productivity. Although this does not necessarily suggest an innovation *failure* on the part of large firms, it does highlight the limits of the economies of scale argument for innovation.

Innovation success in small firms[1]

A corollary of innovation failure in large firms is that small firms should be more innovative than large firms. A significant body of evidence now supports this idea, although it must be carefully interpreted. From a sample of over 8000 innovations in almost 250 industries, Acs and Audretsch (1988) concluded that small firms are 43 percent more innovative; however, they found a substantial sectoral variation in the innovation productivity of small versus large firms. Small firms were found to be 6.64 times more innovative (per employee) than large firms in the *most* innovative industries, i.e. those that have the highest number of total innovations, which includes chemicals, instruments, and electrical equipment. Similarly, Malerba and Orsenigo (1995) found that small innovative firms were highly active in apparatus, industrial equipment, assembling and handling apparatus, metallurgical processes, and textiles.

Large mimic small when innovation is crucial

Given the premise that competitive advantage is increasingly based on the ability to create new value within changing markets and technological environments, firms have looked for mechanisms to promote innovation, flexibility, and adaptability. It is now widely held that mature companies need to increase their ability to innovate, even if it means rendering their existing products obsolete (e.g. Ghoshal and Bartlett 1997). Many managers and academics now urge large firms to try to acquire the characteristics of small firms in order to enhance their innovation capability. Most of these efforts are focused on structural changes, such as disaggregating hierarchies into smaller,

[1] Definitions of small vary considerably: Acs and Audretsch (1988) use less than 500 people while most OECD studies use less than 100 people.

autonomous units (Zenger and Hesterly 1996), creating internal corporate venturing units (Burgleman 1984), de-coupling technology development from product creation processes (Sanchez and Mahoney 1996), and use of cross-functional teams (Jelinek and Schoonhoven 1993). An alternative route has been to create links to the small, innovative firms themselves and use these network-based relationships to supplement the tasks performed by in-house R&D departments (Fairlough 1996; Powell 1990; Rothwell 1983).

EXAMINING THE FIRM SIZE VS. INNOVATION PARADOX

Economic analyses

At the heart of economic arguments explaining the relationship between firm size and innovation lies an assumption of significant economies of scale and scope in innovation. Thus, in a model of innovation dominated by large firms, a virtuous cycle is created; rents from earlier knowledge creation are diverted into R&D which, in an enhanced cumulative fashion, generates further knowledge creation which can be exploited using existing complementary assets in marketing, distribution, and manufacturing, generating further economic rents. This model of large, monopolistic firms making significant expenditures in long term R&D echoes Schumpeter's later analysis of innovation in *Capitalism, Socialism, and Democracy* (1942), in which he defined a vision of innovative activity characterized by a process of "creative accumulation" carried out by large firms that institutionalize innovation processes in their R&D laboratories. Schumpeter's thesis is that, at least in some sectors, the superior capacity of large firms in creative accumulation gives them a great advantage over small firms in both the generation and the application of new knowledge. Since some recent evidence has cast doubt on the validity of the *assumption* of economies of scale in R&D at least in some industries (Graves and Langowitz 1993), however, a more complex theoretical explanation is required. Nonetheless, much academic literature and certainly journalistic analysis[2] still suggest that R&D is subject to significant economies of scale and large firms, such as 3M, often serve as models for innovation.

Scherer (1965) was one of the first to raise doubts about "whether the big, monopolistic, conglomerate corporate is as efficient an engine of technological change as disciples of Schumpeter have supposed it to be." In fact, Schumpeter himself had also defined a contrasting, and more widely known, vision of innovation—creative destruction—in his earlier book *The Theory of Economic Development* (1934). In some sectors Schumpeter suggests that innovation takes place in an environment in which temporary monopoly power is rapidly competed away because all firms—large and small—are fishing in an equally accessible pool of technological opportu-

---

[2] This assumption was highlighted in the recent editorializing over the proposed merger of Glaxo-Wellcome with Smith Kline Beecham which focused on the economies of scale in R&D.

nities, and these sectors are as likely to be dominated by small as large firms because of the relative equality of innovation opportunity.

The multi-sector evidence described earlier in this chapter complements Schumpeter's dichotomous vision of creative destruction by small, innovative, entrepreneurial firms on the one hand, and creative accumulation of large, R&D intensive organizations on the other. However, a theoretical rather than a descriptive understanding of the innovation success of small firms (which clearly cannot be subject to economies of scale or scope) is required. Economic explanations usually rely on the concept of incentives to explain the empirical observation that small firms in some sectors overcome the substantial resources devoted to innovation by their larger competitors. The argument runs as follows: a large firm prefers to maintain a profitable revenue stream from an existing product rather than invest in uncertain innovations that may or may not replace this revenue stream (e.g. Reinganum 1983) while small, entrant firms have greater incentives to invest in radically new technologies. Thus, this economic logic implies that small firms succeed at innovation because large firms choose not to innovate, and therefore small firms succeed only when large firms choose either not to innovate, or not to take their new products to market. A more colloquial version of the same point is that large firms are reluctant to "cannibalize" the certain revenue streams from existing products with the uncertain revenue streams of new products. Large firms may also be constrained by focusing so closely on meeting the needs of their existing customers that they ignore the market for attractive, but more risky, innovations whose market potentials are less immediately apparent (Bower and Christensen 1995).

An incentive-based argument is also used to explain the nature of the firms found to be driving different types of innovation. Systemic innovations are said to be best appropriated by large, integrated organizations, whereas small entrepreneurial firms are most effective in the exploitation of autonomous innovation. To be successful, a systemic innovation requires the orchestration of complex and interconnected elements in the market place—something that can only be accomplished through the coordinated incentives of a (large) single entity (Teece 1996).

The incentives-based argument does not systematically explain the observed *variation* in firm size and innovation. Although an emerging consensus is that small firms are more successful at product innovation, little is known about the origins of this advantage. In part, this is because the economic approach is focused on the appropriation of knowledge rather than its creation. In fact, a broad assumption generally made in the economic approach regarding knowledge creation is highlighted by Cohen and Klepper (1996):

Our explanations for findings such as the apparent comparative advantage of small firms in generating major innovations . . . does not rest on any innate effect of firm size on the productivity of different types of R&D. . . . indeed, in our model small and large firms face exactly the same R&D project productivity schedules and have the same costs of performing R&D. The only way they differ is in terms of their incentives that are the consequence of limited appropriability and growth due to innovation. (p. 242)

Thus, some economic analyses rely on an assumption of *equal* potential for productivity among firms of different sizes and then explain the observed differences in innovation in terms of differential incentives to actually *perform* R&D. Such approaches have not addressed whether the small or the large firm, having decided to spend a dollar on R&D, is more likely to generate innovative output. At the heart of such explanations lies the conflation of knowledge generation and knowledge appropriation, and this has the effect that in most analyses the process of *knowledge generation* is assumed away. A more successful explanation of the firm size vs. innovation paradox requires that processes of both knowledge generation and knowledge appropriation be considered.

Competence-based analysis

The competence view suggests that a firm's abilities in the creation of new knowledge may be more important determinants of competitive success in dynamic markets than the firm's current endowment of resources (Sanchez, Heene, and Thomas 1996). Consequently, sources of variation in innovation performance between large and small firms may be found by studying differences in the way new competences are built through both knowledge generation and knowledge appropriation in large and small firms. The competence view thus extends earlier work in the contingency approach by Burns and Stalker (1966) and Lawrence and Lorsch (1967), who identified different organizational forms and argued that an "organic" mode of organizing was necessary for survival in fast-changing industries.

Competences are ultimately rooted in knowledge, which in turn is generated by a process of learning. It is often argued that the ability to learn depends directly on the amount of prior knowledge an organization has (Cohen and Levinthal 1990). Firms, like individuals, need an existing knowledge base in order to be able to acquire and use new knowledge. Knowledge is stored in memory, which is associative in that it records events through the creation of linkages to pre-existing concepts. For example, in the process of learning a new language, a student usually compares the vocabulary and grammar of the new language to vocabulary and grammatical rules from his or her native language. Once a new language is mastered, the knowledge base for language is enlarged, and learning a third language may become easier, and so on. Learning is therefore subject to cumulative effects, and performance, defined in terms of speed of knowledge acquisition, is generally higher when the object of learning can be related to existing concepts. Thus, for a firm or individual, having a broad and differentiated set of concepts may enhance the ability to acquire new knowledge. In this way, the continuous generation of knowledge through association with an existing knowledge base is the foundation of organizational competence development. This traditional view of learning implies that large firms' greater endowments of knowledge may lead to more innovation. However, looking more closely at the structure of knowledge and the competence building process suggests why small firms may have advantages when it comes to generating new knowledge that supports radical innovation.

COMPETENCE-BASED ANALYSIS OF THE FIRM SIZE VS. INNOVATION PARADOX

Along with Galunic and Rodan (1997) and Moran and Ghoshal (1996), we begin with the view that competence building is essentially a process of combining and exchanging previously unconnected or weakly connected pieces of knowledge within the firm. Re-combination takes place by a process of analogical transfer. Looking at this issue in an engineering design context, Shirley observed:

The ability to generalize is an important means of problem solving in design. Knowledge developed in the solution of one design sub-problem can often be re-used analogically in solving related sub-problems in the same design and for solving similar problems in other designs. (1992: 88)

For example, faced with a new assignment, engineers will first try to see whether the current problem is similar to a previous problem that they have successfully solved (Slusher and Ebert 1992). If there is no relevant solution in their existing knowledge base, they will explore other sources of information within the firm, such as experienced individuals and knowledge repositories stored on electronic networks. CAD systems, for example, may be internal knowledge repositories that contain libraries of available components or procedures and solutions that can be re-used in creating new designs.

The process of solving problems through re-combination may occur at several levels, from the solving of technical problems in component design to the re-combination of previously disconnected organization-level competences. However, a number of factors may inhibit re-combination. Similarities between past problems and current problems may not be recognized, or potentially novel and useful combinations might not be detected. Alternatively, past solutions may be inappropriately generalized and applied to new problems, leading to conservatism and a failure to adapt to external change.

One of the benefits that large and mature firms enjoy is the accumulation of a large stock of knowledge. To the extent that learning occurs through re-combinations of knowledge, one would expect the existence of a large knowledge base to facilitate the process of building new competences, because there are more pieces of knowledge that might potentially be re-combined. However, both the cross-sectional studies of innovation failure by large firms across a range of industries and the more detailed lifecycle studies of large firms in specific industries suggest that a deep knowledge base may also work to inhibit creative re-combination.

Studies on both individual level problem solving (Frensch and Sternberg 1989) and corporate-level adaptation (Anderson and Tushman 1990) suggest that with increased knowledge comes a loss of flexibility and adaptability. In the Frensch and Sternberg (1989) study, bridge players who were either experts or novices played bridge against a computer. As expected, the experts did better than the novices. When superficial structural changes were made to the game, both groups were hurt slightly, but recovered quickly. However, when deep structural changes were made to the game, the experts were hurt more than the novices. Parallels to this effect can be observed in organizations. The deep structural changes in the bridge game experiment are like the competence-destroying innovations that Tushman and Anderson (1986) observed to erode the value of a deep accumulated knowledge base in a firm and to confer relative advantage on new firms with less extensive knowledge. These findings are more easily understood when considering knowledge as a *structure of routines* rather than as a *stock of information* that is being accumulated (Langlois 1997). Knowledge structures are essentially modular sets of categories that allow the organization to generate novelty and change through re-combination. Knowledge acquisition occurs by the creation of new linkages or the strengthening of existing interconnections between the modules in the structure. While it is true that learning depends upon prior knowledge, it is also the case that the existing knowledge base acts as a filter that pre-selects the external events that are going to be perceived and potentially limits both the repertoire of possible responses and the time it takes to respond. This happens because previous learning has strengthened some linkages while making other linkages weaker (Langlois 1997).

We therefore suggest that although small entrepreneurial firms start from a more limited knowledge base, this circumstance may in fact be one of their key advantages—when combined with certain processes and organizational characteristics that facilitate innovation. Figure 7.1 shows the connections between the areas of concern addressed in our four propositions.

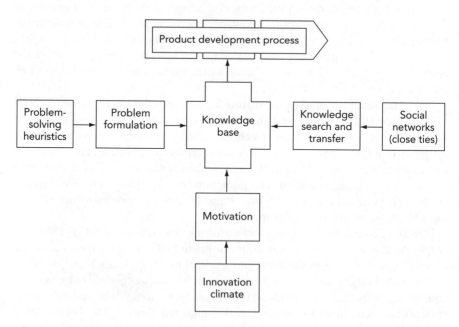

Fig. 7.1   *Factors affecting the likelihood of creative re-combination in small and large firms.*

Our case research into small and large firms has investigated the following factors affecting an organization's capacity for innovation:

(1) problem-solving heuristics that facilitate creative re-combinations of knowledge (Kaufmann 1988);

(2) a flexible product development process that accommodates high uncertainty and ambiguity (Eisenhardt and Tabrizi 1995);

(3) close network ties between individuals and functions that support transfer of non-codified knowledge (cf. Hansen 1997);

(4) an internal organizational climate conducive to innovation (Amabile 1988).

Below we describe each of these factors in more detail and explain how they relate to firm size. We put forward some propositions relating to each of these factors and illustrate the propositions with examples from three small companies and three large companies included in our research (see Table 7.1). Our research findings in each of the small companies are contrasted with observations from a large company in the same industry or product market.

Problem-solving heuristics

The first time we visited MiniTech we were struck by the "frame-breaking" mindset of the founder of this small but fast growing home appliance company, who stated that his goal was to build "the most creative environment in the world." The head of research and development estimated that they had generated at least 100 usable ideas for completely new products, in addition to ideas for incremental improvements to their existing products. He explained their basic attitude when looking at an appliance in the following way: "You can always improve upon existing products." The result

TABLE 7.1 *Characteristics of small and large companies in our research*

AUTOMOBILES

PetitAuto	*GrandAuto*
auto design and development firm;	European car manufacturer;
250 employees;	over 3,000 employees;
source of design expertise for large auto firms;	large product development teams;
wide range of design tools implemented.	substantial depth in a range of engineering functions.

CHEMICALS

ChemMicro	*ChemLargo*
chemical services company;	2,000 employees;
200 employees;	wide ranging expertise in chemical products and
processes;	
recent public offering;	worldwide network of production plants.
specialized process development projects.	

HOME APPLIANCES

MiniTech	*MaxiTech*
900 employees;	6,500 employees;
new entrant in mature market segment;	global leader in home appliances.
introduced product based on new technology.	

has been some radical innovations in both basic technology and product design, both highly successful. During the last few years, MiniTech's products have eclipsed MaxiTech and other established market leaders as the best selling appliances in their segment in the UK. In contrast, although MaxiTech also devotes substantial resources to basic research, the perception among both outsiders and some insiders was that the company was rather conservative and that product designers had failed to improve on the basic architecture of its already established product platforms, causing it to lose its hegemony in the UK market to MiniTech. Our experience at MiniTech was reinforced at PetitAuto, where we saw many examples of rapid and creative problem solving. The design engineers and engine specialists prided themselves on being able to rapidly and decisively solve problems that had eluded GrandAuto and many other large auto companies. PetitAuto is renowned in the industry for its ability to take complex and subtle problems in car performance and solve them using entirely new conceptual approaches. Companies such as GrandAuto value these skills and often work with PetitAuto to find solutions to difficult questions.

These observations led us to consider theoretical perspectives that can shed light on the ability of some product developers to solve problems creatively. We start with the view that the competence building process is a collaborative one that is influenced by the social context in which it takes place (something we will describe in more detail below). However, the essential input to the process is the *ability of individual employees to imagine new combinations* of hitherto unconnected pieces of knowledge. What we observed in both MiniTech and PetitAuto can be described as a "frame-breaking" or "habit-breaking" mindset, which enables engineers and product developers to see problems in new ways.

The most important situations may involve what are called "ill-defined" problems. These can be design problems for which there is no directly applicable pre-existing solution, either in the individual's personal knowledge base or in the firm's knowledge repositories. Ill-defined problems also include a class of "discovered" or "constructed" problems (Kaufmann 1988), i.e. problems which have not been presented as tasks by anybody else, but are initiated on a voluntary basis to improve an already secure situation (see also Mintzberg, Duru, and Theoret 1976). For these situations, the problem solver must first of all find a way to formulate the problem itself. The way problems are formulated and represented critically affects the success or failure of the problem solving process.

A familiar example is the nine-dot problem (see Figure 7.2), which consists of a 3 × 3 grid of dots. The task is to draw four straight lines through all nine dots without lifting the pencil from the paper. This problem is impossible to solve if the problem solver represents it in terms of the original configuration of a square. Several solutions are possible, however, once this assumption is broken. (For example, one can draw lines that extend beyond the square in order to connect the nine dots.) In other words, the problem has to be re-framed before it can be solved.

Cognitive psychologists have identified a number of problem solving strategies—called *heuristics*—that people use to formulate and re-frame representations of problems. Newell *et al.* (1962: 152) defined a heuristic as "any principle or device that

Fig. 7.2 *The nine-dot problem.*

contributes to a reduction in the average search to a solution." Anderson (1975, cited in Kaufmann 1988) identified some common heuristics:

Shifting between concrete and abstract representation. A problem in geometry often becomes obvious once one represents it in concrete terms. For example, understanding that the hypotenuse of a right angled triangle is shorter than the sum of the two sides becomes easier if one asks: Is it shorter to take a path that cuts diagonally across a vacant parking lot than to take the sidewalk that lies on two sides of the lot?

Selectively ignoring parts of the problem. Often the problem representation includes information that is not relevant to the solution and thereby obstructs the problem solving effort. Solving the problem then depends on the problem solver asking him or herself exactly what information the solution requires. In the nine-dot-problem above, for example, hidden assumptions associated with the terms "grid" or "square" get in the way of solving the fundamental problem.

Viewing things from a different perspective. One can deliberately rearrange the way concepts are structured to test whether other problem representations are possible. For example, in chess, looking at the chessboard from the opponent's perspective may suggest new strategies for attack or defense.

Finding distant analogies. The use of analogies has helped solve important problems. For example, the wave theory of light was developed by drawing analogies with sound waves (Glass and Holyoak 1986). Analogies may be found between concepts that superficially seem very distant, but that will prove useful if the "deep structures" of the problems are similar. Drawing analogies between disparate domains requires a more abstract cognitive schemata that illuminates a basic structure that is common to both problems. For example, in one of the firms studied (MaxiTech), the basic technological challenge was represented as "separation"—for example, separating dust from air, or dirt from clothes, or pollutants from water. This was seen as the basic "deep structure" of a problem that exists across different business divisions with different products. Representing a problem in a more abstract cognitive schemata may enable the transfer of solutions between different technological domains that are superficially different but structurally similar.

It is interesting to note that people learn not only solutions to problems, but also these more abstract problem schemas that they acquire through solving problems. These schemas can be stored in the memory and accessed later in an effort to solve new problems. The various problem solving heuristics that are applied in an organization are therefore the source of organizational routines in problem solving that become part of organizational competences.

In general, we propose that product designers in small entrepreneurial firms will utilize more heuristics associated with "creative" problem solving (like those identified by Anderson above) than product designers in large mature firms, who we suggest are more likely to look for available solutions in the existing stock of problem solving schemata within the organization. These creative problem solving heuristics directly underlie the capacity to discover new re-combinations of knowledge—usually at a higher level of abstraction—that generate new and innovative problem solutions and product concepts. Therefore, we propose as follows:

Proposition 1: Product designers and engineers in small, entrepreneurial firms make more frequent use of creative problem-solving heuristics, compared to product designers and engineers in large, mature companies.

Product development processes

We observed the product development process at PetitAuto and were struck by the complex but fluid interrelationships among many highly skilled specialists, each using their own set of product development tools, heuristics, and frames of reference. In contrast to GrandAuto and other traditional car companies, the development process we observed was both fluid and structured; it embodied a rigid timetable with a dynamic underlying process. According to one designer, "everyone knows exactly what they need to get done, but because the overall project timetable is clear, they also know when to interact with other team members." The regular but informal interaction of experts was facilitated by the airy, open plan office space and the strong sense of exploration that we sensed throughout our visits.

The crucial contrasts between the way the teams we observed work at PetitAuto and the norms for good product development often advocated in the academic literature highlight the importance of product development processes in knowledge creation and innovation. A substantial body of literature investigates how the design process is structured and managed in different firms, and proposes relationships between managerial practices and project outcomes (e.g. Brown and Eisenhardt 1997; Clark and Fujimoto 1991; Dougherty 1992; Slusher and Ebert 1992). Some of the research in this area has focused on national differences in the structure of the design process, prompted by the observation that firms in the Japanese auto industry were able to develop comparable cars considerably faster than their US or European competitors in the 1970s and 1980s (Womack, Jones, and Roos 1990). More recently, attention has shifted to understanding the impacts on firm performance of a firm's choice of product development process, and the subsequent development of a contingency-based view of the design process.

Different design situations may be most successfully supported by different design processes and structures. Design situations range from incremental and routine tasks, such as the modification of existing components, to complex and creative tasks, such as the development of a new component or a completely new product (Slusher and

Ebert 1992). Creative tasks are usually poorly structured, and designers are typically faced with higher levels of ambiguity in determining the product concept and its technical and functional requirements. Complex tasks are those that involve many integrated components and subsystems, and require the coordination of many different specialists and functions, including product design, manufacturing, and even marketing.

The range in types of design problems becomes crucial when considering the competences of firms of different sizes to accomplish such tasks in innovation processes. With increasing firm size generally comes increased formalization and bureaucratic differentiation. The traditional bureaucratic model is one of hierarchy with an extensive division of labor between individuals and functions that relies on rules and operating procedures to achieve reliability and efficiency. This would lead one to expect that large firms will, for a given development task, have a more structured and sequential development process. This ought to confer large firms with an advantage in well defined tasks—i.e. when design involves incremental changes to existing components, because traditional sequential techniques for engineering are effective for incremental innovation (Slusher and Ebert 1992). In contrast, we expect small firms to use a different model for product development based less on careful planning and sequencing and more on improvisation, informality, and flexibility (cf. Eisenhardt and Tabrizi 1995; Moorman and Miner 1998). Whereas formal sequential techniques rely on careful planning before executing tasks, improvisation involves planning and execution simultaneously. Indeed, this is what we observed at PetitAuto and MiniTech. The advantage of improvisation is that it is not constrained by prior plans that might have been rendered irrelevant by a changing context. Since unstructured design problems are more amenable to solution through the more "organic" processes often used by small firms, small firms are likely to have an advantage in innovating in such contexts. Thus, we propose:

Proposition 2 (a): Small, entrepreneurial firms use less formal and less structured product development processes than large, mature firms.

Proposition 2 (b): Small firms following less formal and structured product development processes will be more successful in innovating radically than large, mature firms.

Our case studies tend to confirm these propositions. At MaxiTech we generally observed a fairly structured and linear sequential process. The product development process is formalized and standardized company-wide, and a "check point" model specifies how the development process should proceed from concept development to detailed engineering, testing, manufacturing, etc. At both MiniTech and PetitAuto, the coordination necessary between these different functions was typically achieved by means of real-time communication between the various people involved in development processes—for example, the operations director and the research and development director. The use in MiniTech and PetitAuto of direct personal communication was made possible by the fact that the companies have small groups of managers who all work on the same physical premises.

Innovation climate

One designer at PetitAuto, when asked about the social environment there, talked of the "creative team debate focused on clear goals." Another mentioned "the competitiveness of finding the best solution to a problem." The chemists at ChemMicro stressed how interesting the work was and the status within the company that came from solving really "complex chemistry." In both cases, the intellectual challenge for individuals and teams was center stage. In ChemLarge, GrandAuto, and MaxiTech, the social environment and the rewards appeared to value timeliness and efficiency above intellectual contribution.

Research in psychology has documented ways in which the social environment within the firm influences people's motivation and in turn affects the level and frequency of creative problem solving. The research indicates that people who work on ill-defined problems are more likely to be sensitive to certain aspects of social context than people working on routine tasks (Amabile 1988).

Poorly structured or "ill-defined" problems that require creative solutions contain apparently conflicting facts that need to be sorted out, and as a result many of the paths one might pursue to derive solutions will prove ineffective. Individuals working on such problems therefore need high levels of motivation and persistence in order to succeed. A stream of research conducted by Theresa Amabile and associates (1983, 1988, 1996) suggests that social context can have a large impact on individual motivation and creative problem solving. The main finding of this research is that people are more likely to produce creative and useful ideas in an environment where risk taking and innovation are valued. Creativity might be encouraged through explicit mandates to develop new products and processes, through fair and supportive evaluation of new ideas that are proposed, and through rewards and recognition for creativity. It has also been established that creativity is fostered when individuals and teams have relatively high levels of autonomy in how they carry out their tasks and a sense of ownership and control over their own work and ideas (Deci and Ryan 1985). Conversely, factors that are perceived to be constraining will undermine creativity. These may include constraints such as highly critical or threatening evaluations, restricted choice of problem solving schemata, excessive competition, and an instrumental orientation toward work. (Amabile *et al.* (1996) have operationalized these factors in a survey questionnaire that can be used to assess people's perceptions of the work environment.)

Although autonomy and self-management are important aspects of creative processes, leadership also plays a key role in providing guidance and strategic vision for the problem solving effort (Hackman 1986). A clear, engaging direction is not only motivating, but also necessary to coordinate the efforts of diverse teams and individuals and create alignment between overall strategies and specific projects. As pointed out by Dougherty and Cohen (1995), in order for people to have autonomy and exercise choice, there must be a system to compare the choices against. People involved in product development may make inappropriate or unstrategic choices if they do not know what the strategy is.

In short, we suggest that the work environment plays an important role in the competence building process through its effects on people's motivation to undertake and succeed at creative problem solving efforts. In line with models that predict that formalization and differentiation will increase with size, we also expect to find systematic differences between large and small firms with regard to their internal climate for innovation. Hence,

Proposition 3: Small, entrepreneurial firms have a more favorable work environment for creativity compared to large, mature companies.

Social networks

Although individuals supply the basic inputs to the competence-building process, competence is an organizational characteristic that cannot be created by any one person. Innovations depend on a person having a good idea (Amabile *et al.* 1996) and may be sponsored by particular individuals (Dougherty and Hardy 1996), but they require insights from a variety of specialties and collective action by many people from different organizational functions. The breadth and intensity of the social networks that exist among individuals in an organization therefore affect the innovation process. While the traditional bureaucratic model tends to separate different organizational units from each other, research on product development has often found that close and frequent interaction between research and development and other units improves project effectiveness. Hansen (1997) has recently expanded this line of reasoning by distinguishing weak and strong ties between the product development team and other units. Weak ties (i.e. distant or infrequent relationships) can be efficient vehicles for knowledge sharing in that they bridge otherwise disconnected groups and provide access to novel information. Weak ties are therefore beneficial in the early stages of a project when project members are searching for information that will be useful in defining and designing a product. On the other hand, strong links (i.e. close and frequent relationships) have benefits in the later stages of development, when the knowledge of the team must be transferred to and incorporated by other units.

In addition to the breadth and intensity of an organization's social networks, the level of codification of knowledge within an organization also influences the ease with which knowledge can be transferred within the organization and the likelihood of creative re-combination of resources. If knowledge remains tacit and uncodified, it becomes more difficult to detect and to transfer (Sanchez and Heene 1997). Different pieces of knowledge may be scattered widely within and across organizational boundaries, and the contextual specificity of much tacit knowledge often makes it hard to transfer even if it has been detected (Szulanski 1993).

We expect to find some systematic differences in the way knowledge is transferred in big versus small companies as a function of their size. Small companies are generally less differentiated into separate functions, and they generally rely more on tacit (as opposed to codified or well documented) information. In short, interaction and communication are more intensive in small firms, and this leads to the development of strong interpersonal links. Knowledge in small companies is less dispersed, and knowledge transfer is often accomplished through real-time collabor-ation and sharing of non-codified and tacit knowledge.

In sum, we believe that the close network ties within small firms enhance their abil-ity to make creative re-combinations, both by increasing the likelihood that a project team detects relevant tacit knowledge in disparate domains, and by increasing the ease with which a team's outputs (e.g. a product concept) can be transferred to and incor-porated by other units once it has been developed. Hence,

Proposition 4 (a): Small firms possess more closely tied individuals and teams than large, mature firms.

Proposition 4 (b): Knowledge sharing occurs more frequently and efficiently through personal interactions of people in small firms than through functional channels in large firms.

We can also add that individuals in small companies tend to be more strongly tied to individuals *outside* the firm compared to individuals in large companies. For example, ChemMicro is a university spin-out, and its staff retain close ties to the Department of Chemistry and particularly to key academic figures. ChemLarge has entered into numerous university relationships, but these are typically more formal and less personal in nature. The personal ties that span organizational boundaries are much stronger for ChemMicro, which benefits in this regard from its geographical proximity to the university.

DISCUSSION

Taken together, the propositions above suggest that small firms may be better at competence building than large mature firms because they are capable of being more creative in framing problems, managing product development processes more flexibly, and are characterized by a better climate for innovation and more closely tied networks of individuals. We suggest that these elements compensate for the narrow knowledge base that small and new firms start out with. Clearly, future research is required to ascertain the extent of these differences and their impacts on innovation, product development, and firm performance.

In researching these effects, it will be important to control for firm age, because it is possible that some of the characteristics that we have attributed to small firms (e.g. informality) may instead result from an interaction of both age and size. Although we are not aware of studies that follow the evolution of the knowledge-building process over the life of the firm, anecdotal evidence from firms such as Microsoft suggests that a shift from intensive, organic structures to formalized product development structures will occur as product complexity, firm size, and age increase (Cusumano and Selby 1995).

If further research confirms that small companies possess unique knowledge-build-ing processes, it would be interesting to consider whether large companies can effect-ively replicate the characteristics of small firm innovation processes. As suggested by

Busenitz and Barney (1997) and Barney (1991), the type of cognitive and organizational differences that we have described here may, if they are difficult to emulate, be sources of competitive advantage for entrepreneurial firms. Even if larger firms succeed at replicating some of these practices and characteristics, they may actually lose their value when transported into a large company setting. For example, an experiential or improvising style of product development helps a small company to solve ill-defined problems in a more creative way than a more structured process would do. Yet the same product development process might be difficult to mesh smoothly with other processes in larger companies that often have well-established processes for re-using and leveraging their existing technologies and other forms of knowledge. Moreover, small companies may be able to transfer learning from one project to another project by informal means among project members. In contrast, achieving organizational learning in a larger company usually requires a higher degree of codification of knowledge for the learning to be effectively spread among a larger number of people. Processes supporting a high degree of codification may not mix well with more experiential strategies for detecting, using, and creating knowledge.

The studies cited in the introduction suggest that there will be different circumstances under which small firm competence-building processes are more or less effective, depending on such factors as a specific industry context, the current stage in a product cycle, and the nature of the innovation at issue. For example, it may be that innovations that are systemic in nature may be more effectively introduced by large vertically integrated firms (Teece 1996). We propose that detailed analyses of the processes that lie at the heart of building knowledge will better enable us to understand not only the nature of small firm competence-building processes, but also those circumstances in which such processes are more or less effective than the competence-building processes of large firms.

REFERENCES

Acs, Z. J. and D. B. AUDRETSCH (1988). "Innovation in large and small firms: An empirical analysis," *American Economic Review*, 78 (4), 678–90.

AMABILE, T. M. (1983). *The Social Psychology of Creativity.* New York: Springer-Verlag.

——— (1988). "A model of creativity and innovation in organizations," *Research in Organizational Behavior*, 10, 123–67.

——— R. CONTI, H. COON, J. LAZENBY, and M. HERRON (1996). "Assessing the work environment for creativity," *Academy of Management Journal*, 39 (5), 1154–84.

ANDERSON, P. and M. TUSHMAN (1990). "Technological discontinuities and dominant designs: A cyclical model of technological change," *Administrative Science Quarterly*, 35, 604–33.

BARNEY, J. (1991). "Firm resources and sustained competitive advantage," *Journal of Management*, 5, 129–37.

BOWER, J. L. and C. M. CHRISTENSEN (1995). "Disruptive technologies: Catching the wave," *Harvard Business Review*, 73 (1), 43–54.

BROWN, S. and K. EISENHARDT (1997). "The art of continuous change: Linking complexity theory and time-paced evolution in relentlessly shifting organizations," *Administrative Science Quarterly*, 42 (1), 34.

BURNS, T. and G. STALKER (1966). *The Management of Innovation*. Oxford: Oxford University Press.

BURGELMAN, R. (1984). "Designs for corporate entrepreneurship in established firms," *California Management Review*, 26, 154–66.

BUSENITZ, L. W. and J. B. BARNEY (1997). "Differences between entrepreneurs and managers in large organizations: Biases and heuristics in strategic decision-making," *Journal of Business Venturing*, 12 (1), 9–31.

CHANDLER, A. D. (1990). *Scale and Scope: The Dynamics of Industrial Capitalism*. Cambridge, MA: Harvard University Press.

CHRISTENSEN, C. M. and J. L. BOWER (1996). "Customer power, strategic investment, and the failure of leading firms," *Strategic Management Journal*, 17, 197–218.

CLARK, K. and T. FUJIMOTO (1991). *Product Development Performance*. Boston: Harvard University Press.

COHEN, W. M. and S. KLEPPER (1996). "Firm size and the nature of innovation within industries: The case of process and product R&D," *The Review of Economics and Statistics*, 78 (2), 232–44.

—— and D. A. LEVINTHAL (1990). "Absorptive capacity: A new perspective on learning and innovation," *Administrative Science Quarterly*, 35 (1), 128–52.

CUSUMANO, M. and R. SELBY (1995). *Microsoft Secrets*. New York: HarperCollins.

DECI, E. and R. M. RYAN (1985). *Intrinsic Motivation and Self-Determination in Human Behavior*. New York: Plenum.

DOUGHERTY, D. (1992). "Interpretive barriers to successful product innovation in large firms," *Organization Science*, 3 (2), 179–202.

—— and M. COHEN (1995). "Product innovation in mature firms," in E. H. Bowman and B. M. Kogut (eds.), *Redesigning the Firm*. New York: Oxford University Press.

—— and C. HARDY (1996). "Sustained product innovation in large, mature organizations: Overcoming innovation-to-organization problems," *Academy of Management Journal*, 39 (5), 1120–53.

EISENHARDT, K. M. and B. N. TABRIZI (1995). "Accelerating adaptive processes: Product innovation in the global computer industry," *Administrative Science Quarterly*, 40, 84–110.

FAIRLOUGH, G. (1996). "A marriage between large and small: R&D for healthcare products," *Business Strategy Review*, 7 (2), 14–23.

FRENSCH, P. A. and R. J. STERNBERG (1989). "Expertise and intelligent thinking: When is it worse to know better?" in R. J. Sternberg (ed.), *Advances in the Psychology of Human Intelligence*, 5, 157–88.

GALUNIC, C. and S. RODAN (1997). "Resource combinations in the firm: Knowledge structures and the potential for Schumpeterian innovation," INSEAD working paper 97/89/OB/SM.

GHOSHAL, S. and C. BARTLETT (1997). *The Individualized Organization*. New York: Heinemann.

GLASS, A. L. and K. J. HOLYOAK (1986). *Cognition*. New York: Random House.

GRAVES, S. and N. LANGOWITZ (1993). "Innovative productivity and returns to scale in the pharmaceutical industry," *Strategic Management Journal*, 14, 593–605.

HACKMAN, R. J. (1986). "The psychology of self-management in organizations," in M. S. Pallack and R. Perloff (eds.), *Psychology and Work: Productivity, Change, and Employment*. American Psychological Association Master Lectures.

HANSEN, M. T. (1997). "The search/transfer problem: The role of weak ties in sharing knowledge across organizational subunits," Harvard Business School working paper 98-011.

HENDERSON, R. (1995). "Managing innovation in the information age," *Harvard Business Review*, Oct.–Nov. 72 (1), 100–6.

—— and K. CLARK (1990). "Architectural innovation: The reconfiguration of existing systems and the failure of established firms," *Administrative Science Quarterly*, 35, 9–30.

HOUNSHELL, D. (1996). "The evolution of industrial research in the United States," in R. Rosenbloom and W. Spencer (eds.), *Engines of Innovation*. Cambridge, MA: Harvard University Press.

JELINEK, M. and C. B. SCHOONHOVEN (1993). *The Innovation Marathon: Lessons from High Technology Firms*. San Francisco: Jossey-Bass.

KAUFMANN, G. (1988). "Problem solving and creativity," in K. Grønhaug and G. Kaufmann (eds.), *Innovation: A Cross-Disciplinary Perspective*. Oxford: Oxford University Press.

LANGLOIS, R. (1997). "Cognition and capabilities: Opportunities seized and missed in the history of the computer industry," in R. Garud, P. Nayyar, and Z. Shapira (eds.), *Technological Innovation: Oversights and Foresights*. Cambridge: Cambridge University Press.

LAWRENCE, P. R. and J. W. LORSCH (1967). *Organization and Environment*. Cambridge, MA: Harvard Graduate School of Business Administration.

MALERBA, F. and L. ORSENIGO (1995). "Schumpeterian patterns of innovation," *Cambridge Journal of Economics*, 19 (1), 47–66.

MINTZBERG, H., R. DURU, and A. THEORET (1976). "The structure of unstructured decision processes," *Administrative Science Quarterly*, 21, 246–75.

MOORMAN, C. and A. S. MINER (1998). "The convergence of planning and execution: Improvisation in new product development," *Journal of Marketing*, 62 (July), 1–20.

MORAN, P. and S. GHOSHAL (1996). "Value creation by firms," *Academy of Management Best Paper Proceedings*.

NEWELL, A., J. SHAW, and H. A. SIMON (1962). "The process of creative thinking," in H. Gruber, G. Terrell, and M. Wertheimer (eds.), *Contemporary Approaches to Creative Thinking*. New York: Atherton Press.

POWELL, W. (1990). "Neither market nor hierarchy: Network forms of organization," in B. M. Staw and L. L. Cummings (eds.), *Research in Organizational Behavior*. Greenwich: JAI Press.

REINGANUM, J. (1983). "Uncertain innovation and the persistence of monopoly," *The American Economic Review*, 73 (4), 741–48.

ROTHWELL, R. (1983). "Innovation and firm size: A case for dynamic complementarity, or is small really so beautiful?" *Journal of General Management*, 8 (3), 5–26.

SANCHEZ, R. and A. HEENE (1997). *Strategic Learning and Knowledge Management*. Chichester: John Wiley.

—— and J. T. MAHONEY (1996). "Modularity, flexibility, and knowledge management in product and organization design," *Strategic Management Journal*, 17, 63–76.

—— A. HEENE, and H. THOMAS (1996). *Dynamics of Competence-Based Competition: Theory and Practice in the New Strategic Management*. Oxford: Elsevier Pergamon.

SCHERER, F. (1965). "Firm size, market structure, opportunity, and the output of patented inventions," *American Economic Review*, 55, 1097–125.

SCHUMPETER, J. (1934). *The Theory of Economic Development*. Cambridge, MA: Belknap Press of Harvard University Press.

—— (1942). *Capitalism, Socialism, and Democracy*. New York: Harper & Row.

SLUSHER, E. A. and R. J. EBERT (1992). "Prototypes for managing engineering design processes," in G. I. Susman (ed.), *Integrating Design and Manufacturing for Competitive Advantage*. New York: Oxford University Press.

SHIRLEY, G. V. (1992). "Modular design and the economics of design for manufacturing," in

G. I. Susman (ed.), *Integrating Design and Manufacturing for Competitive Advantage*. New York: Oxford University Press.

SZULANSKI, G. (1993). "Intra-firm transfer of best practice, appropriate capabilities, and organizational barriers to appropriation," Best Paper Proceedings, Academy of Management 53rd Annual Meeting, Atlanta, Georgia, Aug. 8–11.

TEECE, D. (1996). "Firm organization, industrial structure, and technological innovation," *Journal of Economic Behavior and Organization*, 31 (2), 193–225.

TUSHMAN, M. and P. ANDERSON (1986). "Technological discontinuities and organizational environments," *Administrative Science Quarterly*, 31, 439–65.

WOMACK, J., D. JONES, and D. ROOS (1990). *The Machine that Changed the World*. New York: Harper Perennial.

ZENGER, T. R. and W. S. HESTERLY (1996). "The disaggregation of corporations: Selective intervention, high-powered incentives, and molecular units," *Organization Science*, 8 (3), 209–22.

PART IV

ORGANIZATIONAL KNOWLEDGE AND THE MANAGEMENT FUNCTION

8

Creation of Managerial Capabilities through Managerial Knowledge Integration: A Competence-Based Perspective

FRANS A. J. VAN DEN BOSCH AND RAYMOND VAN WIJK

INTRODUCTION

During the last few decades, the field of strategic management seems to have lost its emphasis on management. Although different scholars (e.g. Coff 1997; Pennings, Lee, and van Witteloostuijn 1998; Pfeffer 1998) have emphasized human capital as being of strategic importance to firm behavior and performance, the field has largely failed to recognize management capability *per se* as a more specific human asset (Bartlett and Ghoshal 1993; Donaldson 1995; Hilmer and Donaldson 1996). The resource-based view of the firm (e.g. Grant 1991; Wernerfelt 1984) also largely neglects to address thoroughly the role of managers in the competitive equation. The loss of emphasis on management has brought on "a silent, ongoing battle between weak signals from the realm of management practice and strong, well-developed paradigms in established fields of scholarly inquiry" (Prahalad 1995: p. iii). Mahoney and Sanchez (1997) have addressed this issue by proposing an interactive, reciprocating process model to reconnect the domains and theories of strategic management practice and research. Thus, at least within the competence-based view, we now see a return to explicitly considering the role of management itself in organizational competence.

Edith Penrose (1959) commented on the key role of managers more than forty years ago in her seminal work on the resource-based view. In Penrose's view, management's role is two-fold: (1) the management *of* resources, and (2) management *as* a resource *per se*, taking the view that managers carry and employ *managerial resources* and *capabilities*. Both are closely related because managers as resources render services for the management of other resources. In addition, the key role of managers is suggested by the view that "of all various kinds of productive services, managerial services are the only type which every firm, because of its very nature as an administrative organization, must make use of" (Penrose 1959: 48).

An earlier version of this paper was presented at the Fourth International Conference on Competence-Based Management, held June 18–20, 1998, in Oslo, Norway. We gratefully acknowledge the helpful comments and suggestions of Max Boisot, Lex Donaldson, Aimé Heene, and the conference participants. In particular, we would like to thank Ron Sanchez for many constructive criticisms and suggestions.

The theory of competence-based competition builds on the indispensability of management in its view of firms as open systems that are guided by a strategic logic derived from *managerial cognitions* and governed by *management processes* that coordinate asset stocks and flows (Hall 1997; Sanchez and Heene 1996). Most intellectual inquiries building on Penrose's growth theory (e.g. Ghoshal, Hahn, and Moran 1997; Mahoney 1995) and studies arguing for a "managerial action perspective" in resource-based theories (Martens, Vandenbempt, and Bogaert 1997) share similar interests in understanding the management *of* resources. But, apart from the few noteworthy articles treating managers as a key class of resources (e.g. Barney 1994; Castanias and Helfat 1991), insights into managers *as* resources, and the *managerial* resources and capabilities they carry, remain sparse.

The competence perspective has emphasized the importance of *organizational* resources and capabilities, particularly organizational knowledge (Conner and Prahalad 1996; Hall 1997; Sanchez 1997). In investigating the management of organizational knowledge creation processes, the literature on new organizational forms has explicitly focused on management processes and resources at different managerial levels (see e.g. Bartlett and Ghoshal 1993, 1997; Hedlund 1994; van Wijk and van den Bosch 2000*a*). In particular, Bartlett and Ghoshal's (1997) work on management competences treats managerial knowledge as a pivotal managerial resource. Nevertheless, although the concept of managerial knowledge has attracted the interest of management scholars such as Fayol (1949) and Mintzberg (1973, 1994), it remains relatively unexplored. It is by integrating and applying managerial knowledge, however, that managers develop managerial capability (cf. Grant 1996) and render the service of their resource (Penrose 1959). Moreover, managers' own process for learning and capability development play a critical role in organizational knowledge creation processes and in the adoption of new organizational forms that improve dynamic organizational capabilities (Hedlund 1994). Given these key services of managers as a resource, it can be argued that we should now put "*managerial* knowledge at the forefront of competitive advantage" (Floyd and Wooldridge 1996: 23, emphasis added).

This paper focuses on defining what managerial knowledge and managerial capabilities are, what services are rendered by them, how they interrelate with organizational knowledge creation processes, and how front-line, middle, and top managers can contribute to a firm's organizational competences. The agenda of the paper is as follows. The next section examines organizational knowledge creation and the essential role of managerial knowledge creation in that process. The third section defines key categories of managerial knowledge. In the fourth section, the paper explores ways in which individual managers' knowledge becomes integrated to create managerial capabilities in an organization. A conceptual framework for analyzing managerial knowledge integration is developed in the fifth section and applied to three levels of management—front-line managers, middle managers, and top managers.

ORGANIZATIONAL KNOWLEDGE AND ITS CREATION

In the search to explain the competitive successes of firms, management scholars have paid attention to knowledge resources and knowledge creation processes as primary sources of competitive advantage. Because knowledge serves as the base upon which capability is formed, knowledge may create barriers to imitation by rivals. Knowledge may therefore account for the larger part of a firm's value added. Knowledge has been characterized as "the most strategically-significant resource of the firm" (Grant 1996: 375). In dynamic environments, knowledge creation processes are especially crucial, because new knowledge resources enable a firm to respond to the changing demands imposed by the environment over time (Nonaka and Takeuchi 1995).

Inquiries into knowledge and knowledge creation thus far have highlighted the roles of tacit versus explicit knowledge related to products and services. Much less emphasis has been placed on knowledge creation in "higher-order" managerial capabilities (Sanchez and Heene 1996). Furthermore, although knowledge has been recognized as residing at both individual and organizational levels (Spender 1996a), most of what we refer to as higher order capabilities are usually characterized as organizational in nature (e.g. Kogut and Zander 1992; Teece, Pisano, and Shuen 1997; van den Bosch, Volberda, and de Boer 1999). As we shall now argue, however, higher order capabilities may also reside at the level of the individual manager.

Tacit versus explicit knowledge

Following Penrose (1959) and Polanyi (1958), management research generally makes a distinction between explicit and tacit forms of knowledge. Arguments have been offered for the strategic importance of both explicit and tacit knowledge (e.g. Nonaka and Takeuchi 1995; Sanchez 1997; Spender 1996b; Winter 1987). In contrast to explicit knowledge, tacit knowledge is difficult to articulate, codify, and teach since it emanates from context-specific personal experience and learning-by-doing. Tacit knowledge is also relatively immobile and subject to limited appropriability and significant causal ambiguity (from an organizational knowledge perspective). Tacit knowledge, therefore, inhibits imitation by rivals, but it also retards internal transfer and replication. Explicit knowledge, because it is articulated, codified, and teachable, is easier to transfer internally, but it may also be susceptible to diffusion and imitation by rival firms.

The relative strategic value of explicit or tacit knowledge depends on the content of the knowledge and the process and context in which each must be utilized (e.g. Liebeskind 1996). Nevertheless, the knowledge *creation processes* of firms require interaction between *both* tacit *and* explicit forms of knowledge. According to Nonaka and Takeuchi (1995), the knowledge creation process of firms is a four-phase process in which tacit knowledge is converted into explicit knowledge, and vice versa. Similarly,

Boisot (1995, 1998) points out that the knowledge creation process of a firm may be seen as a "social learning cycle" (SLC) in which knowledge cycles through three dimensions in the "information space" of firms: abstraction, diffusion, and codification of knowledge.

Besides absorbing new external knowledge (van den Bosch, Volberda, and de Boer 1999), two additional ways of creating knowledge at the organizational level are the replication of knowledge among organizational members without alteration of its content (Kogut and Zander 1992; Nelson and Winter 1982) and the integration of different kinds of knowledge into a new body of knowledge (Grant 1996). In knowledge integration processes, individuals' specialized knowledge serves as the basis of their ability to perform individual tasks. These specialized capabilities of individuals must be integrated to create *organizational* capabilities (Grant 1996). Tsoukas argued that in this process "[t]acit knowledge is the necessary component of *all* knowledge . . . to split up tacit and explicit knowledge is to miss the point—the two are inseparably related" (1996: 14, original emphasis). Tacit knowledge often takes the form of rules and routines (see also Nelson and Winter 1982), and much explicit knowledge is built on a foundation of tacitly shared knowledge.

Organizational level knowledge: products and services knowledge

As we have noted, much of the literature on knowledge and knowledge creation focuses on *organizational* processes. In so doing, discussions of knowledge and knowledge creation are often focused on the way in which knowledge makes it possible to earn profits and rents through its deployment and application to products and services. For example, Grant (1996) illustrates the need for knowledge to be integrated to form an *organizational* capability by analyzing processes of knowledge integration in a manufacturer of private-branch telephone exchanges.

Related to Grant's notion of knowledge integration is Henderson and Clark's (1990: 10) proposition that organizational "innovations that change the way in which the components of a product are linked together" require creation of new kinds of "architectural" product knowledge. Elaborating on the impact of knowledge about architectural linkages between components in products, Sanchez (Ch. 11, this volume) and Sanchez and Mahoney (1996) propose that creating modular architectures for product designs can improve organizational knowledge creation processes, as well as making possible significant flexibility and modularity in organizational design. They argue that modularity is therefore an important form of *architectural* knowledge about how to interrelate components in a design. Grant and Baden-Fuller (1995) argue that new forms of product knowledge are most likely to be created through interorganizational collaborations when the knowledge domains and product domains of firms are not congruent, thereby allowing new combinations of knowledge to be discovered.

Higher-order capabilities

When individuals perform activities, they are often guided by rules and practices that are taken for granted (Tsoukas 1996). The same goes for knowledge creation. Even though knowledge creation is likely to be based upon a tacitly shared background (Tsoukas 1996), codification processes in knowledge creation must be governed by "a coding repertoire . . . as well as a body of accumulated experience guiding the use of that repertoire—i.e. a coding convention" (Boisot 1995: 168) that serves as a vehicle for articulating and structuring knowledge. Similarly, socialization, externalization, internalization, integration, and replication require an infrastructure of organizational processes, both formal and informal. In organizational knowledge creation, managers who organize, coordinate, and lead provide an essential infrastructure for the learning organization (Hedlund 1994; Nonaka and Takeuchi 1995; Penrose 1959).

The competence perspective views firms as open systems in which asset stocks and flows, including knowledge and knowledge creation processes, are coordinated and governed by *management processes* and a strategic logic derived from *managerial cognitions* (Sanchez and Heene 1996). Management processes that support the creation and use of organizational knowledge are essential in a "firm's abilit[ies] to integrate, build, and reconfigure internal and external competences to address rapidly changing environments," and thus are an important contributor to a firm's dynamic capabilities (Teece, Pisano, and Shuen 1997: 516). Therefore, in addition to managing resources, management processes *are* a resource (cf. Penrose 1959). It is in this sense that *managerial knowledge* is "a different kind of knowledge" (Sanchez 1997: 177) that enables a firm to integrate, build, and renew other forms of organizational knowledge. Thus, managerial knowledge *creation* processes that are essential in developing the strategic logic of a firm (Sanchez, Heene, and Thomas 1996) are "higher-order" capabilities that can create dynamic capabilities in an organization, and therefore may be considered metacapabilities (Collis 1994).[1]

MANAGERIAL KNOWLEDGE: SOME ANTECEDENTS

Mahoney (1995: 97) argues that besides "competition between heterogeneous 'bundles of resources' . . . competition between heterogeneous 'mental models' needs to be considered in order to understand competitive advantage." Barney (1994) proposed at a more general level that managers' experiences, intelligence, and cognitive style may stand the tests of value, rareness, imperfect imitability, and imperfect substitutability necessary to be considered a strategic resource. Castanias and Helfat (1991) propose that top management may constitute a resource in terms of managerial skills from

---

[1] Here the principle of infinite regress apparently can be applied as well, which is the capability to develop the capability to create managerial knowledge, and so forth. Nevertheless, as Collis (1994: 150) suggests, "although the source of sustainable competitive advantage can be found in any one of the—very large—number of levels, valuable capabilities are dependent on the context of industry and time." We share that view in arguing that the value of creating new knowledge is dependent on time and context.

which differential rents may flow, and therefore may be a source of sustainable competitive advantage. Both Barney and Castanias and Helfat thus acknowledge that managers—and in particular their knowledge—do matter in the competitive equation.

The fields of organization theory and organization behavior also offer another perspective on the nature of managerial knowledge. Following Koontz's notion of managing, managerial knowledge may be defined as knowledge regarding "the art of getting things done through and with people" (1964: 15). Earlier, Fayol (1949: 7) referred to managerial knowledge as comprising general education "not belonging exclusively to the function performed," special knowledge "peculiar to the function," and experience "arising from the work proper." More recently, Mintzberg (1994) has argued that managers have

> values . . . [together with] a body of *experience* that, on the one hand, has forged a set of skills or competences, perhaps honed by training, and on the other, has provided a base of *knowledge* . . . [which] is, of course, used directly, but . . . also converted into a set of *mental models* . . . [that] determine . . . his or her *style* of managing. (p. 12, original emphasis)

Paralleling Ewing (1964), Mintzberg treats executive experience, skills and competences, and knowledge separately. The perspective of Grant (1996) and Nonaka and Takeuchi (1995) on knowledge creation and integration, however, suggests that all these aspects of managing are intermingled and build upon each other. But the conceptual distinction between skill and knowledge remains important: "skill" refers to something one "does," while "knowledge" is something one may "have" but does not necessarily act upon (cf. Simon 1985).

MANAGERIAL KNOWLEDGE INTEGRATION

The intermingling of skill and knowledge is essential in integrating managerial knowledge into managerial capabilities and competencies (Grant 1996). As suggested in Figure 8.1, at the most basic level, several forms of managerial knowledge components (know-why, know-what, know-how, know-who, know-where, know-when) are the building blocks of managerial knowledge domains relating to functional, technical, company-specific, and environmental matters. In turn, these knowledge domains are the building blocks of the integrated managerial knowledge that each individual manager develops in performing his or her job. When integrated organizationally, individual managers' capabilities collectively constitute a firm's managerial capabilities.

Knowledge components

To manage knowledge and knowledge creation effectively within an organization, "managers need to understand not just the stocks of knowledge within the firm . . . but also how to manage the actual and potential transfers and diffusions (flows) of knowledge within and across the boundaries of the organization," (Sanchez 1997: 174). Accomplishing this requires recognizing the basic differences in the *contents* of various

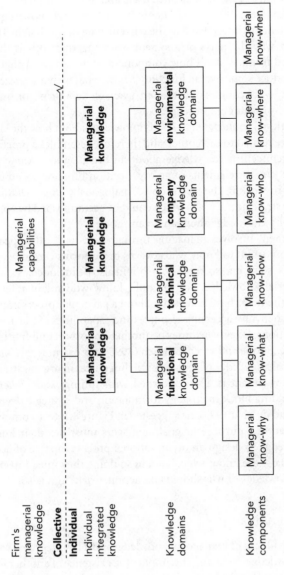

Firm's
managerial
knowledge

Collective
Individual

Individual
integrated
knowledge

Knowledge
domains

Knowledge
components

FIG. 8.1 *A conceptual framework of managerial knowledge integration.*
Source: adapted from Grant 1996.

kinds of knowledge. For example, Sanchez (1997) distinguishes know-how, know-why, and know-what forms of knowledge that correspond to state, process, and purpose forms of knowledge about a system, respectively. Sanchez then develops the concept of a product as a system, but of course, the concept of a system can also include any technical method or function, the firm itself, and its environment.

According to Sanchez (1997: 176–7), know-how is practical knowledge about "how elements of a system are interrelated in the current state of the system." Know-why is knowledge about why the parts of a system work together; this is the theoretical knowledge needed to understand how component parts can be configured in a system design to produce some overall function. Know-what is characterized as strategic knowledge about "what courses of action are available to a firm" for using its know-how and know-why forms of knowledge.

In an organizational context, *know-how* is knowledge about how the elements of an existing system are related to each other, and therefore resembles a practical or procedural form of architectural knowledge about an organization. *Know-why*, then, is knowledge about why the elements of an organization function together and enable the organization to work in the way it does. Analogously, *know-what* is managerial knowledge of the strategic purposes which could be accomplished by applying know-how and know-why knowledge about an organization.

Since management involves managing through and with other people (Koontz 1964), it is also important to know *who* governs or performs certain elements of the organization as a system, and so *know-who* should also be included as a basic building block of managerial knowledge. For example, know-who might refer to knowing which R&D staff members have knowledge about a particular process. Similarly, since managing may also involve accessing resources and capabilities of the firm in different geographical locations, *know-where* may be another important building block of managerial knowledge. Boone and van den Bosch (1996), for example, discuss the importance of managerial knowledge of geographical differences in organizations in Europe. Finally, since management is also concerned with timing, *know-when* constitutes another basic building block in strategy formulation and strategic decision-making (van den Bosch and de Man 1997). As suggested in Figure 8.1, to accomplish a new (or existing) organizational purpose or goal, managers must use their know-*how* and know-*why* knowledge to design an organizational process capable of accomplishing the purpose or goal—the know-*what*—and in so doing they must integrate into this design specific knowledge of *who* should take action, *where*, and *when*.

Knowledge domains

The basic building blocks of managerial knowledge must be integrated within a number of specific knowledge domains. This implies the existence of another form of managerial knowledge at a higher level, a form of managerial knowledge that interrelates the basic knowledge building blocks within the several kinds of activities a manager must perform (see Figure 8.1).

In explaining the emergence of cultural resources and an unique set of organizational capabilities, skills, and abilities, Castanias and Helfat (1991) employ Katz's (1955) classification approach for identifying the skills of a manager. Katz identifies *technical skills* as "an understanding of, and proficiency in, a specific kind of activity, particularly one involving methods, processes, procedures, or techniques" (p. 34). *Human skills* are characterized as the "ability to work effectively as a group member and to build cooperative effort within a team" (p. 34). *Conceptual skills* are described as "the ability to see the enterprise as a whole" (p. 36). However, because this classification does "not distinguish between different organizations and environments in which the skills are employed," Castanias and Helfat (1991: 159) proposed an alternative classification configured around "generic skills," "type of business or industry-related skills," and "firm-specific skills." Given our premise that organizational skills and capabilities are formed by managers' activities in integrating knowledge, we find it useful to combine the framework of Katz with that of Castanias and Helfat to identify technical, human, and conceptual forms of *managerial* knowledge, as well as generic, industry-related, and firm-specific managerial knowledge.[2,3]

The knowledge a manager must use in performing his or her function is the result of simultaneously integrating generic knowledge, industry-related knowledge, and firm-specific knowledge. This is reflected in Simon's (1985:17) conjecture that

managerial knowledge falls into two main categories: on the one hand, knowledge about human behavior in organization and about how organizations operate, and, on the other, knowledge about the content of the organization's work—knowledge that may be largely specific to an industry or even to a particular company or plant.

Adding Simon's distinction between, in essence, *process* and *content* forms of knowledge, we now have the essential dimensions of a useful framework for the classification of *knowledge domains* in managerial work.

As illustrated in Figure 8.1, the knowledge domains within which managerial knowledge is formed can be arranged in four domains: (1) managerial *functional* knowledge, (2) managerial *technical* knowledge, (3) managerial *company* knowledge, and (4) managerial *environmental* knowledge. In this classification, Fayol's (1949: 7) notion of functional knowledge is adopted to address knowledge "peculiar to the function" of the manager. This form of knowledge includes knowing what roles a manager needs to play in scheduling, leading, controlling, and communicating with other people. (For a review of managerial roles, see e.g. Drucker 1973; Mintzberg 1973, 1994.) This essentially coordinating role of managers requires knowledge of how to interrelate effectively the functional areas making up a firm, such as R&D, manufacturing, human resources, marketing, and finance. Technical knowledge, in turn, requires knowledge about the methods, processes, procedures, and techniques specific to each area of functional activity.

---

[2] As will be explained later in this chapter, Castanias and Helfat (1991) argue that generic skills, industry-related skills, and firm-specific skills have an increasing potential for generating managerial rents.

[3] An additional classification is provided by Sternberg (1997), who distinguishes analytical, practical, and creative intelligence to show that IQ (as commonly measured) is only one part of managerial intelligence. This classification takes us beyond the scope of this paper, but clearly suggests an interesting direction for further expansion of our framework.

Company-specific knowledge here reflects Katz's (1955) and Simon's (1985) notion of knowledge about how a specific organization operates. Expanding their observations, we add the perspective that this form of managerial knowledge also includes knowing what the organization stands for, and what values are held by various individuals and groups within the firm. Environmental knowledge includes understanding how to work with external providers of key resources (van den Bosch and van Riel 1998), as well as market knowledge of customers' preferences, relevant macroenvironmental developments, and competitors.

Individual managerial knowledge

At the highest level of individual knowledge, management knowledge domains are integrated in the form of an individual's managerial knowledge. This knowledge may be in tacit form, because as managers gain experience in managing over time, they may develop and follow personal routines for managing (Nelson and Winter 1982). Although managers often create documents in various forms to communicate processes to be followed in their organization, they often do not rely exclusively on such documents while "doing" their job. Therefore, this form of managerial knowledge remains to some extent, and for some managers to a large extent, in tacit form.

In performing his or her job, a manager must integrate the four knowledge domains into a coherent set of knowledge that may be idiosyncratic to a particular context. In the context of organizational knowledge creation, therefore, individual managers apply a "code" of personal integrated knowledge in which "a personal element, to some extent incommunicable, remains [as] a source of individuation and differentiation in the skill with which the code is applied" (Boisot 1995: 170). As managers develop and integrate knowledge domains over time, "this increase in knowledge not only causes the productive opportunity of a firm to change in ways unrelated to changes in the environment, but also contributes to the 'uniqueness' of the opportunity of each individual firm" (Penrose 1959: 52–3).

A firm's managerial capabilities

A firm's managerial capabilities are created over time by integrating the knowledge of the individual managers on a management team in ways that "enable them to provide services that are uniquely valuable for the operations of the particular group with which they are associated" (Penrose 1959: 46). Consequently, "they become individually and as a group more valuable to the firm in that the services they can render are enhanced by their knowledge of their fellow-workers, of the methods of the firm, and of the best way of doing things in the particular set of circumstances in which they are working" (Penrose 1959: 52). In a collective setting, managers should be able to complement and leverage each other's individual knowledge, both at the level of the specific knowledge components and at the level of the knowledge domains shown in Figure 8.1.

When a management collective is more or less permanent, managers are able to specialize, and thereby to build upon the competences available to a firm (Sanchez and Heene 1996). Since knowledge and mental models are to some extent irreducibly individual and thus heterogeneous (Mahoney 1995), changes in the managers who make up an organization's management teams may lead to reconfiguring and reintegrating managerial knowledge in ways that give rise to new combinations of knowledge—and therefore to new managerial capabilities at the firm level.

Thus, to sum up the above analysis, integration of various identifiable forms of individual managerial knowledge is a prerequisite for the creation of organizational managerial capabilities. Moreover, the managerial capabilities of an organization will depend on the composition and the degree of integration of the knowledge of individual managers and the stability of the management team.

MANAGEMENT LEVELS AND MANAGERIAL KNOWLEDGE INTEGRATION

In this section we apply our conceptual framework of managerial knowledge integration to different levels of management within a firm. Following Bartlett and Ghoshal (1993), we focus on three levels: front-line management, middle management, and top management. Although in each of these levels of management many of the same set of roles and tasks are performed by managers, there are differences in the relative importance of each to the overall organization. This view goes back to Fayol (1949), who stated that all activities within firms can be divided into six groups. Five of these groups of activities relate to functional areas of management. Management activities *per se* are identified as the sixth group of activities. Fayol observed that most of these activities will be present in most managerial jobs, although to varying degrees. Fayol stressed that "pure" managerial activities increase in importance in senior jobs and are least important (or perhaps even absent) in direct production or other functional jobs.

With the recent emergence of new organizational forms and the ongoing decentralization of processes in organizations, traditional boundaries between management levels are breaking down (Bartlett and Ghoshal 1993; Hedlund 1994; van Wijk and van den Bosch 1998, 2000*a*, 2000*b*; Volberda 1998). Notwithstanding this development, Bartlett and Ghoshal (1993) usefully build on Fayol's approach in describing different levels of management activities, and the differences in their relative importance by level. Figure 8.2 illustrates the relative importance of knowledge components and knowledge domains at the front-line management level.

Front-line management

Front-line managers occupy themselves mostly with functions like production (Fayol 1949) and with the creation of new (managerial) knowledge within particular functional areas or organizational units (Bartlett and Ghoshal 1993). Although they need to possess some organizational knowledge about other people in their departments and about their senior managers, and some environmental knowledge in order to identify

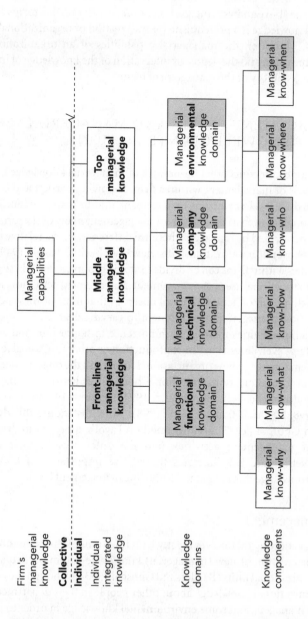

Firm's managerial knowledge

Collective
Individual

Individual integrated knowledge

Knowledge domains

Knowledge components

Managerial capabilities

Front-line managerial knowledge · **Middle managerial knowledge** · **Top managerial knowledge**

Managerial functional knowledge domain · Managerial technical knowledge domain · Managerial company knowledge domain · Managerial environmental knowledge domain

Managerial know-why · Managerial know-what · Managerial know-how · Managerial know-who · Managerial know-where · Managerial know-when

Fig. 8.2   *A conceptual framework of managerial knowledge integration: the case of front-line management.*
Source: adapted from Grant 1996.

Note: Shared areas indicate relative importance of knowledge domains and knowledge components for a specific level of management.

appropriate capabilities and knowledge, as illustrated in Figure 8.2, their managerial knowledge is largely based on technical and functional knowledge domains. Thus, the managerial knowledge components upon which the managerial knowledge domains of front-line managers are built pertain particularly to know-how and know-who— i.e. with *how* a particular task is being performed, and with *who* is doing or can do it.

Middle management

In traditional organizations, middle managers are the implementers of resource allocation decisions made at the top. In more contemporary organizational forms, however, middle managers provide a strategic coordinating level of management— the "boosting level" of management as described by Vila and Syvertsen (2000)—in linking the firm's resources, skills, and knowledge (Bartlett and Ghoshal 1993; Mintzberg 1994). Thus, in more contemporary forms of organizations (Pettigrew and Fenton 2000), a middle manager's individual knowledge is mostly built on the knowledge domains of company knowledge and environmental knowledge, and less directly on the functional and technical knowledge domains. Of course, middle managers require a certain level of understanding of technical and functional knowledge before they can understand possibilities (and constraints) in linking different resources and knowledge (Leonard-Barton 1995). Yet it is environmental and company-specific forms of knowledge that enable middle managers to craft implementation designs for linking required resources and knowledge effectively, and that enable them to determine when to do so, whom to involve, and where to find essential resources.

The relative importance of environmental *versus* company-specific knowledge depends on the scope of decision making accorded to middle managers by top management. This scope may range from a strict focus on implementing a well-defined and precisely bounded part of a strategic plan formulated by top management (as in a traditional hierarchy) to being active participants with top management in defining an evolving set of strategic goals (as in an organization with a more decentralized and "empowered" form of strategic management, see e.g. van Wijk and ven den Bosch 2000*a*). Functional and technical knowledge predominate in the former case, while company-specific and environmental knowledge gain importance in the latter case.

Top management

Top management's function in organizations is mainly to articulate a vision of the firm's future, and the strategic logics and strategies that can bring the firm to its intended future (Bartlett and Ghoshal 1993; Mintzberg 1994; Sanchez, Heene, and Thomas 1996). Since the strategies of firms must ultimately achieve an alignment of organization and environment, the knowledge domains relating to the company and environment are central to top management capability.

As contemporary strategies increasingly become defined in terms of processes that span across traditional functions and boundaries of organizational units, the relative importance of specific functional and technical knowledge in the top management function has decreased. Of course, to have an understanding of the organization adequate to identify the most appropriate strategic logics and strategies to adopt, top managers still require a certain level of company-specific know-who, know-where, and know-when. The most important company-specific knowledge component for top managers, however, will be know-why knowledge regarding why the organization works the way it does, from which top managers can develop insights into the limits of the organization for competence leveraging in the near term and its prospects for competence building in the longer term (Sanchez, Heene, and Thomas 1996).

Managerial competences

Since "knowledge is fundamental to organizational competence" (Sanchez and Heene 1997: 5), so then is managerial knowledge fundamental to managerial competency. From a competence perspective, *managerial competency* can be defined as a collective ability of managers to lead an organization's competence building and leveraging by sustaining their *own* coordinated deployments of managerial resources, managerial knowledge, and managerial capabilities in ways that help their organization achieve its near-term and long-term goals. In this regard we recall Sanchez and Heene's (1996) characterization of competition as "a contest between managerial cognitions," in which managers "face the unique challenge of learning how better to manage their own cognitive processes"—and as we point out here, learning to do so *both individually and collectively.*

From this perspective, managerial competences occupy the highest level in our conceptual framework of managerial knowledge integration, in which managers must collectively apply and integrate their individual managerial capabilities in support of the wider goals of the organization depicted in Figure 8.3. Taken together, Figures 8.2 and 8.3 depict systemic interdependencies among specific knowledge components, specific knowledge domains, individual managers' stocks of knowledge, the ability of each manager to integrate his or her knowledge to create individual managerial capabilities, and the ability of an organization's managers collectively to integrate their individual managerial capabilities into a management competency. Because these systemic interdependencies include path dependencies, contextual variation (Dijksterhuis, van den Bosch, and Volberda 1999), and idiosyncratic managerial mental models and cognitive processes, managerial competences are likely to be highly firm-specific forms of

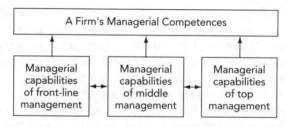

FIG. 8.3 *Managerial competence building.*

knowledge that go beyond any generic or industry-specific knowledge and capabilities managers of the firm may have (Castanias and Helfat 1991). As systemic interdependencies between idiosyncratic knowledge and capabilites within a firm are built up over time, a firm's managerial competences become increasingly firm-specific, difficult to imitate, and (when also effective) therefore a key determinant of sustainable competitive advantage.

CONCLUSION

Managerial knowledge has thus far been a relatively unrecognized and unexplored aspect of the creation of sustainable competitive advantage. In this chapter we have elaborated the ways in which various forms of managerial knowledge, when appropriately integrated at individual and collective levels of management, serve as the foundation for an organization's managerial competences. This view is consistent with competence-based management's emphasis on developing a dynamic, systemic, cognitive, and holistic view of management processes. We hope that the conceptual framework we have developed here will contribute to a more complete understanding of what managers at various levels of an organization must know, and what forms of integration of managerial knowledge are critical to the achievement of managerial competency, organizational competence, and competitive advantage.

REFERENCES

BARNEY, J. B. (1994). "Bringing managers back in: A resource-based analysis of the role of managers in creating and sustaining competitive advantages for firms," in A. T. Malm (ed.), *Does Management Matter?* Lund: Lund University, Institute for Economic Research, 1–36.

BARTLETT, C. A. and S. GHOSHAL (1993). "Beyond the M-form: Toward a managerial theory of the firm," *Strategic Management Journal,* 14 (Winter Special Issue), 23–46.

——— (1997). "The myth of the generic manager: New personal competencies for new management roles," *California Management Review,* 40 (1), 92–116.

BOISOT, M. H. (1995). *Information Space: A Framework for Learning in Organizations, Institutions, and Culture.* London: Routledge.

——— (1998). *Knowledge Assets: Securing Competitive Advantage in the Information Economy.* Oxford: Oxford University Press.

BOONE, P. F. and F. A. J. VAN DEN BOSCH (1996). "Discerning a key characteristic of a European style of management," *International Studies of Management & Organization,* 26 (3), 109–27.

CASTANIAS, R. P. and C. E. HELFAT (1991). "Managerial resources and rents," *Journal of Management,* 17 (1), 155–71.

COFF, R. W. (1997). "Human assets and management dilemmas: Coping with hazards on the road to resource-based theory," *Academy of Management Review,* 22 (2), 374–402.

COLLIS, D. J. (1994). "Research note: How valuable are organizational capabilities?" *Strategic Management Journal,* 15 (Winter Special Issue), 143–52.

CONNER, K. R. and C. K. PRAHALAD (1996). "A resource-based theory of the firm: Knowledge versus opportunism," *Organization Science,* 7 (5), 477–501.

DIJKSTERHUIS, M. S., F. A. J. VAN DEN BOSCH, and H. W. VOLBERDA (1999). "Where do new organizational forms come from? Management logistics as a source of coevolution," *Organization Science*, 10 (5), 569–82.

DONALDSON, L. (1995). *American Anti-Management Theories of Organization: A Critique of Paradigm Proliferation*. Cambridge: Cambridge University Press.

DRUCKER, P. F. (1973). *Management: Tasks, Responsibilities, Practices*. New York: Harper & Row.

EWING, D. W. (1964). "The knowledge of the executive," *Harvard Business Review*, 42 (2), 91–100.

FAYOL, H. (1949). *General and Industrial Management*. London: Pelman (originally translated from *Administration Industrielle et Générale*, published by Dunod, Paris).

FLOYD, S. W. and B. WOOLDRIDGE (1996). *The Strategic Middle Manager: How to Create and Sustain Competitive Advantage*. San Francisco: Jossey-Bass.

GHOSHAL, S., M. HAHN, and P. MORAN (1997). "An integrative theory of firm growth: Implications for corporate organization and management", INSEAD Working Paper 97/87/SM, Fontainebleau, France.

GRANT, R. M. (1991). "The resource-based theory of competitive advantage: Implications for strategy formulation," *California Management Review*, 33 (3), 114–35.

—— (1996). "Prospering in dynamically competitive environments: Organizational capability as knowledge integration," *Organization Science*, 7 (4), 375–87.

—— and C. BADEN-FULLER (1995). "A knowledge-based theory of inter-firm collaboration," in *Best Papers of the Academy of Management*. Vancouver: Academy of Management.

HALL, R. (1997). "Complex systems, complex learning, and competence building," in R. Sanchez and A. Heene (eds.), *Strategic Learning and Knowledge Management*. Chichester: John Wiley, 39–64.

HEDLUND, G. (1994). "A model of knowledge management and the N-form corporation," *Strategic Management Journal*, 15 (Summer Special Issue), 73–90.

HENDERSON, R. M. and K. CLARK (1990). "Architectural innovation: The reconfiguration of existing product technologies and the failure of established firms," *Administrative Science Quarterly*, 35 (1), 9–31.

HILMER, F. G. and L. DONALDSON (1996). *Management Redeemed: Debunking the Fads that Undermine Corporate Performance*. New York: The Free Press.

KATZ, R. L. (1955). "Skills of an effective administrator," *Harvard Business Review*, 33 (1), 33–42.

KOGUT, B. and U. ZANDER (1992). "Knowledge of the firm, combinative capabilities, and the replication of technology," *Organization Science*, 3 (3), 383–97.

KOONTZ, H. (1964). "Making sense of management theory," in H. Koontz (ed.), *Toward a Unified Theory of Management*. New York: McGraw-Hill, 1–17.

LEONARD-BARTON, D. (1995). *Wellsprings of Knowledge*. Boston, MA: Harvard Business School Press.

LIEBESKIND, J. P. (1996). "Knowledge, strategy, and the theory of the firm," *Strategic Management Journal*, 17 (Winter Special Issue), 93–107.

MAHONEY, J. T. (1995). "The management of resources and the resources of management," *Journal of Business Research*, 33 (2), 91–101.

—— and R. SANCHEZ (1997). "Competence theory building: Reconnecting management research and management practice," in A. Heene and R. Sanchez (eds.), *Competence-Based Strategic Management*. Chichester: John Wiley, 43–64.

MARTENS, R., K. VANDENBEMPT and I. BOGAERT (1997). "The limits of the resource-based view on strategy and beyond: Causality thinking versus action perspective," Working Paper 97–245, UFSIA, University of Antwerp, Belgium.

MINTZBERG, H. (1973). *The Nature of Managerial Work*. Englewood Cliffs, NJ: Prentice-Hall.

—— (1994). "Rounding out the manager's job," *Sloan Management Review*, 36 (1), 11–26.

NELSON, R. R. and S. G. WINTER (1982). *An Evolutionary Theory of Economic Change*. Cambridge, MA: Belknap Press.

NONAKA, I. and H. TAKEUCHI (1995). *The Knowledge-Creating Company: How Japanese Companies Create the Dynamics of Innovation*. Oxford: Oxford University Press.

PENNINGS, J. M., K. LEE, and A. van WITTELOOSTUIJN (1998). "Human capital, social capital, and firm dissolution: A study of professional services firms," *Academy of Management Journal*, 41(4), 425–40.

PENROSE, E. T. (1959). *The Theory of the Growth of the Firm*. Oxford: Basil Blackwell.

PETTIGREW, A. M. AND E. M. FENTON (eds.) (2000). *The Innovating Organization*. London: Sage.

PFEFFER, J. (1998). *The Human Equation: Building Profits by Putting People First*. Boston, MA: Harvard Business School Press.

POLANYI, M. (1958). *Personal Knowledge: Toward a Post-Critical Philosophy*. Chicago: University of Chicago Press.

PRAHALAD, C. K. (1995). "Weak signals versus strong paradigms," *Journal of Marketing Research*, 32 (3), pp. iii–viii.

SANCHEZ, R. (1997). "Managing articulated knowledge in competence-based competition," in R. Sanchez and A. Heene (eds.), *Strategic Learning and Knowledge Management*. Chichester: John Wiley, 163–87.

—— and A. HEENE (1996). "A systems view of the firm in competence-based competition," in R. Sanchez, A. Heene, and H. Thomas (eds.), *Dynamics of Competence-Based Competition: Theory and Practice in the New Strategic Management*. Oxford: Elsevier Pergamon, 39–62.

—— —— (eds.) (1997). *Strategic Learning and Knowledge Management*. Chichester: John Wiley.

—— —— and H. THOMAS (eds.) (1996). *Dynamics of Competence-Based Competition: Theory and Practice in the New Strategic Management*. Oxford: Elsevier Pergamon.

—— and J. T. MAHONEY (1996). "Modularity, flexibility, and knowledge management in product and organizational design," *Strategic Management Journal*, 17 (Winter Special Issue), 63–76.

SIMON, H. A. (1985). "What we know about the creative process," in R. L. Kuhn (ed.), *Frontiers in Creative and Innovative Management*. Cambridge, MA: Ballinger, 3–20.

SPENDER, J.-C. (1996*a*). "Making knowledge the basis of a dynamic theory of the firm," *Strategic Management Journal*, 17 (Winter Special Issue), 45–62.

—— (1996*b*). "Competitive advantage from tacit knowledge? Unpacking the concept and its strategic implications," in B. Moingeon and A. Edmonson (eds.), *Organizational Learning and Competitive Advantage*. London: Sage, 56–73.

STERNBERG, R. J. (1997). "Managerial intelligence: Why IQ isn't enough," *Journal of Management*, 23(3), 475–93.

TEECE, D. J., G. PISANO and A. SHUEN (1997). "Dynamic capabilities and strategic management," *Strategic Management Journal*, 18 (7), 509–33.

TSOUKAS, H. (1996). "The firm as a distributed knowledge system: A constructionist approach," *Strategic Management Journal*, 17 (Winter Special Issue), 11–25.

VAN DEN BOSCH, F. A. J. and A.-P. DE MAN (1997). *Perspectives on Strategy: Contributions of Michael E. Porter*. Dordrecht: Kluwer Academic.

—— and C. B. M. VAN RIEL (1998). "Buffering and bridging as environmental strategies of firms," *Business Strategy and the Environment*, 7, 24–31.

—— H. W. VOLBERDA, and M. DE BOER (1999). "Coevolution of firm absorptive capacity and knowledge environment: Organizational forms and combinative capabilities," *Organization Science*, 10 (5), 551–68.

VAN WIJK, R. A. and F. A. J. VAN DEN BOSCH (1998). "Knowledge characteristics of internal network-based forms of organizing," in S. Havlovic (ed.), *Academy of Management Best Paper Proceedings*, BPS: B1–B7.

—— —— (2000a). "Creating the N-form corporation as a managerial competence," in R. Sanchez and A. Heene (eds.), *Implementing Competence-Based Strategy*. Greenwich: JAI Press.

—— —— (2000b). "The emergence and development of internal networks and the impact on knowledge flows: The case of Rabobank Group," in A. M. Pettigrew and E. M. Fenton (eds.), *The Innovating Organization*. London: Sage, 144–77.

VILA, J. and C. SYVERTSEN (2000). "Towards the business federation: Organizational arrangements in management consulting firms in Norway and Spain," in R. Sanchez and A. Heene (eds.), *Implementing Competence-Based Strategy*. Greenwich: JAI Press.

VOLBERDA, H. W. (1998). *Building the Flexible Firm: How to Remain Competitive*. Oxford: Oxford University Press.

WERNERFELT, B. (1984). "A resource-based view of the firm," *Strategic Management Journal*, 5 (2), 171–80.

WINTER, S. G. (1987). "Knowledge and competence as strategic assets," in D. J. Teece (ed.), *The Competitive Challenge: Strategies for Industrial Innovation and Renewal*. Cambridge, MA: Ballinger, 159–84.

9

A Pragmatic Analysis of the Role of Management Systems in Organizational Learning

PHILIPPE LORINO

INTRODUCTION

This research is based upon the personal experience of the author as project leader in charge of redesigning management accounting and control systems in the French computer company Groupe Bull at the end of the 1980s.[1] This is not a case study, in the sense of, for instance, ethnological case studies, but rather an experience of research-action, in which the author was a fully involved actor. Given my personal involvement, it was desirable to let some time (eight years) pass to improve the objectivity of analysis. In addition, this story has been written after discussion of the case with other researchers who had no personal role in Groupe Bull.

In this study, I analyze the role played by management and control systems in the ability of an organization to learn from environment and experience. This analysis starts with two premises:

1. The capacity of an organization to learn is somehow related to the learning capacity of the individuals who belong to it; so some link should exist between the individual learning of actors and organizational learning processes, but there is no reason why this link should be a simple transposition of individual learning processes to organizational learning.

2. Any organization produces many kinds of formal representations of its own organizational action (action processes, objectives, results, and resources) in the form of explicit and supposedly shared mental models. Those formal representations include management systems for financial and management accounting, budgeting and planning, performance scorecards, investment and project management, task definition and so on.

In particular, I attempt to illustrate the interaction between formal management systems and individual mental schemes, viewed from a management perspective of

---

[1] This case study in no way involves present Bull management. Strategies, policies, and persons have changed and the author left the company in the early 1990s. Thus, this study must be seen as historical with respect to Groupe Bull.

interpreting organizational action as value-creating action. In this attempt, we face at least three difficulties:

1. A large part of the literature about organizational learning is based upon strong but implicit assumptions about the link between individual and organizational learning (for instance, the assumption that organizational learning is based upon shared representations or common individual learning processes).
2. There are relatively few links between organizational learning research, on one side, and accounting and control research, in which management systems are often seen either as "positive accurate copies of reality" or "behavioral engineering tools," a controllable way for omnipotent/omniscient managers to influence actors' behaviors.
3. Research into management systems often has difficulty reconciling the opposition between positivism (in which management systems are described as autonomous objective artifacts which influence and constrain subjective action and knowledge) and subjectivism (in which management systems have no other reality than the subjective content actors invest in them).

I attempt to overcome these difficulties by developing a pragmatic, interpretive, and instrumental theory of organizational learning and the role of management systems in organizational learning.[2] In this effort, Charles S. Peirce's theory of triadic interpretation is used to represent the collective learning process as a constant interaction between formal representations and individual interpretation processes. This interaction process is part of organized action, since as John Dewey's pragmatic theory of inquiry and Jean Piaget's cognitive psychology tell us, acting and learning are inseparable. This approach leads us to an instrumental theory of management systems as "instruments" that combine both subjective schemes of action and objective artifacts. This approach helps us to see learning strategies as requiring changes in systems of representation, in individual schemes of interpretation, *and* in the interactions of the two. Changes in all these aspects are necessary to break out of "cognitive circularity" and create new cognitions.

GROUPE BULL AT THE END OF THE 1980s: A CASE OF ORGANIZATIONAL NON-LEARNING

A new strategic context

As part of my induction into Groupe Bull in 1987, I was informed about Bull's market and competitive background. The computer industry at that time was moving from design and production of highly "customerized" machines (mainframes) to design and assembly of standard machines, with a growing percentage of sales and profits coming from software and service sales. Hardware was still important, representing

---

[2] By "management systems" I mean a complex combination of elements, including "management tools" such as the accounting or the budget systems, but also the managerial practices which "surround" the use of management tools—for instance periodic meeting and review rituals, formal and informal channels to disseminate information, formal and informal reporting habits, etc.

TABLE 9.1 *Changing strategic context in the computer industry in the late 1980s*

Previous strategic context	New strategic context
almost exclusively "hardware" business	growing importance of software and services
professional market	professional and mass consumer markets
hardware direct distribution	hardware indirect distribution + direct distribution of solutions and services
highly customerized hardware, small lots, short series, small volumes	standardized hardware, big lots, large series, large volumes
"proprietary" operating systems hardware	standard operating systems hardware
semi-captive customers	open and competitive market
high manufacturing value added	low manufacturing value added
high gross margin rates	low gross margin rates
long life cycle	short life cycle
heavy manufacturing investment (complex testing equipment)	moderate manufacturing investment (simplified testing machines)
hardware sales, supported by software and services	service sales, "solution" sales, hardware sales, with autonomous market positions

around 70 percent of sales, but the growth rate of software and services was two to three times higher than hardware growth. Bull was fast to develop sales of services and built some technological strongholds, such as artificial intelligence applications, network architectures, and distributed systems. In addition, a growing part of production and sales was provided by "standard" hardware (PCs, UNIX[3] workstations). The share of mainframes and mini-computers was regularly decreasing.

In hardware activity, the competitive situation in 1987 can be summarized as follows (see Table 9.1):

1. The market ceased to be exclusively professional and began to gradually include both a professional segment and a fast-growing consumer segment.
2. Distribution ceased to be exclusively direct and began to become increasingly indirect (distributors, resellers, OEMs). Direct customers were mostly companies buying a large amount of services (system and network engineering) and "solutions" (combinations of application software for specific customer requirements, hardware platforms, and engineering/customerizing/training services), rather than stand-alone machines. Therefore, in this market segment, hardware sales were mostly a consequence of "solution" sales.
3. Hardware was becoming less and less "customerized" and more and more standardized (the number of versions and models decreased from hundreds to less than twenty).
4. Hardware was becoming less and less "proprietary"[4] and more and more "standard." As a consequence, it was becoming easier for customers to change

---

[3] UNIX is a trademark registered by AT&T company.

[4] "Proprietary" hardware is equipped with operating systems which are the exclusive property of the manufacturer; by contrast "standard" hardware is equipped with operating systems which are open to any producer.

hardware suppliers. The market was becoming much more competitive and open, and product profit margins were decreasing substantially (gross margins decreased from 70 percent to 30 percent). This evolution was reinforced by a decrease in manufacturing value-added: standard computers became pure assembly products, with very low manufacturing value-added.

5. Product life cycles were getting shorter and shorter, decreasing from six to seven years for a mainframe in the 1970s to ten months for a PC at the end of the 1980s. Consequently, obsolescence risks were increasing and market prices steadily declining (at least 10 percent per year), for assembled computers as well as for electronic components.

Towards new value chains

In the value chain structure, value creation was drifting from proprietary hardware design and assembly to "upstream" activities (design and production of electronic "chips," design of operating systems) and "downstream" activities (services such as system engineering, network engineering, data administration, system customerization, installation, user training). In the service area, Bull was trying to become a major European actor. The company had already become the eighth largest in Europe in sales of computer services without a specific policy towards that segment, and had strong potential for growth because of its technological competences and strong network of partnerships with application software houses, universities, and research centers.

Hardware, software solutions, and services were also becoming more autonomous markets: independent actors were beginning to offer application software and all types of services. A single value chain providing computers, software, and services was being replaced by different value chains for computers, software, and services.

Managerial consequences and Bull operational problems

The new strategic situation at the end of the 1980s created new managerial requirements:

1. The growing share of software and services in sales and profits required that the reporting system identify, measure, and analyze the specific performance of each of the three businesses (computers, software, and services).
2. In the hardware business, the growing importance of purchased components in the total cost of sales and the increased risks of obsolescence of components due to short life cycles led to a clear need to adopt "Just-In-Time" manufacturing and logistics strategies. "Just-In-Time" requires close coordination between production, distribution, and sales (for instance, quick communication of sales forecasts to manufacturing and purchasing, fast and accurate communication of customer order modifications, strict control of production and distribution lead times, etc.).

Bull, however, suffered from a traditional lack of cooperation between manufacturing and commercial units.

3. Fast paced technological innovation and short product life cycles required high performance in engineering processes: quick development (because profit margins are much higher in the starting phase of the product life), successful product start ups (because problems in start ups damage the economics of the whole life cycle, no time being available to "catch up"), and close integration between technological innovation and market developments. These kinds of performance require very effective cooperation between engineering, manufacturing, procurement marketing, and marketing. Here again, Bull suffered from traditionally tense relations between engineering and manufacturing and between engineering and marketing.

These problems, which were evident in Bull, called for deep changes in culture, organization, and systems, and many Bull managers had a clear perception of necessary changes. The situations described below are examples of efforts to achieve some necessary changes. Some of the changes were successful, but most were abandoned before final implementation.

Software and service sales

When I met the manager of the software business (let's call him Mr Soft) for the first time, he complained about the lack of reliable reporting and performance control systems for the software business. He explained that the Bull product list included a growing number of application software programs, either developed by Bull (for example, MRP[5] solution IMS-7), or developed by partner software houses but distributed by Bull.

"We have a problem," Mr Soft commented. "Any software sold by our commercial network is considered as a complementary feature of hardware sales. So the software sale is recognized in the P&L statement of the hardware product line which supplied the machine on which the software will be used. For instance, if you sell 500,000 dollars of IMS-7, it will be included in the income of the UNIX product line if IMS-7 is sold on a UNIX machine, in the income of the G-COS7 product line if IMS-7 is sold on a G-COS7 machine, etc. Consequently I hardly know the total sales of IMS-7. I know how much we invest to develop the software, but how can I measure the corresponding return?"

"Isn't it possible to extract the sales figures from the product lines reporting?" I asked.

"That's what we try to do, but it is not easy, all the more as the hardware product lines keep software sales fairly unclear. As a matter of fact, they usually use software and service as a selling argument for hardware. So they provide them to customers with highly variable and discounted prices. Therefore actual sales figures are not meaningful."

---

[5] MRP = Material Requirements Planning, or in later generations of systems, Manufacturing Resources Planning.

"Why don't you account for software sales at standard prices? The number of software packages sold would be multiplied by the standard price of the package in the price list."

"That is difficult, too. Most software solutions are modular, with ten to twenty different functional modules. For instance, IMS-7 MRP software has fifteen modules, including Requirements Planning, Inventory Management, Procurement Planning, Master Schedule, Customer Order Planning, Just-In-Time Scheduling, etc. Our management system does not recognize a difference between selling one or selling ten modules of IMS-7. Every sale will be counted as *one* sale of IMS-7. If your proposal were implemented, it would make the true financial cost of software commercial discounts very clear. I do not think Bull's commercial networks would like such transparency! Actually, I think that the management system is designed to make it impossible to manage software as a 'normal' product line! It is the same situation in selling services, I can tell you."

"This is strange and worrying, since the corporate strategy points to software and service as critical businesses for the future of the company!"

"Yes, in theory. In practice, the commercial networks are hardware sellers, they use software and services as sales support and promotion tools, and they do not want to lose such commercial power. Of course, their view is supported by the hardware product lines. They do not express it in a very explicit way, but the fact is that all my attempts to change this situation have failed."

As part of my mission to improve management accounting and control systems, I proposed creating software and service product lines with their own reporting and P&L systems (see Figure 9.1).

However, the Corporate Financial Manager refused this proposal and explained that, for the time being, most of the profit margin was originating in the hardware business, and that it would be dangerous to de-motivate and to hamper the commercial networks' sales efforts by preventing them from using an important commercial tool for hardware sales. His opinion was supported by the Marketing Manager.

Manufacturing cost accounting

I was asked to audit Bull's manufacturing cost management systems. I went to the company's most important factory, located in the west of France. At Bull headquarters, before I left for the factory, I was told that the final assembly cost there was 18 percent higher in the first months of this year compared to last year. On the other hand, the cost of manufacturing printed circuits had diminished. At the factory, I interviewed the factory manager, Mr Anjou, who presented his Just-In-Time manufacturing strategy.

"The new competitive environment makes costs related to inventory and work-in-progress higher and higher. Due to short and unpredictable product life cycles, obsolescence risks are significant if final assembly inventory is high. At the same time, computer and component market prices are decreasing, which steadily reduces the

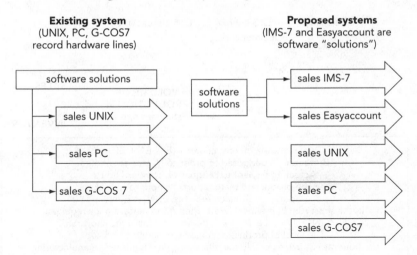

Fig. 9.1   *Accounting systems proposed for software and service businesses.*

value of inventory at a rate of more or less 10 percent per year. Last, the final market is very volatile, because customers can easily move from one supplier to another if the right machine is not available at the right moment. So it is necessary to have very short response times. Given these circumstances, I am very satisfied with the remarkable performance of the final assembly workshop, but I have problems with the printed circuit workshop." I was surprised when I heard this, because I knew that the cost of final assembly had substantially increased while the cost of printed circuits was quite low.

"That is easy to understand," Mr Anjou said. "*Your* costing system has been designed so that any progress towards Just-In-Time results in higher manufacturing costs. (See Figure 9.2.) Manufacturing expenses are divided by manufactured volumes (measured in standard hours), to determine the average hourly cost rate for manufacturing. All manufactured quantities are taken into account, whether intended for immediate delivery or for inventory. Now most expenses are fixed in the short run (especially since manufacturing printed circuits is a capital-intensive activity). So to improve manufacturing performance as measured by manufacturing costs, you have to maximize volumes and productivity. Our machines require long set up times when we change production lots. Small and complex lots are postponed until there are possibilities to combine several similar orders in one production run, to justify the long set up time and to keep a good level of productivity. So we tend to be late in manufacturing small and complex lots, while we tend to be fast in manufacturing large, simple lots, because they are 'good for productivity.' However, we must often hold these long production runs in inventory for some time.

"What's worse," Mr Anjou added, "a large part of the costs related to inventories are not accounted for in manufacturing costs, like costs of write-offs for obsolescence, costs of financing, and opportunity costs for decreased market prices. To reduce costs under this accounting system, it is better to increase inventories than to diminish them.

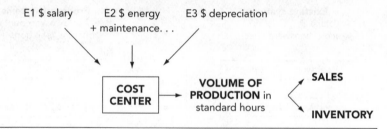

Total expenses of cost center = E = E1 + E2 + E3
Budget: E_0 \$ budgeted to produce N_0 standard hours
Actual: E_a \$ spent to produce N_a standard hours
The production team reports its hour rate: E/N
Good performance requires: $E_a/N_a < E_0/N_0$
In the short run, E_a is almost fixed. Then good performance requires:
$N_a > (N_0.E_a) / E_0$, i.e. $N_a > k$, k being constant in the short run.
The level of production must be maximized to keep
the hour rate as low as possible in the short run. That is why manufacturing
engineers and supervisors try to maximize local productivity.

FIG. 9.2   *Cost accounting system for manufacturing.*

As a result, Just-In-Time champions get reprimanded by controllers because their average accounting cost increases.

"The accounting control system is heavily skewed in favor of volume and productivity maximization, whereas Just-In-Time policies subordinate productivity to reactivity. With Just-In-Time the 'golden rule' is: 'Produce *what* you are asked *when* you are asked.' However, the present control system imposes the rule: 'Produce *as much as* possible, preferably of the same thing.'"

I proposed a modification in the manufacturing costing system to make it more consistent with the objectives of Just-In-Time. An inventory-carrying cost would be introduced, based upon interest costs, market price downtrends, and obsolescence costs. Recognizing these costs would discourage production that only contributed to high levels of inventories.

The Corporate Manufacturing Manager and the Finance Manager opposed such a reform, however, each for his own reasons. The Corporate Finance Manager, an accountant, did not want to include "non-accounting elements" (like inventory-carrying cost) in manufacturing cost, because this would provide a "biased picture" of the "true" production costs and would create variances between financial reporting and internal management control. The Corporate Manufacturing Manager, a former factory manager, strongly asserted that an efficient manufacturing team is a team which manufactures. It would therefore be difficult to keep up the morale or efficiency of manufacturing people in periods of low demand and low workload if they did not produce for inventories. They would then have little to do, and "idleness is the root of all evil." Though manufacturing people could be usefully employed in tasks other than production (such as maintenance, cleaning, training, and quality analysis), the Manufacturing Manager did not want to encourage "non-productive" tasks which would deteriorate the key performance ratio "productive cost versus non-productive cost."

Inventory valuation rules

The factory manager, Mr. Anjou, also complained about the work schedule of his ten-person control team. They seemed to be absorbed by very formal tasks and to have no time to dedicate to real improvement issues, particularly Just-In-Time and Total Quality. I met with the factory controller, and we analyzed the actual workload of the control team. Fifty percent of their time was dedicated each month to evaluating the book value of inventories, with a fairly complex method of FIFO[6] smoothed over the year to avoid important short run variations due to volume fluctuations. The factory controller felt that this sophisticated method, developed ten years ago, was no longer suited to present performance issues.

"Assembly value added is now less than 8 percent of material cost. I think that the effort we dedicate to evaluating assembly tasks is out of proportion. Suppose we use a very rough calculation method and incur 30 percent error (which is not probable) in calculating the value-added of inventories. That would mean 30 percent of 8 percent, or less than 2.5 percent error in determining the inventory value. Now, thanks to Just-In-Time policies, we should soon have less than one month inventory as an average. The maximum error risk would then be 2.5 percent on one-twelfth of yearly production—i.e. a maximum error of 0.2 percent of assembly value-added each year. Does that justify five full-time employees?"

"What would you suggest then?" I asked.

"Before working here, I was the controller of a small Bull factory in Scotland, which had never done anything other than assembly. We had a very simple system for manufacturing cost accounting: manufacturing cost was apportioned to lots and products as a fixed percentage of purchased material value. We had copied the costing systems of mass distribution. Errors if any were small, and we saved a lot of time. If we adopted such a system here, my team could devote much more time to Just-In-Time implementation and Quality improvement."

I proposed adopting such a system of "surcharges" in which all manufacturing costs would be considered as surcharges added to the purchased material value (see Figure 9.3). The Corporate Financial Manager (CFM) objected, "You cannot compare our small assembly unit in Scotland with the main factory of the group, which is our flagship and a high tech unit." I commented that one of the best competitors of Bull had already adopted such a system in all its factories. The CFM then said he would not object if the Corporate Manufacturing Manager (CMM) agreed. However, the CMM

---

[6] FIFO: "first in, first out." To evaluate the value of an inventory composed of parts which were manufactured in different periods with different costs, the following rule is adopted: the parts leave the inventory in the same order as they went in.

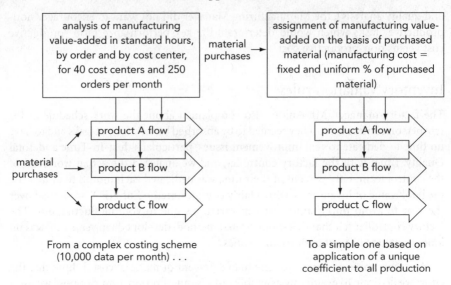

FIG. 9.3   *Proposed change in cost accounting for assembly value-added.*

reacted strongly: "Do you believe we are in a Department Store? I need to know our true costs to control manufacturing performance! If we become a distribution company, we can re-discuss it—but I might be far from here then. I am an engineer, not a dealer!"

The CEO's perspective

Disappointed at finding it so difficult to change the management systems of the company, I asked for an interview with the CEO, who had hired me. I wanted to explain to him my view of the situation: managing new performance factors requires measurements that are critical in the new strategic situation, and in many cases the existing management systems had negative effects. The CEO carefully listened to me. He asked me to prepare a formal and complete proposal to change the accounting and control systems in order to make them more coherent with the new strategic orientations of the company. He said he would present my recommendations to the Executive Committee. I prepared a presentation focused on:

1. the simplification of the manufacturing costing system;
2. the establishment of specific P&L reports for software and service product lines;
3. costing and performance measurement in manufacturing to support implementation of Just-In-Time.

But, on presenting my recommendations, the skeptical faces of most members of the Executive Committee, including the CEO, suggested that the battle was already lost. Failure seemed clear after my presentation when the CEO asked the Financial Manager to present a big project, named "The Economic Model," which perfectly contradicted my analysis. This model based Bull management on a profit center model in which

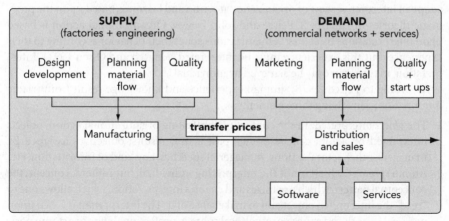

FIG. 9.4 *"The Economic Model" proposed to Bull management.*

engineering and manufacturing would be grouped in one profit center (called the "Offer"), while commercial networks and services would be grouped in a second profit center (called "Demand"). A transfer price system was to be introduced between the two profit centers (see Figure 9.4).

After presentation of "The Economic Model," I warned the Executive Committee that this model leaves the company organized around the hardware production-distribution channel, and does not improve the strategic identification and monitoring of "software" and "service" activities as autonomous businesses. I also advised that in the hardware business, the model even aggravates the existing separation between upstream and downstream phases of material flow (commercial forecasts and order management planning on one side, production planning and control on the other side), which would be disastrous for Just-In-Time policies. In addition, the model further separated upstream and downstream phases of the product life cycle (market research and functional specifications definition on one side, product design and product and process engineering on the other side), which would be disastrous in an industry characterized by shortening life cycles and requirements for predictable and quick product developments. Transfer prices and profit centers as defined in the model were also likely to reinforce local optimization and work against cooperation between functions.

INTERPRETATION—AND ISSUES OF INTERPRETATION— OF THE BULL CASE

A theory of interpretation

A lack of communication among colleagues is obvious in the Bull story, though all involved were reasonably clever and well-disposed individuals. It seems that everyone's respective sense-building processes diverged significantly. To analyze this situation, I adopt an interpretive view of organizational action and learning, based upon the pragmatic theories of Charles S. Peirce and John Dewey. Organizational action is based upon interpretations by actors: "Organizations adapt their behavior according to their experience, but this experience must be interpreted" (March and Olsen 1991). Interpretation, in turn, can only be achieved by individuals.

According to Peirce (1978), human experience and knowledge result from triadic interpretations involving three elements:

1. The *object* interpreted: In the context of controlling organizational action, objects interpreted by actors can be events, past action results, objectives assigned by managers, other actors' actions, managerial speeches, any kind of information, etc.
2. An *interpretant*, which is not the interpreting individual, but rather a concept, the conceptual pattern which organizes and enables interpretation, which allows one to "read" the interpreted object and to make sense of it. The interpretant is based upon personal history and experience, cultural context, professional state of art, and position in the organization. I will use the expression *actor's interpretive scheme* for Peirce's "interpretant." Though both concepts can be seen as slightly different ("interpretant" is more general and can point to concepts which are less structured than what we generally call "scheme"), they can be seen as equivalent for the study presented here.
3. The *sign* produced to "translate" the interpreted object into the particular field of significance which has been selected through the interpretive scheme. In our context (organizational action), signs can be actions, speeches, gestures, written figures or texts, orders, indicators, information, etc. For instance, starting from the *object* "event," the *sign* can be the verbal formulation of the causes of the event (i.e. translation of the event into formulated explanations, through interpretive schemes). Results of past actions can be translated into written causes in a report. Assigned objectives can be translated into action plans which are believed effective. Action plans can be translated into actions. Other actors' actions can be translated into supposed motives (see Figure 9.5). The sign emitted becomes an object to be interpreted by the same actor who originated the sign (learning process based upon a chain of interpretations) or by other actors (through communication processes linking different actors' interpretations).

Peirce's triadic theory of interpretation replaces the Cartesian dyad "object/sign," "reality/representation," by the triad "sign representing object *for someone or something.*" Any learning process then appears as a *semiotic* process, in which *knowledge*

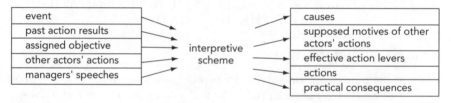

FIG. 9.5   *Objects, interpretive schemes, and signs.*

production takes the form of sign production and circulation within the context of action.
The production and interpretation of signs can either facilitate or impede potential
action by providing a framework of sensemaking—never in an abstract way, but always
in reference to specific actions, specific actors, and specific interpretation schemes in
practical situations.

For instance, Mr Anjou and I selected the same interpretation objects: the evolution of manufacturing costs in the final assembly and the printed circuit workshops.
Initially, my interpretive scheme conformed to "Fordian" theories of action: If manufacturing cost diminishes, final product cost diminishes, and product margins
increase, which enables a firm to invest, or selling price diminishes, which enables an
increase in market share. In either case, a manufacturing cost decrease is good news.
My interpretive scheme is based upon my academic studies and my previous experience in Fordian industries. Mr Anjou, closer to operations and better informed about
their complexity, interpreted the situation in quite a different way. To increase productivity, production to inventory is undertaken in order to use equipment and
human labor in an intensive way. Thus inventories pile up, and production cycles
get longer because of longer waiting queues. Production to support uncertain market forecasts—rather than firm orders—increases. Mr Anjou knew that expenses,
particularly the cost of working capital, will increase when production becomes disconnected from market demands. Mr Anjou and I then emit signs about our interpretation of manufacturing cost evolution, including contradictory judgments about
workshop performance (verbal or written signs), actions (reports I required from the
"low-performance" final assembly workshop, strict instructions given by Mr Anjou
to the stockpiling printed circuit workshop, etc.).

Theories of value-creating action to interpret organizational action

To study the learning process of a firm, we are interested in a specific kind of interpretation process: the interpretation of organizational action that produces new
organizational action. The respective interpretive schemes of actors (Peirce's "inter-
pretants") are *theories of action* as defined by Chris Argyris and Donald Schön
(Argyris and Schön 1978)—i.e. models which provide conditional causal links: "in
situation S, if you want to achieve consequence C, under assumptions a, . . . n, do A."
Such schemes are based upon the actor's personal experience, the specific position of
the person within the organization, and the specific culture of the social groups he
belongs to (as characterized, for instance, by professional values, state-of-the-art
practice, and ethics). We therefore focus our attention on actors' interpretations of
organizational action, which link actions with consequences (and consequences with
their causes) and give meaning to action ("action for . . ."). Thus, a central question in
the learning of an organization is: "Knowing what we know from experience, what do
we currently do to reach a given objective, or what should we be doing in our present
and foreseeable contexts?"

There are hundreds of ways to interpret the same action. If we observe the
movement of handling and transport vehicles on the shop floor, for example, we can

interpret it as a ballet, as a more or less efficient logistic system, as a financial investment, as a safety issue, as a technological achievement, as the scene of a film, etc. If we
are interested in management systems, then for us the firm may be viewed as a type
of organization that survives and grows by creating value for stakeholders. Then the
particular interpretations of interest are interpretations of action (theories of action)
as *value creation*. From this perspective, the central question underlying interpretive
schemes in management may be stated as, "Knowing what we know from experience,
what do we do, what should we do, to create value in present and foreseeable contexts?" Thus, we are essentially interested in actors' interpretations of organizational
action as value-creating action.

   Such interpretation can occur in many different types of situations and at various
levels, from the interpretation of machine behavior on the shop floor ("when the
drilling tool has this color or smells so, it has to be changed because it is going to break
soon") to the interpretation by a CEO of competitors' actions in deciding the firm's
own actions. One of the main purposes of management systems is to ensure at least a
minimum level of coherence between multiple kinds and levels of interpretation
processes within the organization—not for the sake of achieving cognitive/interpre-
tive coherence, but to ensure a requisite level of coherence in organizational action.
Moreover, this coherence must be achieved in a dynamic context: coherence of actions
achieved through coherence of interpretations must be continually rebuilt in constantly evolving situations.

What was the shared representation of organizational action as value-creating action in Bull?

To guide the actors' actions and to give sense to them, it is necessary to have some theory of action that achieves value creation. There can be global representations of how
the firm as a whole creates value for its stakeholders, and such representations may be
at least partly shared by most of a firm's actors. Such common interpretive schemes
involve a perception of collective identity: "What do we do, as a firm? For what purpose
do we exist? Through which kinds of actions do we express and build our identity and
our purpose? How are our multiple activities organized to create value, or how should
the value chain be organized to create value? What kind of value chain (Porter 1985) do
our actions compose?"

   Such "higher-order" interpretive schemes (Sanchez and Heene 1996, 1997) are particularly important when they exist in an organization, because the coherence and
coordination of organizational action can be partly ensured by the relative congruence
of individuals' answers to these questions. As we shall see below, this congruence can be
improved by creating formal management models. Such higher-order, more abstract
schemes of interpretation about the identity and purpose of the firm as a collective system of action thus frame and influence more local, concrete, and specific schemes of
interpretation. Of course, the multiple interpretive schemes in an organization are
unlikely ever to be perfectly coherent.

   In the case of Bull, a relatively congruent higher-order interpretive scheme existed at the time of the situations described above. This scheme could be summarized as follows:

Bull creates value because it is a manufacturing company that is able to design, produce, and sell computers. Bull is the central element of a value chain that provides information processing hardware characterized, as any manufacturing activity, by a sequence of material transformations. To transform matter, which is the "noble" way to create value, Bull implements capabilities acquired through its long history as a manufacturer. We believe in the importance of, and thus nobody wants to repudiate, our manufacturing and technical capabilities, such as the effective use of sophisticated equipment, the skill of highly qualified operators, the implementation of advanced product and process technologies, and so on.

In the strategic context of the 1970s, such a manufacturing-oriented interpretive scheme was appropriate: A computer was a manufactured product with a high content of manufacturing value-added; each producer had its own product technology with its own "personality." The implementation of the product by or for the customer required a high level of expertise. Indeed, sometimes machines were made to implement application software developed by the customer firm itself and tailored to its specific requirements. The value chain of the industry was truly a manufacturing-driven value chain (see Figure 9.6).

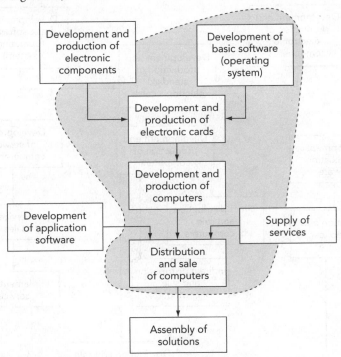

FIG. 9.6 *Value chain for mainframe computer industry, 1970s.*
Note: The grey zone within the dotted line identifies the parts of the value chain directly achieved by Groupe Bull. The remainder of the value chain consists of activities performed by other firms (suppliers, subcontractors, software houses, license owners, etc.).

In the new strategic context of the late 1980s, however, the value chain split up into several distinct value chains that were sometimes only loosely linked:

1. Software and services became their own markets, progressively more independent from the hardware market, which meant that, besides the computer value chain, there appeared service and software value chains.
2. Although hardware was still sometimes bought by customers on a stand-alone basis, it increasingly became an element of integrated solutions that included software and services, which meant that the computer value chain decomposed into a "stand-alone hardware" value chain (often leading to "indirect sales" through third party value-added vendors), and "solutions" sold by a computer firm that bundled its own hardware with software and services.

Coming from outside Bull, I was not especially influenced by Bull's history, culture, and traditional interpretive scheme. I was therefore relatively open to considering heterodox interpretations proposed by actors in the company, and I developed a view of the value-creating system of activity that differed from the dominant manufacturing-driven scheme in Bull (see Figure 9.7).

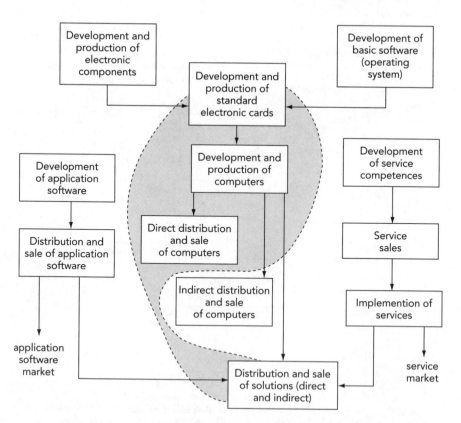

FIG. 9.7   *My heterodox interpretive scheme of Bull's value-creation process.*

This difference between Bull's and my interpretive schemes was important in understanding the first situation described (software and service sales). The software and service managers appointed to develop the software and service businesses were influenced by "position effect" (Boudon 1986) and developed the view that Bull had multiple value chains. Their interpretive scheme, however, was not congruent with the schemes of other Bull executives, who held to interpretive schemes in which any action that would "scatter" attention and efforts over objectives other than making and selling hardware could have disastrous short-run consequences for the company.

Hardware value chain: A Galilean revolution

There were also important differences within Bull in the interpretive schemes concerning the hardware business itself. Most managers seemed to view this activity as the "surviving" quintessence of the traditional manufacturing model of performance—the last activity which justified the manufacturing identity of Bull. So the preservation of the traditional manufacturing interpretive schemes was a particularly sensitive issue. Several operational managers, facing difficult problems in improving the logistics flow or the engineering design cycle, benefited from a "position effect" (Boudon 1986). Their daily efforts to overcome lack of cooperation and coordination within the existing manufacturing context compelled them to question the traditional manufacturing model. As for me, I benefited from a "disposition effect" (Boudon 1986). Thanks to my previous experience outside Bull, I could manage to keep my distance from the dominant interpretive schemes and build a different vision of Bull's value-creating process.

The members of the Executive Committee (in situation #4, pp. 186–7), more or less consciously based their analyses and decisions upon the dominant interpretive scheme, in which the "hardware business" was essentially a "process of transforming material," and was "supported" by "support activities," including logistics and engineering (see Figure 9.8).

The model in Figure 9.8 was the "map of the world" for the "Bull way of thinking." It defined how the world should be viewed from the company perspective, with

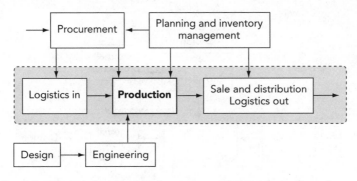

Fig. 9.8   *The "hardware business" as a process of material transformation.*

production (the "material transformation process") in the center and other activities as peripheral supports, in the same way as European maps of the world "make us see" Europe in the center, with America to the west and Asia to the east.

Actually, material carrying costs become more important than the costs of transforming materials. Computer production handles a flow of costly and depreciating components (due to price erosion and technical obsolescence), and physical transformations of materials are quite minor. In this regard, Bull activity should be seen as basically a logistics activity, in which internal manufacturing transformations are a minor action. In a real sense, Bull functioned as a "value-added distributor" of component assemblies (see Figure 9.9).

This interpretive scheme could particularly be observed in Mr Anjou's (the factory manager) view when he proposed formally accounting for inventory carrying costs and simplifying the manufacturing cost accounting system by considering manufacturing cost as simply a fixed rate of material cost. This view, however, "turned upside down" the dominant interpretive scheme of the Bull world, in the same way as turning a world map upside down would upset our usual vision of the planet.

A radical change in the value chain representation could also have taken another turn. Since the computer product life cycle was continuously shortening, quick, predictable, and reliable product development became a critical competence, since it was more and more vital to be first to market to capture any economic profits. Consequently, the management of technical and marketing data in advancing new product concepts through successive stages of development (first draft, prototype, start up, midlife, engineering changes, phasing out) could be seen as the essential chain of actions in the computer business (see Figure 9.10). This view is supported by the fact that performance in operations was strongly influenced by design and planning decisions (standardization of components, number of component and computer versions available, and assembly schemes making possible late-point differentiation of the product).

In such an interpretive scheme, handling a material flow is seen as only a logistics "support activity" that supports a primary flow of technical data and market concepts in an extended product and component development process (cf. Sanchez 1995). Production then appears as a "second-tier" support activity, planned and designed to

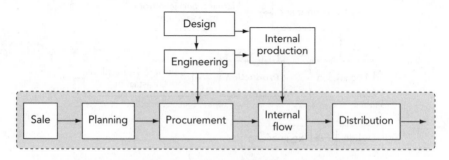

FIG. 9.9   *View of Bull's value-creation process as assembly of components.*

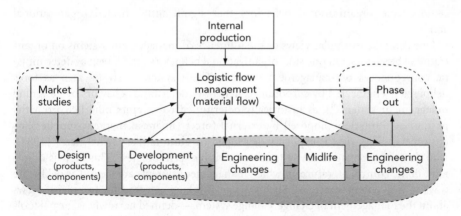

FIG. 9.10 *Bull's value-creation process seen as a product development process.*

optimize logistics flows of components as they are assembled into products. The decision to make or buy may then become subordinate to logistics considerations (lead time optimization, delivery time requirements, etc.). In effect, production becomes a part of a logistics design that is itself designed to support the overall engineering life cycle of the firm's products. In this case, all elements of the dominant hardware interpretive scheme are upset, since the basic action process no longer handles tangible objects, but rather information and concepts (Clark and Fujimoto 1991) through the technical life cycle of the product. In this new "world map," metaphorically speaking, Europe has moved to a peripheral location on the border.

Three visions of the world, three sets of interpretive schemes, three theories of action—each with broad and fundamental strategic and operational implications for Bull. But two of these three interpretive schemes were "unthinkable" for most decision-makers in the company. They were essentially "unseen" schemes, unconsciously excluded from the field of conceivable, arguable, and debatable theories of organizational action.

TOWARDS A PRAGMATIC MODEL OF ORGANIZATIONAL LEARNING

Organizational behaviors result from hybrid systems

Organizational behaviors may be explicit or implicit, deliberate or emergent, and lead to attitudes and decisions that have significant influence on organizational actions, on the technical processes which underlie those actions, on the rules and conventions which regulate them, and on the actual products which result from organizational actions. For instance, in the Bull story, the conservation of production rules which prioritized "local" productivity, the use of software as a commercial tool to sell hardware, the rejection of new costing concepts, and the definition of functional profit centers were organizational behaviors that significantly affected organizational action.

One can take two polar views of the influence of management systems on organizational behaviors. On one side, organizational behaviors can be seen as deterministic consequences of management systems. These systems may be seen as tools deliberately engineered by corporate leaders ("we determine behaviors by designing management systems"), as historically determined constraints inherited from the past, or as limitations imposed by external forces (financial markets, suppliers, or customers). This view is explicitly developed by authors like Michel Berry (1983), who describes management systems as "invisible technologies." This view is dominant in the control literature, in which management systems are viewed as deliberate ways to implement strategies. Such ways of thinking can lead to "technicist" views about the management of change. Change systems—defined narrowly as formal tools or even software—may be conceived as capable of changing organizational behaviors. This can prove to be a dangerous illusion in many cases.

On the other side, organizational behaviors can be seen as independent from systems, or even as determining the actual content of management systems. Systems can be "twisted" by actors in opposite directions, in the same way as a hammer can be used to break a window to save people from fire, or as a weapon to harm someone. In this view the systems have no inherently necessary purpose *per se*, since they are manipulated by actors. This position is quite common among the organization sociologists who see organizations mainly as games of power (Crozier and Friedberg 1977; Friedberg 1983) or in some "human resources" and change management literatures, where culture is seen as the main or exclusive determinant of organizational behaviors. This polar view may dangerously underestimate the influence of managerial tools and practices.

The view developed here is a midground view that organizational behaviors result from a complex interaction between formal management systems and actors' schemes of interpretation. This interaction is similar to what Michel Calon and Bruno Latour call "hybrid systems" (Calon 1988; Latour 1991). In hybrid systems, human subjects act and learn here and now in a framework of networks constrained by artifacts (for instance, management systems such as the accounting system) that are not infinitely plastic and offer some resistance to actors' intentions. For instance, scientific research results from hybrid networks combining scientists, scientific equipment, information tools, and communication channels.

The artifacts are not passive or "interpretively neutral," because other actors in other times or places have implanted aspects of their own interpretations into them. The architecture of a building, for example, can impose aspects of schemes of interpretation (of social or family life or of workplace) on users long after the architect has departed. Actors must then blend their own theories of action with the elements of theories of action that the artifacts (such as management systems) embody and preserve through time and space.

Artifacts reproduce and maintain interpretive elements and impose them on actors in present actions. However, the word "maintain" here can be misleading. Actually the original purpose of the artifact and the purpose it supports in new contexts can be quite different, because the artifact is not *per se* an interpretive scheme, but rather an object for interpretation at any moment by actors. Any residual purpose effect embodied in an artifact that cannot be modified or ignored by actors in a new context becomes, *de facto*, part of their "hybrid" interpretive scheme.

Hybrid interpretive systems can be found in all types of social situations. Calon and Latour give the example of a New York highway built in the 1950s to go to Long Island beaches. Calon and Latour allege that the engineer who designed the highway was a racist. Since non-white people in New York used to go to the beaches by bus, they suggest that he designed low bridges to prevent buses from using the highway. Forty years later, the engineer is gone, but the low bridges are still there and still prevent buses from using the highway. The low bridges continue to affect how people think about going to the beaches—and about many other activities in which bus transportation could potentially play a role.

The theory of hybrid systems is convergent with instrumental theories (Vigotsky 1934/1997) which analyze relations between subjects and instruments. "The instrument is an artifact, situated outside the subject, but its use requires some scheme of utilization built by the subject. The subject transforms himself by inserting the artifact into some activity making sense for him" (Cerratto 2000). An instrument's perceived usefulness results from the characteristics of an artifact and from the interpretation process by which the subject employs the artifact in some pattern of action. One could say that an "instrument" is the product of an "artifact" combining with a "scheme of interpretation."

In our analysis of management accounting and control systems, hybrid systems consist of existing management systems combined with actors' schemes of interpretation. It is therefore difficult and perhaps impossible to change organizational action if management systems and interpretive schemes are not transformed *concurrently*. Any attempt to change organizational actions simply by modifying one of these two elements will collide with the inertia of the other element. Significant changes in the norms of organizational action require changes in both management systems and actors' schemes of interpretation, and in the ways they interact.

Budgeting systems, for example, define areas of responsibility and control, management accounting undertakes to establish causal links between cost drivers and costs, planning systems develop causal flows between action plans and objectives, performance control systems posit chains of causality linking local action and corporate

TABLE 9.2 *Management systems and schemes of interpretation*

Management systems	Schemes of interpretation
Cost accounting	"We are manufacturers, we produce and sell machines"
Budget practices	"We have to reduce non-productive overhead"
Mission statements	"Any time shop floor teams lack workload, we have problems"
3-year plan	"To be responsible and motivated, managers must commit on bottom line"

performances, and so on. Due to their formal nature, these systems create (i) certain forms of inertia to change and (ii) standardization that constrains local modulation. Organizational systems therefore impose some degree of organizational uniformity and stability. But these systems do not directly determine behaviors, since they can only act as artifacts that are subject to individual interpretation. Their embedded purposes may constrain and guide, but cannot dictate the patterns of action they will be used in, nor the "hybrid purpose" they will serve in a given individual's interpretive scheme.

What is the genesis of management systems? To carry out a process of organizing, there is a purely practical need to ensure at least some measure of convergence between actors' interpretive schemes, particularly between individual theories of action, because some degree of compatibility in beliefs about causal links between actions and results is necessary before actors can take part in coordinated collective action. There is also a practical need to ensure continuity of interpretive schemes and knowledge over time to provide a measure of cognitive stability and institutional memory. Actors engage in various processes that can take quite different political forms, from imposition by leaders to professional community choices, to produce management systems that embed explicit, formalized, and generally acceptable interpretive schemes. These systems are then used as:

- standards and routines for action
- coordination and communication tools
- aids for maintaining memory and continuity.

Management systems therefore appear as "stocks of interpretations and stocks of interpretive schemes" that were designed in a specific historical context, framed by interpretions of contemporaneous situations. Formalization of systems then creates inertia that limits ongoing and real time adaptation. This is not altogether unfortunate, however. Inertia has an important cognitive function of protecting organizations from high dispersion of action norms and from organizational amnesia leading to continual "reinvention of the wheel." The achievement of organizational coherence is therefore importantly dependent on the creation of at least some forms of organizational inertia. Interpretive schemes crystallize into explicit representations of action (rules, standards, procedures, key indicators, models, measurement techniques) and become organizational "objects" in the sense of Peirce's semiotic framework. Today's schemes of interpretation, those being developed by present actors, interact with these formalized artifacts of prior interpretive schemes.

In the Bull story, for example, the factory manager Mr Anjou wished to change managerial practices and to promote Just-In-Time behaviors. He failed to manage to make this change, however, partly because of the inertia of existing Bull control systems—inertia that he is able to understand and to criticize, but not to overcome. The Bull controller wants to change management control systems in some key areas, but cannot manage to do so because of a lack of influence on the interpretive schemes of corporate leaders. Bull's existing management systems (management accounting, product line reporting, performance management) act as stocks of hidden and frozen interpretive schemes that resist adoption of new interpretive schemes. Such a situation only persists, however, when existing interpretive schemes of key actors coherently interact with existing management systems, both elements contributing to maintain each other in a high level of mutual coherence (particularly with respect to representing how organizational action creates value for stakeholders).

Knowledge and representations are experience-based and pragmatic

The individual members of an organization are actors in organized processes of action (design, produce, sell, service). Each actor in a process of action makes decisions and controls his own action by interpreting the process and his specific role in and contribution to it. Action processes require two functions (Lorino 1996) to be viable:

(1) coordination, to ensure at least a "satisficing" (Simon 1982) level of coherence between different actors' actions within the same process;
(2) "equilibration" (Piaget 1970) between processes of *adapting* interpretive/action schemes to new contexts (which Piaget calls "accommodation") and processes of *applying* existing interpretive/action schemes to new situations (which Piaget calls "assimilation").

Both coordination and equilibration are achieved through management systems as *signs* of organizational action processes. Management systems thus contribute both to monitoring ongoing actions by individuals and groups and to guiding the interpretive mental activities of an acting and learning subject and thereby steering his or her current activity. Both types of interpretive schemes—those that have become embedded in management systems, and those evolving schemes of individuals that now populate an organization—exist to both enable and constrain, to stimulate and to limit organizational action.

This analysis now leads to a very general observation: Knowledge is based on action. That is the conclusion of both Piaget's (1970) cognitive psychology and the pragmatic philosophies of Dewey (1938/1967), Peirce (1978), and James (1907). These philosophers reject any dualism between reality and discourse, between action and knowledge, and assert that knowledge is necessarily contextual. *Signs* produced by actors are bound to give purpose and sense to action and, as a result, to make action possible. Therefore, interpretive schemes should be evaluated by the test of their practical effects. Peirce even goes as far as to identify the object of a concept with the sum of all the practical effects of the concept: "We must consider the practical effects that, to our mind, can be induced by the object of our concept. Conceiving all those practical effects is the same as completely conceiving the object itself." This means that the sign produced in an interpretive process (Peirce's "representamen") is not a (Platonic) pre-existing "idea" to be discovered—for instance, there is no such thing as the "true" cost of something—but rather a sign produced to build (or sometimes to limit) potentials for action. Thus, in a costing system, there will be representations of the "relevant costs" for a type of action envisaged: direct, variable, standard,

Philippe Lorino

marginal, and differential costs that vary according to the specific action. For example, marginal-cost-based analysis and direct-cost-based analysis will produce different representations of costs and may lead to different "make or buy" decisions. Thus, the only test of a system like costing is validation through action—i.e. does this representation lead to useful results in our overall scheme of interpretation and action?

According to John Dewey (1938/1967), mental schemes are always produced in a context of "problem solving," of "building practical solutions," and of "bringing a specific inquiry to conclusion." Dewey rejects the dualistic view of classical Logic, which considers "truth" as an attribute of the syntax of logical propositions itself, independent of context. In his pragmatic view, action and knowledge are inextricably interrelated. The formal (universal, generic) and contextual (relative to specific biological, material, psychological, cultural environments) conditions for an inquiry to be effective are intertwined. Knowledge is essentially procedural, is based upon an individual's own experience, and is validated by experience and frames new experience.

If we apply the pragmatic philosophy to business management, there is only one way to test and prove management concepts: by implementing them. Any managerial "idea" rests, either implicitly or explicitly, on an action plan. Its implementation is the only possible test of its validity. An already tested management idea can at any time be questioned by, and needs to be tested in, a newly evolved context. Thus, validation of management ideas is never completed. The expression "truth" of management ideas is never more than a hypothesis, a more or less risky bet. Of course, a hypothesis that has already been tested in the past in a fairly stable context is less risky than a new hypothesis, but it is still a hypothesis, and will remain so forever. Thus, truth "lives on credit," as James put it.

The cognitive and pragmatic perspective developed here asserts that managerial knowledge is always experimental and procedural. Its focus should be on inquiry methods and rules (for instance: how to interpret results, how to solve problems, how to sort out causes), and the results of any given process of inquiry should not be mistaken for a "truth" that can be independently and ontologically isolated from the original context of inquiry. The key question in managing organizational knowledge is thus the *inquiry procedure*—i.e. how to develop a representation that experience might validate, and how to test it—not the intrinsic value of a given representation. The "good manager" therefore does not fix on the content of past decisions, but rather learns from past situations how to define action procedures that enable the generation and testing of new representations.

Organizational learning is based upon the interaction between "management models" and "interpretation schemes"

Interpretive schemes are essentially individual. But individual interpretations usually occur in collective processes of action. Collective action must achieve some degree of coherence. So must individual interpretive processes, too. In this "action constrained" frame, organizational learning may take two different forms:

1. At the individual level, new knowledge may appear as new schemes of interpretation in actors' mental activity, derived from their personal and practical experience.

2. At the organizational level, knowledge appears in the form of management systems that may be more or less formalized.

Both forms of learning are complementary. Management systems support collective problem solving and help groups to analyze problems and to communicate. They also support the adaptation of individual interpretive schemes and influence individual learning and sense-building in many ways—for instance, by providing problem-solving routines, they help organize actors' attention. In turn, individual interpretive schemes interact with individual experience, which enriches and modifies them, and management systems, which both support and constrain them. These two types of interactions (individual interpretive schemes with individual experience, individual interpretive schemes with management systems) build cognitive dissonances and tensions between adaptation or conservation of schemes (i.e. the need for "equilibration") and between organizational uniformity or diversity of schemes (i.e. the need for "coordination"). In so doing, the interactions fuel organizational learning by producing cognitive dissonances. (See Figure 9.11.)

At the individual level, management systems orient and constrain actors' perception of situations. They provide routines that guide action. They propose models of organizational action which influence individual schemes to some extent. For instance, management accounting systems include cost and activity drivers that:

(1) establish economic similarity (similar cost behaviors) between the activities that have the same driver; and

(2) establish functional definitions of activities (an activity that is represented by the output measure "number of parts" becomes perceived as a part producing activity).

The representations embodied in a cost accounting system therefore provide a model of economic flows within the value chain and orient productivity analyses.

At the organizational level, actors' interpretive schemes interact through management systems that support their communication and provide a common frame of reference for sense-making. Interactions between actors' interpretive schemes and management systems contribute to coordination and resolving conflicts between individual viewpoints. (See Figure 9.12.)

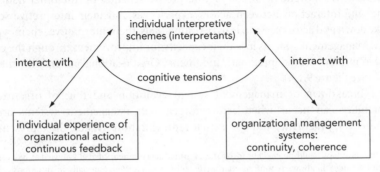

FIG. 9.11 *Management systems, individual experience, and organizational learning.*

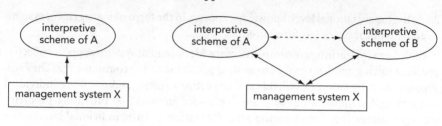

Example:

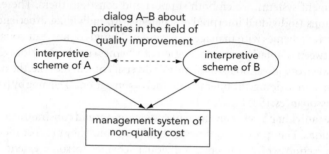

FIG. 9.12 *Management systems, individual interpretations, and coordination.*

Loss of representation adaptability: from sign to "specular" representation

Learning processes may falter when, for various reasons, actors' schemes of interpretation freeze. Management systems are material or immaterial artifacts which cannot by themselves, by their own will, build and trigger change. Management systems, in short, cannot interpret experience.[7] Only actors' interpretive schemes evolve with experience and can develop perspectives that enable them to criticize and adapt or replace management systems. In other words, in the interaction between interpretive schemes and management systems, adaptation or innovation dynamics can only come from the evolution of actors' schemes of interpretation. There is a permanent tension between a management system's inertia and coherence on the one hand, and the more or less chaotic movement of actors' interpretive schemes on the other hand. If by chance the interaction between actors' experiences and their interpretive schemes breaks down and actors cease to learn as individuals, their interpretive schemes tend to ossify. Management systems lose their capacity for improvement through the exercise and evolution of actors' "pragmatic judgment." Organizational adaptability then vanishes. (See Figure 9.13.)

The breakdown of management system evolution and thus of organizational adaptability can occur when actors forget that management systems are only hypothetical, pragmatic, and contextual representations. When the representations

[7] This comment could be challenged by the eventual development of real knowledge-based systems, though learning will always require human intelligence at some level, especially in situations calling for innovation.

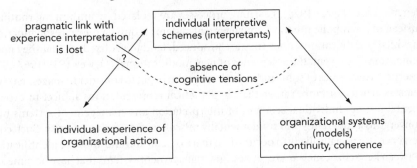

FIG. 9.13   *Loss of experience-based learning.*

"stored" in the management system are no longer regarded as hypotheses that live "on credit" and are subject to ongoing validation through experience, management models become mistaken for some "objective" scientific truth with a right to prevail over actors' "subjective" schemes of interpretation. In such circumstances, there is no longer any reason why actors' mental interpretation schemes should interact with their experience, since actors' interpretive schemes are validated only by conformance to existing management systems. In organizations caught in the grip of such cognitive paralysis, contradictions in interpretations arising from actors' practical experiences will usually lead to complex and tortuous interpretations intended to support existing models and schemes, rather than a decision to revise them. Interpretive schemes begin passively to mirror management systems. Creative tensions and iterative interaction between mental interpretation schemes and management models disappear. The only basis for organizational adaptation—feedback from individual experience—is lost.

From sign to specular representation

The interactions between actors' interpretive schemes and their experience will be broken if the epistemological status of management systems changes from "pragmatic hypothesis" to an "accurate mirror of reality"—i.e. to *ontological truth* (Rorty 1979). In other words, a management system is no longer subject to modification through experience once it has been validated as an exact reflection of "reality." This occurs when, for instance, the "cost relevant for such or such type of action in this or that context" is replaced by a notion of the "true cost" of some action. In this case, the representation "cost" ceases to be a triadic sign that builds sense for action (A is *a* representation of B *for* C), but rather becomes a dyadic representation that is *"the" mirror of reality* (A is *the* representation *of* B). When this happens, management systems are no longer open to discussion and argumentation, and thus become relieved of their need to demonstrate pragmatic relevance.

When management systems are elevated to the status of ontological truth, they cease to be temporary and contingent interpretive models. They become mere "habits" in

Peirce's sense (Peirce 1978). Learning processes are replaced by unthinking routines. Instead of a symbolic function, management systems acquire a mechanistic function, in which "modifications, once they are produced, tend to get fixed, so that they postpone, or even prevent, the emergence of new modifications" (Dewey 1939/1967). The interpretive schemes of some individuals may even begin to consider management systems as articles of faith, rather than hypothetical representations subject to experimental testing. Individual schemes of interpretation and management systems may converge to a coherent—but fundamentally misconceived—image of truth. Such convergence is especially likely to occur when there is a cultural and affective identification between key actors, such as executives, and management systems that have become key features of their professional and cultural identities.

Let me give two examples:

1. When attributing costs to computers, Bull managers defined themselves as manufacturers of sophisticated technological objects. This sense of identity was reflected in the exhibits of historic models of computers in the hall of the Bull factory in Angers.
2. Management based on profit centers promoted decision-makers from the status of "managers" to the status of "entrepreneurs" with full responsibility to account for profit.

The circularity of inquiry and learning

The risk of getting trapped in static, rigid interpretive schemes results from the very nature of human learning processes. According to Dewey (1938/1967), representations ("logical models") arise through *inquiries*, such as processes of problem solving. Dewey observes that representations can simultaneously have two distinct aspects.

1. Representations may provide *generic solutions* that can be applied in future inquiries *in similar contexts*.
2. Representations may acquire a more general cognitive power that extends, beyond any specific context to become *universal forms* (theoretical norms) of reasoning that can be used to design, control, and validate future inquiry procedures.

Interpretive schemes that emerge from experience may therefore be implemented as *routines*—pre-formed conclusions applied in later experience. They also become "metarules" used to build and structure later inquiries and experiences. Dewey therefore stresses the intrinsic *circularity* of learning: "Conceptions, whereas they need to be tested and revised according to observed facts, are also required to control the selection, the arrangement, and the interpretation of facts." The means to both produce *and* control interpretive schemes is *action*. Experience-based interpretation schemes thus have the ability to frame new experience and, therefore, to manage themselves.

The Bull story reflects these dual aspects of representations. Management systems were originally built to help actors in Bull control organizational processes of action (for instance, to solve problems). The manufacturing cost accounting systems in Bull (based on concepts of direct cost, overhead, overhead/direct ratio, standard costs, actual costs, variance, volume-based allocation, hour rates, etc.) were derived from manufacturing accounting experience and culture as a means to improve organizational action performance by pricing products, valuing inventory, and prioritizing marketing efforts. Once established, they became generic concepts used in *supposedly* similar situations to price future products, to evaluate future stocks, and to prioritize future marketing efforts.

Moreover, Bull's manufacturing cost accounting concepts and systems were also used to indoctrinate people to manufacturing culture, and to define rigor in problem-solving procedures in cost control. Bull's cost system provided the basis for validating organizational actions by asking questions such as

1. Does factory reporting clearly respect our cost accounting rules?
2. Does investment justification clearly integrate overhead in conformance with our cost accounting procedures?
3. Does the budget respect the structure of our cost accounting standards?

Once Bull's costing systems became enshrined as the "universal form" for correctly representing costs, any effort to propose new management costing systems that would represent costs in a new way would be criticized and rejected as "wrong." A new *activity-based costing* (ABC) system, however, would have demonstrated that products viewed as profitable in the traditional direct costing (DC) system were not profitable when viewed within the ABC system, and vice versa. In short, an ABC system would suggest that the DC system is wrong, and the DC system would suggest that the ABC system is wrong.

The *circularity* inherent in learning through interpretive schemes need not lead to a perverse stasis, although we have seen that it clearly can. Rather, the circularity of learning processes that Dewey elaborated simply reflects the fact that interpretation and action belong to the same sense-building process. In essence, interpretation requires action, and action requires interpretation. For instance, management interpretive schemes (as experience-based schemes) must be continuously validated by affirming (experiencing) the effectiveness of the organizational actions that they inspire, but as control procedures they are used to assess and measure the effectiveness of organizational actions.

To prevent the circularity of interpretation–action from becoming a cognitive trap calls for systematic vigilance. It is not enough to confirm through action that some facts organized by interpretive scheme X seem to confirm scheme X. Managers must also be willing to wonder whether some scheme Y exists which would organize facts in a way that would invalidate scheme X. Interpretive schemes in organizations should be practical frames for action-based learning-by-doing and *should* generate *generic* frames that help an organization understand other situations, as long as they are not "falsified" by experience. But interpretive schemes and their artifacts like management systems should never be elevated to *universal* frames used to understand all situations or held to be valid forever as ontological truths.

The difficult issues in managing organizational learning are:

1. How can we organize efforts to test organizational interpretive schemes at the same time that we make practical use of those schemes?
2. How can we avoid making "the logical mistake of methods which consider the conceptual object as if it consisted of first and ultimate truths, norms and principles, valid *per se*" (Dewey 1938/1967)?

As Mahoney and Sanchez (1997) have argued, managers must also be capable of building better "local theories" by testing the limits of the usefulness of current schemes. The challenge in using management systems is, as Dewey put it, not to lose sight of "the three essential logical conditions of conceptual object in the scientific method, i.e. (a) the status of theoretical conceptions as hypotheses which (b) have a function in the control of observation and ultimate practical transformation of phenomena and which (c) are tested and continuously revised on the basis of the consequences they produce in implementation."

According to Dewey, in the process of hypothesizing, testing, and revising, there are two possible causes for cognitive deadlock:

1. loss of flexibility and creativity in the production of hypotheses;
2. failure to maintain continuous and close review of the interpretive schemes which guide action.

To avoid cognitive deadlock, firms should therefore develop two explicit management functions:

1. Provide ways to generate, incubate, and test different interpretive schemes, whose effectiveness can be compared to that of existing interpretive schemes. This is essential to maintaining "flexibility and creativity in the production of hypotheses."
2. Make the organization's interpretive schemes—both individuals actors' mental schemes and the schemes that underlie management systems—explicit, visible, and arguable, in order to be able to discuss, criticize, and improve on them. This is essential to maintaining continuous and "close review of the interpretive schemes which guide actions."

CONCLUSION

Summarizing the conceptual basis of this study, organizational learning can be seen as a complex combination of "individual learnings" *about* organizational action. This combination is based upon the interaction between individual interpretive schemes and individual experience, on one side, and interpretive schemes and organizational artifacts ("management systems"), on the other side. Management systems may be viewed broadly as any kind of formal modeling of organizational action. More than representations *of* organizational action, they are signs *about* organizational action. In this sense, interpretive and pragmatic views of management methods and practices enable organizational learning better than positivist and specular views. The Bull study suggests how firms that do not adopt this pragmatic interpretive view of management systems can fall into this cognitive trap, even when facing drastic changes in their strategic environments.

The interpretive approach to organizational learning and organizational acting therefore has significant consequences in several areas.

Managerial measurements, rules, and controls must be regarded as belonging to the domain of action interpretation; therefore they are intrinsically debatable and arguable issues. There is no inherently best—indeed, not even inherently "good"— management systems relevant for a given situation, but only management systems that are "effective" in a given situation *for* something or somebody (triadic relevance). Therefore the design and development of management systems should be undertaken with a clear view to their impacts on individual and organizational acting and learning.

In the context of interpretive theories of organizational learning, a manager's main functions are more procedural than substantive, more focused on questions such as "how to organize interactions between interpreting individuals, between interpreting individuals and managerial artifacts, how to reveal interpretive schemes," than "what to do in such and such situation, what course of action to adopt." The managerial function should therefore be oriented towards organizing inquiries (heuristics), interpretations (hermeneutics), and learning processes (pedagogics).

Understanding an organization as a system of action may also point the way to building coherent concepts joining competence-based management theory and control theory. In both theory areas, competence and learning can then be seen to reside at the nexus of performance and to be inseparable from organizational action.

Management methods should be viewed as just one element within broader interpretive systems, including an organization's general or specific languages, codes, communication styles and channels, and knowledge management techniques. There is therefore a multitude of interactions in collective interpretation and collective activity to be researched. These interactions involve processes of individual acting and learning, management control, organization, and semiotics, the latter of which offers a theoretical frame that links both individual and organizational levels. Within this perspective, there are many specific research questions to explore, such as:

1. How do representations of organizational action influence interpretive schemes and future action? What is the precise role of management systems in the process of interpretation for action, and is there a typology of management systems from this point of view?
2. How can interpretive schemes be made visible and arguable?
3. What is the effect of organizational attributes (cross-functionality, cultural homogeneity or heterogeneity, the status of symbolic and metaphoric thought) on the process of interpreting for action?
4. What guidelines for the design of management systems might be inferred from the study of interpretation processes? Is it possible to develop "a new generation of management systems" integrating knowledge engineering techniques with traditional approaches to control?
5. How does the interpretive theoretical framework discussed here facilitate the study

of the links between competence-based management and competence/action-based management control?

REFERENCES

ARGYRIS, C. and D. SCHÖN (1978). *Organizational Learning: A Theory of Action Perspective.* Reading, MA: Addison-Wesley.

BOUDON, R. (1986). *L'idéologie.* Paris: Fayard.

BERRY, M. (1983). "Une technologie invisible," research document of Centre de Recherche en Gestion de l'Ecole Polytechnique, Paris.

CALON, M. (1988). "La protohistoire d'un laboratoire," in *La Science et ses réseaux.* Paris: La Découverte.

CERATTO, M. (2000). "Analyse instrumentale des transformations dans l'écriture collaborative, suite à l'utilisation d'un collecticiel," communication to IC 2000, Francophone Symposium on Knowledge Engineering, Toulouse.

CHANGEUX, J. P. (1984). *Neuronal Man: The Biology of Mind.* New York: Pantheon.

CLARK, K. and T. FUJIMOTO (1991). *Product Development Performance.* Boston, MA: Harvard Business School Press.

CROZIER, M. and E. FRIEDBERG (1977). *L'acteur et le système.* Paris: Editions du Seuil.

DE GEUS, A. (1988). "Planning as learning," *Harvard Business Review,* Mar.–Apr., 66 (2), 70–5.

DEWEY, J. (1938/1967). *Logic: The Theory of Enquiry.* London: Henry Hold, published in French as *Logique: la théorie de l'enquête,* Paris: P.U.F., 1967.

FRIEDBERG, E. (1983). *Le pouvoir et la régle.* Paris: Editions du Seuil.

HEENE, A. and R. SANCHEZ (eds.) (1997). *Competence-Based Strategic Management.* Chichester: John Wiley.

JAMES, W. (1907). *Pragmatism.* London: Longmans Green.

LATOUR, B. (1991). *Nous n'avons jamais été modernes.* Paris: La Découverte.

LORINO, P. (1996). *Comptes et récits de la performance. Essai sur le pilotage de l'entreprise.* Paris: Editions d'Organisation.

MAHONEY, J. T. and R. SANCHEZ (1997). "Competence theory building: Reconnecting management research and management practice," in A. Heene and R. Sanchez (eds.), *Competence-Based Strategic Management.* Chichester: John Wiley.

MARCH, J. and J. OLSEN (1975). "The uncertainty of the past: Organizational learning under ambiguity," *European Journal of Political Research,* 3.

—— —— (1991). *Décisions et organisations.* Paris: Editions d'Organisation.

PEIRCE, C. S. (1932–54). *Collected Papers of C. S. Peirce.* Boston, MA: Harvard University Press.

—— (1978). *Ecrits sur le signe.* Paris: Editions du Seuil.

PIAGET, J. (1970). *L'épistémologie génétique.* Paris: P.U.F.

PORTER, M. (1985). *Competitive Advantage.* New York: The Free Press.

RORTY, R. (1979). *Philosophy and the Mirror of Nature.* Princeton, NJ: Princeton University Press.

SANCHEZ, R. (1995). "Integrating technology strategy and marketing strategy," in H. Thomas and D. O'Neal (eds.), *Strategic Integration.* Chichester: John Wiley.

—— and A. HEENE (1996). "A systems view of the firm in competence-based competition," in R. Sanchez, A. Heene, and H. Thomas (eds.), *Dynamics of Competence-Based Competition.* Oxford: Elsevier Pergamon.

—— —— (eds.) (1997). *Strategic Learning and Knowledge Management*. Chichester: John Wiley.

SENGE, P. (1990). *The Fifth Discipline*. London: Century Business.

SIMON, H. (1969). *The Sciences of the Artificial*. Cambridge, MA: MIT Press.

—— (1982). *Models of Bounded Rationality*. Cambridge, MA: MIT Press.

VARELA, F. (1989). *Connaître les sciences cognitives*. Paris: Editions du Seuil.

VIGOTSKY, L. S. (1934/1997). *Pensée et Langage*. Paris: Messidor.

10

To Own or to Possess? Competence and the Challenge of Appropriability*

MAX BOISOT AND DOROTHY GRIFFITHS

INTRODUCTION

For the most part, the information systems approach to knowledge management focuses on the capturing, storage, and dissemination within the firm of useful employee knowledge. Supporting knowledge management with information technology is thus often characterized as primarily a technical challenge—one of devising an information system in which only those people entitled to use a given piece of knowledge can gain access to it, and then making it as easy as possible for those people to do so. In this discussion, we move upstream from this issue and argue that the changing nature of the employment relationship poses a real challenge in getting employees to freely contribute their knowledge in the first place. Doing so requires the creation of an incentive structure that will induce employees to contribute their knowledge freely to the organization's information system. In the information age, knowledge workers, like pre-industrial workers, are the owners of the critical means of production. Are these knowledge workers now being asked to give away their assets through an ill-adapted employment relationship?

The answer to this question has implications for the way that we manage the development and management of competences within the firm. In particular, it leads us to hypothesize that when a competence is characterized by a high degree of tacit forms of knowledge, property rights to that knowledge will be difficult to capture by an organization. On the other hand, we argue that when a competence is based on well articulated knowledge that is well diffused within a company, it may become difficult for the firm to appropriate such knowledge. In both cases, extracting full economic profits from knowledge potentially on offer becomes problematic for a firm. We call this dilemma the *paradox of value*.

In this discussion we first present our fundamental conceptual framework—the Information Space or I-Space—as a framework for the examination of information flows among agents within a firm. We then use the framework to highlight the distinc-

* This chapter draws heavily on "Possesion is Nine-Tenths of the Law: Managing a Firm's Competence in a Regime of Weak Appropriability" by Max Boisot and Dorothy Griffiths, *International Journal of Technology Management*, 1999, vol. 17, No. 6, 662–76.

tion between owning and possessing knowledge and to show how the paradox of value operates. We also indicate how recent developments in information technology are likely to exacerbate the paradox of value, and we consider what our analysis implies for how a firm manages its competences.

Recent developments in computing and telecommunications have brought us the realization that information goods can no longer be produced and exchanged by relying solely on the mechanisms that have been appropriate for the production and exchange of physical goods (Gilder 1989; Boisot 1998). It is also becoming clear that the challenge of managing the intellectual property rights associated with the rapid generation of new knowledge is of central importance to many organizations. Consider the following examples of this challenge:

• A large oil major, aware of how rapidly a knowledge-based competitive advantage erodes in its industry, aims to share best technical practice as fast as possible. To achieve this, it has created virtual teams and invested substantially in the creation and distribution of a sophisticated IT infrastructure to support virtual teamworking. Nevertheless some of the technical teams that are meant to work in this way have revealed in informal discussions with the authors that critical items of know-how will not always be shared with other members of the firm. Team members consider such items to be a possession of the team itself, to be made accessible to outsiders only with the prior consent of all team members.

• Evan Brown's former employer, DSC Communications of Texas, is suing him to find out what he thinks. While driving home one day, Brown claims he figured out a method to reverse engineer computer software into higher level source code. His solution, he believed, could apply not only to DSC's own outdated code, but to virtually any code—allowing company around the globe to modernize their software in a snap. DSC finally offered to partner his venture and share the profits, Brown says, but then DSC withdrew the offer and demanded that he reveal his idea, citing a 10-year-old employment agreement. When Brown refused to tell, DSC promptly fired him and filed suit . . . "Generally, if an employee signs a contract to give the employer ownership of all the inventions he conceives while employed . . . the employer owns the invention rights," says Herbert Wamsley, executive director of Intellectual Property Owners. But Brown, who worked in the switch products group of DSC, claims his idea was neither conceived on the clock, nor within the scope of DSC's telecommunications business or his job description. ("Not a Penny for Your Thoughts," Joe Nickell, *Wired Magazine*, October 1997).

• Over the years, Silicon Valley's Wagon Wheel Bar has achieved a certain notoriety as a place where employees from competing companies can indulge in an informal kind of "knowledge trading"—in many cases without their employing firms knowing about it (von Hippel 1988). In such reciprocal arrangement, employees are able to access a kind of knowledge that is normally not available within their respective organizations. The Wagon Wheel Bar offers little purchase to priority claims or intellectual property rights as conventionally understood. The patrons of the bar conduct their knowledge trades according to a logic of knowledge trading rather than that of the usual commercial exchange (Mauss 1990). Interpersonal processes rather than interorganizational ones guide the knowledge trading process, with the result that in Silicon Valley the half-life of proprietary knowledge is short indeed.

● Publishing in a refereed scientific journal stakes out a priority claim over an item of new knowledge that has met tests of quality and relevance established by a given professional community. Yet the actual utility of some knowledge cannot be established by the act of publication itself. Rather it is established by colleagues and peers referring to the publication in which it first appears (Hagstrom 1965). Getting a paper accepted for publication by a peer-reviewed journal is an arduous and time-consuming process. A growing number of academics are asking themselves why they should go through this process when today their papers can be disseminated cost-lessly and with much greater speed by electronic means like the Internet? In such changed conditions, electronic publication becomes an alternative means to archive knowledge, although, without the "quality control" filter of the journal review process. In this new mode of knowledge dissemination, the burden of separating the wheat from the chaff now falls on the recipient, rather than the sender, as a result of which the noise to signal ratio may increase in many academic disciplines.

What lessons in knowledge management can we learn from the above examples? Consider the difference between the academic publication case and the first two cases. In the academic publication case, the creator wants to share with peers what he or she regards as knowledge as quickly as possible. The creator of the knowledge may be so concerned to establish a priority claim on the knowledge created that he or she is prepared to bypass the procedures established by peers to validate new knowledge. In this case, sharing knowledge offers high returns for its creator when new knowledge is used and cited by peers, earning the knowledge creators the esteem of their peers and the career benefits that go with it. Yet there is clearly a conflict of interest between some-one who wants to establish a priority claim over new knowledge and a community of potential recipients who would rather have such knowledge validated by a review process before deciding to accept and use it. And as the wrangle over the "discovery" of cold fusion in the late 1980s reminds us, a peer-review process can help to improve the quality and reliability of what is presented as new knowledge.

Knowledge sharing is also the issue in the Wagon Wheel Bar case, but the process of informal knowledge trading suggests the many ways in which the intellectual property interests of individuals and the organizations they work for can diverge. The Wagon Wheel Bar provides a venue for individuals to operate outside the official institutional framework in which they work, possibly at the expense of their respective employers. As in the academic publication case, new knowledge may leak out in ways that circumvent all the institutional mechanisms designed to protect intellectual property rights.

The issues are more subtle in the oil company case and with respect to the inventive Mr Brown. Both cases concern knowledge hoarding rather than knowledge sharing. An individual or group may possess knowledge that may be an employer's legal property, which is likely if such knowledge is the fruit of on-the-job learning. But as the legal owner of some knowledge, an employer can only effectively exercise his intellectual property rights if he is in a position to make good that claim. As long as employees can keep such knowledge concealed in their heads, discovering and establishing a legal claim to that knowledge may prove impossible. In other words, to *own* knowledge is not necessarily to *possess* it. The adage that "possession is nine-tenths of the law" applies with particular force in matters of knowledge.

The four cases raise the question whether it is better for individuals to hoard or to share knowledge. It is easier to answer this question for physical assets than it is for knowledge assets. Physical assets have unique and spatiotemporal locations and instantiations. In other words, if I possess a physical asset, then you cannot possess the same asset at the same time. We could, of course, cut the asset in two, but then we would each end up with only half the asset. Knowledge assets are different. If I have some knowledge and share it with you, I can still have the knowledge in its entirety. And if I then go on to share the knowledge with a third party, then all three parties will have it in its entirety. In effect, the miracle of the loaves and the fishes—a horizontal supply curve with virtually zero marginal cost—applies first and foremost to information goods. Yet this miraculous ability of knowledge to occupy a virtually unlimited number of spatiotemporal locations simultaneously is so commonplace that we hardly notice it—until we attempt to trade knowledge assets. We then realize that extracting value from knowledge assets may not be so easy.

To profit from knowledge assets, we must first control the proliferation of knowledge to bring it under our control—in other words, we must be able to *appropriate* the knowledge. As in the case of physical goods, we must try to make knowledge assets stay in one place—and at least initially, *our* place. How do we manage this? Through certain institutions like the patent system, we may be able to obtain a temporary monopoly in the use of knowledge that we can show we have created. Thus, while we may not always be able to control the diffusion of our knowledge, we may be able to decide who can legally make use of it and on what terms. Institutional protection for knowledge works best when the knowledge in question can be clearly articulated and documented. However, much of our knowledge is not easily articulated. Some of what we consider knowledge may be rather fuzzy and ambiguous. Such "fuzzy knowledge" is easier to possess than it is to own legally, and consequently, difficult to articulate, "fuzzy" forms of knowledge do not lend themselves to being managed as though they were physical goods.

Fuzzy knowledge in various forms may be a basic ingredient of a firm's "core competences," and this may be one of the reasons that core competences have proved so difficult to identify and manage (Dierickx and Cool 1989; Prahalad and Hamel 1990; Reed and DeFilippi 1990). Fuzzy knowledge cannot be disseminated as readily as well codified, more abstract forms of knowledge. Fuzzy knowledge remains viscous and specific, either to firms or to individuals within firms. In the following discussion, however, we argue that information technology is now capable of greatly facilitating the transmission of fuzzy knowledge and therefore has the potential to dramatically change the process of managing this critical form of knowledge (Boisot 1998).

In this discussion we do not attempt to provide all the answers to the challenges of managing knowledge assets. Rather, we seek to clarify some central issues in managing knowledge assets. In the next section, we present a conceptual framework, the

Information Space or *I-Space*, that can be used to study flows of knowledge within and between organizations (Boisot 1995, 1998). In Section 3 we use this framework to explore the issue of information-hoarding versus information-sharing by individuals in organizations. In Section 4 we look at the ways that information technology is both expanding and accelerating information flows within and across firms. We then ask what implications this development holds for the management of a firm's knowledge assets. We conclude the discussion in Section 5 with a call for the development of a theoretical approach to knowledge management that recognizes technological possibilities of the information age.

THE CONCEPTUAL FRAMEWORK: THE I-SPACE

Data, information, and knowledge

To analyze how knowledge flows within and between organizations, we must first distinguish between *data, information,* and *knowledge.* We take *data* to be states of nature as discerned by an observer by means of energy inputs that reach the observer through his or her senses. Information is a subset of such data that is extracted by observers from the entirety of received data because of its apparent or potential relevance to them ("the difference that makes a difference"). *Information* is what is extracted from data when incoming data can be related in a meaningful way to an observer's prior expectations. *Knowledge* can then be thought of as an observer's beliefs that dispose him or her to act on the receipt of new information (Popper 1983). Knowledge consists of a set of probability distributions which orient an individual's behavior and which in turn are modified by information extracted from data (Arrow 1984). In sum, data is something "out there" that an observer notices, the observer constructs what he believes is information in the form of an interpretation of data that modifies the beliefs that reside "in him" and constitute his or her knowledge.

If we accept the above definitions of, and relationships between data, information, and knowledge, then we can see that only data can flow or be stored within organizations. Data may or may not be informative, depending on its relationship with a receiving person's prior expectations—i.e. his or her knowledge base. Strictly speaking, information and knowledge, being constituents of a person's cognitive dispositional stance, do not flow. Thus, the best we can hope for in an organization is to set up resonances among the belief systems of the different people in an organization. Much current work on competence and knowledge management overlooks this basic epistemological issue. In this discussion, therefore, when we talk about "knowledge flows" between agents, we are always referring to data flows that resonate with the belief systems of the people in an organization, in the sense that the people exposed to the data flows will extract comparable interpretations from those data.

We learn about the world by receiving and interpreting data. Yet given our limited cognitive capacity to receive, process, store, and transmit data (Simon 1957), we are forced to economize on the amount of data we notice and possess. One effective way of economizing in handling data is to filter out superfluities—i.e. data that are perceived as unlikely to be informative. Communication engineers describe this filtering process as boosting the "signal to noise ratio," something that can be achieved through judicious data coding and structuring strategies (Shannon and Weaver 1948). The I-Space framework takes as its point of departure the need to economize on data processing and transmission by devising data coding and structuring strategies.

The basic concepts

The key proposition that underpins the I-Space framework is that our ability to share data with others in an organization is largely dependent on our ability to structure data. Data structuring requires two quite distinct activities:

1. *Codification*: creating categories to which data (observations of phenomena) can be readily assigned for further processing.
2. *Abstraction*: establishing a minimum number of categories needed to efficiently codify data (i.e. to assign observed phenomena to appropriate categories for further processing).

An observed phenomenon can be said to be well codified when its assignment to a relevant category or set of categories is unproblematic, which is to say that both the observation of the phenomenon and the category or categories to which it is assigned are unambiguous and clear. An important measure of the effectiveness of a codification schema in categorizing an observed phenomenon is the number of bits of data needing to be processed before an assignment to relevant categories can be made. A phenomenon which does not readily fit any established category will require more data processing (interpretation) than one which seems to fit into an existing category in a codification schema. In this sense, mystical states are more difficult to codify than, say, traffic lights. Clearly, effective codification is critical to economizing on data processing costs, and, by implication, on transmission costs.

To be sure, effective codification is one way of economizing on data processing and transmission costs, but if we still need a large number of categories to make sense of some phenomenon, we may not be much advanced. The real world, after all, presents us with a potentially infinite number of possible categories. If we are to make good use of them, we need to be selective. We achieve selectiveness through a process of abstract conceptualization (Kolb 1976) that is influenced by our understanding of both the phenomenon itself and what we may want to do with it. By keeping to a minimum the number of categories that we need to draw on to apprehend phenomena, abstraction becomes the second strategy available to us to economize on data processing and transmission costs.

By placing phenomena within clear boundaries, codification lends structure and order to the process of abstraction. And abstraction in turn, by establishing categories that are relevant to an agent's purpose and should therefore be applied to phenomena, channels efforts at codification into useful, meaningful areas. By reducing the volume of data to be processed, both abstraction and codification also reduce the volume of data that needs to be transmitted from one agent to another. Working together, abstraction and codification speed up the diffusion of data within an organization. The structuring and the sharing of data are thus intimately related. The relationship between structuring and sharing data can be described as a curved plane in three dimensional space (see Figure 10.1) that we call an Information Space or I-Space. In the figure, codification and abstraction make up two of the three dimensions, and a population of data processing agents (explained below) make up the third "diffusion" dimension. The curved line schematically depicts the relationship between codification, abstraction, and diffusion. It indicates that the greater the degree of codification and abstraction of the data—i.e. the more data can be made compact through structuring—the larger the population of agents to whom data can be disseminated in a given time.

The data processing agents in Figure 10.1 may be many and varied, ranging from individual human beings to collections of people, such as firms in industry or departments within firms. All that is required of agents is that they be capable of receiving, processing, storing, and transmitting data. Locating agents on the diffusion scale in Figure 10.1, however, requires care and selectivity. At a minimum, agents need to have in common at least some potential interest in the data flowing in the I-Space.

Learning in the I-Space

Forms of knowledge in the I-Space vary according to their data processing characteristics. Some knowledge, for example, is well codified, abstract, and *proprietary,* by which we mean that barriers to its diffusion exist. Other knowledge, by contrast, is relatively uncodified and concrete but widely diffused. This form of knowledge describes the taken-for-granted, "common-sense" views of things that people in an organization share but rarely bother to articulate. Over time, these different forms of knowledge are modified by learning. What starts out as a fuzzy intuition gradually gains in form and structure—i.e. it becomes increasingly codified and abstract and

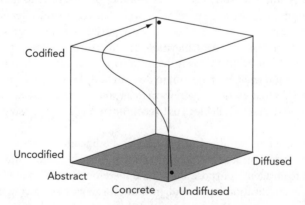

FIG. 10.1   *The codification–diffusion–abstraction curve in the I-Space.*

thus moves upwards towards the back of the I-Space. When this happens, of course, such knowledge can be more easily shared. But learning can also move knowledge down the I-Space, as for example when people acquire well structured knowledge that gradually becomes internalized by being embedded in practice. Eventually such knowledge develops a penumbra of relatively uncodified and concrete insights, leading to personal intuitions that reflect the history of our interactions with streams of data. Such "experiential" knowledge is not easily shared.

New knowledge appears in the I-Space either through new agents that bring new knowledge with them when they enter the I-Space, or through the cyclical movement of existing knowledge in the space. We can decompose this cyclical movement into six phases (Boisot 1995), as indicated in Figure 10.2 and briefly summarized in Table 10.1. We label the cycle of Figure 10.2 the Social Learning Cycle or "SLC." As shown in the figure, the SLC is purely schematic. Many different cycle shapes are possible—tall ones, flat ones, etc.—some of which may create blockages in the social learning process.

The paradox of value

Moving knowledge around the SLC incurs costs of time and resources. Presumably, individuals and firms will only invest in moving through such learning cycles if the benefits of doing so exceed the costs. How does one extract value from a learning process? How should we conceive of value in relation to a learning process? The value of an economic good is a function of its utility and scarcity (Walras 1926). In the I-Space, the utility of an item of knowledge can be related to how far that item has been moved up the codification and abstraction scales. Knowledge is useful insofar as it has been debugged, made reliable, standardized (well codified), and is applicable across a wide domain (abstract). Such knowledge, however, is only scarce insofar as it has *not* been diffused too widely—i.e. beyond the boundaries of the firm. Thus, we conclude that an item of knowledge reaches its maximum potential value in the I-Space in the region labeled MV (maximum value) in Figure 10.3.

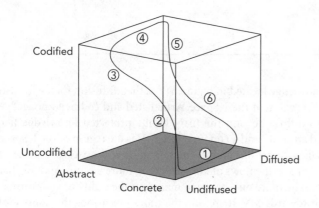

Key: 1. Scanning
2. Codification
3. Abstraction
4. Diffusion
5. Absorption
6. Impacting

FIG. 10.2 *The six steps of an SLC.*

TABLE 10.1   *The six phases of the Social Learning Cycle description*

1. Scanning
Identifying threats and opportunities in generally available but often fuzzy data—i.e. weak signals. Scanning patterns such data into unique or idiosyncratic insights that then become the possession of individuals or small groups. Scanning may be very rapid when the data is well codified and abstract and very slow and random when the data is uncodified and context-specific.

2. Problem solving
The process of giving structure and coherence to such insights—i.e. codifying them. In this phase they are given a definite shape and much of the uncertainty initially associated with them is eliminated. Problem-solving initiated in the uncodified region of the I-Space is often both risky and conflict-laden.

3. Abstraction
Generalizing the application of newly codified insights to a wider range of situations. This involves reducing them to their most essential features—i.e. conceptualizing them. Problem-solving and abstraction often work in tandem.

4. Diffusion
Sharing the newly created insights with a target population. The diffusion of well codified and abstract data to a large population will be technically less problematic than that of data which is uncodified and context-specific. Only a sharing of context by sender and receiver can speed up the diffusion of uncodified data; the probability of a shared context is inversely achieving proportional to population size.

5. Absorption
Applying the new codified insights to different situations in a "learning by doing" or a "learning by using" fashion. Over time, such codified insights come to acquire a penumbra of uncodified knowledge which helps to guide their application in particular circumstances.

6. Impacting
The embedding of abstract knowledge in concrete practices. The embedding can take place in artifacts, technical or organizational rules, or in behavioral practices. Absorption and impacting often work in tandem.

The problem with knowledge located in region MV is that diffusion forces are also at their maximum in this region of the I-Space. Articulated and codified knowledge has greater potential to diffuse beyond the firm; legally protected knowledge like patents can be "invented around," and so on. In effect, MV is the region of the I-Space in which knowledge behaves most like an information good and least like a physical good. Elsewhere in the I-Space, the flows of knowledge are more viscous, and for that reason, easier to control. The more one strives to maximize the utility of an information good by moving it towards MV, therefore, the more precarious the control of

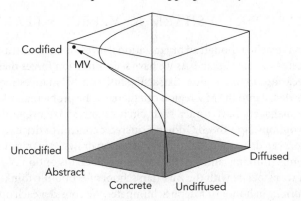

Fig. 10.3 *Maximum value (MV) in the I-Space.*

knowledge—and thus its scarcity—becomes because of the increased potential for knowledge diffusion. *Thus, the value of knowledge in region MV is inherently unstable.* This is another way in which information goods differ from physical goods, and it is a crucial one. Enhancing the utility of an information good through abstraction and codification increases its potential for faster diffusion, reduced scarcity, and thus reduced value. With an information good we face a difficult trade-off. We can maximize utility or we can maximize scarcity; we cannot maximize both. In this sense, the management of knowledge faces a *paradox of value.*

Both economic theorists and practitioners in the burgeoning field of knowledge management have developed a somewhat schizophrenic response towards the paradox of value. On the one hand, both theorists and practitioners continue to conceive of data, information, and knowledge as if, with minor adjustments, they can be treated as physical goods that are easily appropriable. One explanation for the persistence of this approach is that the appropriability regimes for artificially maintaining the scarcity of information goods—patents, trademarks, copyrights, citations, etc.—have not worked too badly in past years. Royalties often get paid, and original work usually gets cited. On the other hand, both theorists and practitioners also view data, information, and knowledge as "public goods" that often escape all attempts at appropriation.

With the rapid evolution of information technology and particularly with the emergence of the Internet, we are about to see our current understanding of and ways of managing knowledge goods tested as never before. With the conceptual tools for managing knowledge currently in use in many organizations, we are, in effect, attempting an ocean crossing with navigation instruments appropriate for coastal waters. In an effort to provide a better set of conceptual tools for managing knowledge in modern times, in Section 4 we shall explore modern information technology using the I-Space. Before we do so, however, we need to briefly look at the strategies available to us for dealing with the paradox of value.

TO HOARD OR TO SHARE? N- VERSUS S-LEARNING

The MV region is reached though an organizational investment in learning and therefore can be located on a SLC plane. As we have seen, diffusion forces make control of knowledge precarious in that region. Extracting full value from investments incurred in moving knowledge into the MV region can therefore be problematic. What options do knowledge managers have under such circumstances? We argue that there are essentially two options: slow the SLC down to increase control, or drive your SLC faster than competitors can drive their SLCs. The first option draws its inspiration from neoclassical economic thinking, and for this reason we label this option *N-learning*. The second option we associate with the Austrian school of economic thinking, and thus we label it *S-learning* in honor of Joseph Schumpeter. We consider each option in turn.

N-learning

N-learners base their approach to the region MV on the logic of the diffusion curve in Figure 10.1. Once the new knowledge has completely diffused in an industry, it has become a common possession of all competitors, and the potential for extracting economic rents from it is exhausted because it has lost its scarcity. The end point of the diffusion curve is thus a world of efficient market equilibrium where knowledge diffuses instantaneously. The only viable strategy for agents to follow in this metaphor is to slow down the diffusion process as much as possible to contain knowledge flows in secrecy as long as they can. This is also what the patent system attempts to do. Although patenting cannot actually block the diffusion of new knowledge, by granting its originators a monopoly on the use of knowledge, patents may be able to remove incentives for direct imitation.

The root metaphor for N-learners is the dam, a barrier for containing the flow of knowledge. The wider and more solid the dam a firm builds, the more easily it can keep knowledge inside the firm or allow it to diffuse in a controlled fashion. The taller the dam, the greater the depth of the stock of knowledge that a firm can accumulate over time. In this metaphor, knowledge is fluid and divisible and thus can be released in discrete units. This representation of knowledge lends itself to portfolio-type thinking: the rate of flow out of the portfolio must be balanced by the rate of flow into the portfolio. Building a dam to contain knowledge diffusion is thus in some sense a bold attempt to tame the forces of nature in the hope that the flow of knowledge can be better controlled and managed. IBM's strategy for managing knowledge in the days before the personal computer can readily be interpreted as an N-learning knowledge management strategy.

S-learning

Unlike N-learners who primarily follow the logic of the diffusion curve, S-learners follow the logic of the SLC. This logic differs from that of the diffusion curve by continuing to push quickly down the I-Space once the diffusion curve has reached market equilibrium. N-learners believe that common knowledge in a market equilibrium creates no strategic opportunities to use that knowledge, so that the prospect of securing economic rents is absent. Not so for S-learners, who see scope for further learning and knowledge renewal in the SLC processes of absorption, impacting, and scanning. These three processes in the SLC involve learning by doing, learning by using, and the discovery of novel patterns in events through these activities. These processes therefore constitute a source of new tacit, contextual knowledge for those who are willing to invest the necessary time and effort to develop insights into ways that available knowledge can be further applied and developed. For S-learners, to dam up knowledge flows as N-learners do is to dam up the learning process itself. Learning is often destructive of old knowledge, but it is also creative (Schumpeter 1934). The strategy of S-learners is therefore not to slow down the SLC, but to flow through the SLC faster than competitors.

The root metaphor for the S-learner may be one of shooting the rapids. The S-learner is participating in a learning race (Prahalad and Hamel 1990) and riding the flow of knowledge as fast as possible wherever it may go. The S-learner tries to learn faster than competitors and in order to win the learning race, willingly shares some current knowledge with outsiders to learn something from observing how they use the shared knowledge. Thus, S-learners add to their own knowledge base by sharing knowledge with others. This learning strategy calls for both flexibility and opportunism. How does the S-learner extract value from this fast-moving learning strategy? By passing through the MV region of the I-Space more frequently than competitors do and collecting rents for at least short periods of time during each passage through the MV region.

In contrast to the N-learner, the S-learner does not view knowledge as fluid and divisible, but rather as reticular, moving through a network of relations, frequent knowledge exchanges, and learning through inferences. This view of learning invites systems thinking rather than portfolio thinking. In some parts of such learning systems—those located in and around the MV region in the I-Space—knowledge will be fluid, while in other regions knowledge will remain viscous and hard to diffuse. Selectively sharing with outsiders knowledge in some elements of the network can increase the value of related knowledge in elements where knowledge is not so easily diffused and shared. Thus, sharing some knowledge can increase the value of a firm's overall knowledge network. The S-learner, in essence, does not think about how to extract value from discrete knowledge *items* in a portfolio, but rather how to extract value from a knowledge *system*. Knowledge sharing in this strategy, while more generous than in the N-learner's strategy, nonetheless remains judicious.

Neither N-learning nor S-learning is inherently correct or strategically superior in all cases. Much depends on the potential speed of the SLCs in firms in a given industry, which in turn depends on the characteristics of the technology, markets, and competition in an industry. A strategy of "shooting the rapids" may not be possible or may not make much sense when operating well downstream in the Mississippi River, just as it is hardly sensible to try to navigate a paddle steamer through torrential streams of the Rocky Mountains. There is therefore potential for both kinds of learning strategies to create competitive advantage. The advent of information technology, however, is speeding up actual or potential SLCs in many industries, as well as changing the nature of data flows in the I-Space itself. Managers conditioned to operate paddle steamers are increasingly being asked or required to shoot the rapids. Many managers are ill equipped to do so, and do not like the prospect of this new way of working. We turn next to the impacts of information technology on the management of knowledge.

THE IMPACT OF INFORMATION TECHNOLOGY

Information technologies (which we also take to include telecommunication technologies) greatly affect the flows of data within and across organizations. Following the convergence of computing and telecommunications, information technology can greatly increase both data processing (interpretation) and communication processes, impacting both how knowledge is structured in an organization and how it is disseminated within and between organizations. Thus one could say, simplifying somewhat, that technological developments have increased the volume of data that can be processed and transmitted per unit of time, while significantly increasing the number of people that can be reached per unit of time. These two developments, when taken together, create the effect depicted in Figure 10.4. As the figure indicates, the data processing and dissemination now possible shift the diffusion curve to the right and towards the front of the I-Space.

What consequences follow from such a shift? First, as indicated by line A in Figure 10.4, at any given level of codification and abstraction, a message can reach more people per unit of time than was previously possible, thereby accelerating processes for diffusing knowledge. Second, as shown by line B in Figure 10.4, for a given percentage of the population within a given time frame, communication may occur with a lower requirement for codification and abstraction of knowledge than before. In effect, with every increase in available bandwidth for communication, the exchange of messages between agents can become what may be characterized as "media-rich."

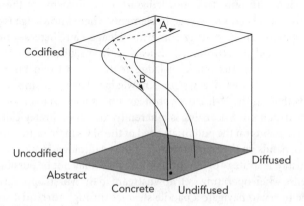

Fig. 10.4   *IT shifts the diffusion curve in the I-Space.*

With videoconferencing, low-cost and mobile telephony, e-mail, and so on, intensive personal communication outside a face-to-face context has become increasingly possible and common, thereby making it possible to disseminate less codified and abstracted forms of knowledge.

Information technology's impact on the paradox of value

Economists might interpret the curve shift in Figure 10.4 as a shift in the supply curve for data. More data becomes available, and its price goes down. Note, however, the impact of the curve shift on the point MV (cf. Figure 10.3). With developments in information technology making data ever more diffusible, it becomes more difficult to reach the MV region of the I-Space, or to stay there if one does reach it. Knowledge now begins to diffuse when it is still in a relatively uncodified and concrete state—and thus before it can be made appropriable through mechanisms such as patent or copyright. Expected returns to hoarding knowledge or pursuing an N-learning strategy thus can be expected to decline. But do returns from sharing knowledge or pursuing an S-learning strategy thereby go up? In other words, is the MV region now more accessible to knowledge sharers than it is to knowledge hoarders?

Consider once more the shifted curve of Figure 10.4. Both codification and abstraction now occur at higher levels of diffusion, as reflected in the rightward shift along the diffusion dimension of the I-Space. One implication of the curve shift is that the cost of investing in knowledge structuring—i.e. in codification and diffusion—can now be shared out among several agents. Thus, although the returns from knowledge sharing may decline because the MV region becomes less accessible, with an appropriate collaborative strategy and information technology support, the costs of pursuing a sharing strategy may go down even more and thus boost overall returns to knowledge sharing.

Devising suitable collaborative strategies challenges our existing notions of intellectual property rights. When knowledge creation is collaborative and occurs at low levels of codification and abstraction, how can we determine clearly who is doing what and thereby match contributions and rewards? If knowledge is indeed a "network good," then we face the problem of establishing boundaries for our knowledge creation networks in the lower region of the I-Space, where boundaries are fuzzy, ambiguous, and well-nigh unspecifiable.

Implications for the management of organizational competences

Many proponents of the resource-based view (RBV) of the firm have yet to recognize and address the network nature of much knowledge today. RBV theorists think of organizational competences as consisting of skills and knowledge that are hard to imitate—and hence tacit and hard to diffuse—but that are somehow well distributed and integrated across networks of people within firms. What happens when the organizational reach of a firm spreads beyond its legal boundaries, as when the knowledge that a firm needs to integrate becomes more loosely coupled as the firm seeks to work through alliances or outsourcing? Who actually owns the fuzzy knowledge created through collaboration in a loosely coupled network, and how can ownership claims on knowledge be made in such a network? These questions apply to intraorganizational as well as interorganizational knowledge management. Employees may be viewed by some firms as their most important asset, but to some employees it may be the firm that is viewed as an asset, one whose knowledge assets may be exploited for personal ends—perhaps at the Wagon Wheel Bar!

If the current evolution of information technology continues to facilitate the diffusion of new knowledge at lower and lower levels of codification and abstraction, then it is likely that firms will encounter the paradox of value at progressively lower levels of codification and abstraction. In this situation, a firm may pursue two strategies.

1. A firm can articulate its competences so as to better exercise its property rights over them. This would involve moving its competence base further along the codification and abstraction dimensions of the I-Space, making its knowledge more visible and thereby more subject to explicit ownership claims. Much current work in knowledge management is intended to support this strategy, which essentially tries to get employees to articulate their knowledge in a form that can be incorporated in the codification system of a computerized database accessible to the firm as a whole. A firm may pay a price for following this strategy, since by being articulated much of the knowledge in its competence base may lose important aspects of its tacit quality (Boisot 1995), while making it easier for the articulated aspects to diffuse. This knowledge management strategy can only succeed if the firm is able to rapidly renew its competences—i.e. if the firm is a fast learner.

2. A firm can maintain its competence base in the lower regions of the I-Space, but recognize that "competence carriers" within the firm own an ever larger proportion of the means of production (i.e. useful knowledge). A firm pursuing this knowledge management strategy must then be willing to share any returns on those competences with its competence carriers. Given the causal ambiguities associated with tacit know-how (Reed and DeFilippi 1990), such sharing would have to be done on a team or a collective basis and would require managers to have a clear sense of the activities and groups in which the firm's competences effectively reside. This second strategy seems to characterize the way many management consulting firms manage the knowledge in their businesses.

Under both strategies a firm's shareholders will receive a declining proportion of its returns on investments in knowledge. Under the first strategy, rents are likely to be dissipated among external players, while under the second strategy rents are distributed among internal players. Both strategies invite a firm to compensate for lower returns to specific investments in learning by accelerating its rate of learning—i.e. by becoming a fast and frequent S-learner. It is an interesting and important question for further investigation whether rapid S-learning is easier to achieve through the first or second learning strategies.

CONCLUSION

The above analysis of knowledge management is still preliminary and needs to be further investigated empirically. The analysis we have presented here is built on the premise that a political economy of information will require intellectual foundations that differ in important ways from those that characterize a political economy of physical goods. Similarly, the "ground rules" for the effective practice of knowledge management in building organizational competences will differ from many current norms in management. Here we briefly discuss the implication of our analysis for the management of organizational competences.

We have argued elsewhere that the modern industrial firm emerged in the last decades of the nineteenth century with a governance structure appropriate to the production and exchange of goods in which energy is the critical resource. Indeed, economic theorizing about firms at the time drew explicitly on the energy concept for its root metaphors (Maturana and Varela 1980). Throughout the twentieth century, however, information has increasingly been substituted for energy in both the production and the composition of economic goods. As the information content of goods increased, they became lighter and more mobile, but harder to fully appropriate. The advent of the "new economy" in the last decade of the twentieth century merely accelerated a process that had already been underway for decades.

The growing substitution of information for energy in the economic order has not been matched by adaptations in the governance structures of economic organizations. We are thus entering the new information economy with institutions largely conceived to serve the requirements of an industrial economy. Managing knowledge in the information economy will require new concepts of knowledge, learning, and organizations, as well as new management structures, processes, and norms.

With the radical speeding up of information flows now possible with information technology, we may find that the firm as conceived in the twentieth century is no longer the most appropriate institution for fostering and exploiting competences. We have long assumed that firms and economic organizations were co-extensive—i.e. that they share the same boundaries. With the increasing transactional reach of organizations made possible by information technology in general and the Internet in particular, however, this assumption has become questionable. Productive activity now spreads out kaleidoscopically through networks that lie largely outside the boundaries of the traditional firm. Under these circumstances, competence becomes an emergent—and elusive—property of recurrent interactions within such networks, rather than something which is produced within a firm's boundaries and which can therefore be legitimately appropriated by the firm. New concepts are needed for the creation and management of competences when the sources of competence span across the boundaries of many organizations.

REFERENCES

ARROW, K. J. (1984). "Information and economic behaviour," in K. Arrow, *The Economics of Information: Collected Papers of Kenneth J. Arrow.* Cambridge, MA: The Belknap Press of Harvard University Press.

BOISOT, M. (1995). *Information Space: A Framework for Learning in Organizations, Institutions, and Cultures.* London: Routledge.

—— (1998). *Knowledge Assets: Securing Competitive Advantage in the Information Economy.* Oxford: Oxford University Press.

DIERICKX, I. and K. COOL (1989). "Asset stock accumulation and sustainability of competitive advantage," *Management Science,* 35 (12), 1504–14.

GILDER, G. (1989). *The Quantum Revolution in Economics and Technology.* New York: Simon & Schuster.

HAGSTROM, W. (1965). *The Scientific Community.* New York: Basic Books.

KOLB, D. (1976). *The Learning Style Inventory: Technical Manual.* Boston: McBer and Co.

MATURANA, H. and F. VARELA (1980). *Autopoiesis and Cognition: The Realization of the Living.* Boston: D. Reidel.

MAUSS, M. (1990). *The Gift: The Form and Reason for Exchange in Archaic Societies.* London: Routledge.

POPPER, K. R. (1983). *Realism and the Aim of Science.* London: Hutchinson.

PRAHALAD, C. K. and G. HAMEL (1990). "The core competence of the corporation," *Harvard Business Review,* May–June, 68 (3), 79–92.

REED, R. and R. J. DeFILIPPI (1990). "Causal ambiguity, barriers to. imitation and sustainable competitive advantage," *Academy of Management Review,* 15 (1), 88–102.

SCHUMPETER, J. A. (1934). *The Theory of Economic Development: An Inquiry into Profits, Capital, Credit, Interest, and the Business Cycle.* London: Oxford University Press.

SHANNON, C. E. and W. WEAVER (1948). *The Mathematical Theory of Communication.* Urbana: University of Illinois Press.

SIMON, H. A. (1957). *Administrative Behavior: A Study of Decision-making Processes in Administrative Organization.* New York: The Free Press.

VON HIPPEL, E. (1988). *The Sources of Innovation.* Oxford: Oxford University Press.

WALRAS, L. (1926). *Elements of Pure Economics: Or the Theory of Social Wealth.* Philadelphia: Orion Editions.

11

Product, Process, and Knowledge Architectures in Organizational Competence

RON SANCHEZ

INTRODUCTION

The ability of an organization to succeed in a competitive environment ultimately depends on its ability to provide product offers that are perceived as valuable and attractive by potential customers. Firms differ greatly in their approaches to meeting this basic "market test" of organizational competence, but all firms have in common the need to sustain effective processes for creating and realizing product offers. This discussion considers the fundamental impacts on a firm's competence of the *architectures* of the products a firm creates and of the processes a firm uses to create and realize its products. We consider in particular how a firm's product and process architectures shape the structure and content of the knowledge that a firm accumulates as it creates and realizes products—in effect, how its product and process architectures determine the *knowledge architecture* a firm acquires and uses to create new products in the future.

In this discussion, we especially investigate how adopting *modular* product and process architectures can significantly enhance a firm's ability to identify and manage its organizational knowledge in creating and realizing products. We consider both "supply side" and "demand side" impacts of modularity on knowledge management. On the supply side, adopting a disciplined modular approach to creating products and processes can greatly improve an organization's ability to identify the nature and extent of its technological knowledge. This leads to greater clarity about what an organization does or does not know technically and thus what it may or may not be capable of achieving in its strategies for product creation and realization. Greater clarity in understanding what technological capabilities an organization has enables managers to use an organization's current knowledge more effectively and to focus organizational learning on developing or accessing new knowledge that will improve the organization's options for creating and realizing new products. We also consider how modular architectures can help a firm access knowledge and coordinate learning processes beyond its own boundaries. In these ways, the adoption of a modular approach to creating and realizing products can greatly improve the *systemic flexibility* of a firm to respond to change and diversity in the markets it serves and the technologies it uses.

On the demand side, we consider how the flexibility of modular architectures to configure many product and process variations can be used to support new forms of market exploration, learning, and development. We consider the essential role of modular architectures in processes of real-time market research, in developing more fine-grained understanding of market preferences at the component level of products, and in supporting e-business strategies for mass customization and product personalization.

This discussion of the fundamental role of product, process, and knowledge architectures in organizational competence is organized in the following way. We first define the concept of an architecture and apply that concept in explaining the terms *product architecture, process architecture,* and *knowledge architecture.* We then introduce the concept of modularity and explain why adoption of modular product and process architectures can improve—often very significantly—an organization's ability to identify and use its own knowledge assets, to access and leverage specific forms of knowledge in other organizations, and thereby to improve its supply-side processes for creating and realizing products. Next we consider how modular architectures can be used as drivers of demand-side processes for organizational learning about market preferences and for defining an organization's options for serving those preferences. We explain how these supply-side and demand-side processes can be integrated in a modular architectural framework for planned organizational learning and for effective leveraging of current knowledge assets. We then consider how the use of a modular architectural framework for knowledge management helps to improve the *dynamic, systemic, cognitive,* and *holistic* dimensions of organizational competence. Concluding comments suggest two important but counterintuitive ways that the definition and discipline inherent in modular architectures can improve organizational flexibility and creativity.

THE ARCHITECTURES OF PRODUCTS, PROCESSES, AND ORGANIZATIONAL KNOWLEDGE

An *architecture*—whether it be for a physical product, a service product, a process, an artistic image, or whatever—is created when (i) a design is decomposed into component parts and (ii) the ways that the component parts will interact in the design are determined.

The *decomposition* of a design into specific kinds of component parts may be motivated by any number of objectives for the design, but leads to a segmenting of the design into *functional parts* that must work together in providing the overall function desired from the design. The functional decomposition of a design is most evident in an assembled product like a personal computer (typically decomposed into a microprocessor, memory card, hard disk, monitor, keyboard, and so on), but designs of services and other processes are also decomposable into specific activities that collectively provide a desired function. The vertical stack of blocks in Figure 11.1 represents the decomposition of a product design into functional components, while the L-shaped array of blocks represents the decomposition of a process design—in this case, the

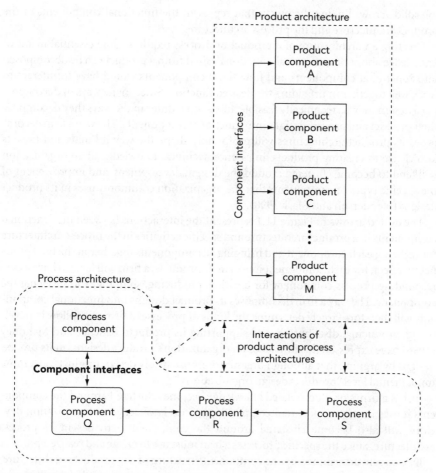

Fig. 11.1 *Functional components and component interfaces in product and process architectures.*

overall process for creating and realizing products—into its functional components (i.e. specific activities).

Determining the ways that the functional components of a design must interact to work together requires specifying what is most commonly referred to as the *interfaces* between components. Interface specifications determine the way one component attaches to another, the spatial position one component will occupy relative to others, the way in which the output of one component is transferred to another component, the way in which one component communicates with and controls or is controlled by another component, and other ways in which the functioning of one component may affect the functioning of another component within a design (Sanchez 1999). In effect, component interfaces define and control the way the component parts of a design fit and work together *as a system*. Component interfaces are indicated in Figure 11.1 by the solid arrows linking the blocks that represent the functional components of the product architecture and the process architecture.

Creating an architecture of a product or process requires some essential forms of knowledge about how an overall function desired from a product can be decomposed into functional components and how those components would have to interact to work well together in providing the desired function. Since many ways of decomposing a design may be technically feasible, firms often differ in the ways they decompose their product and process designs into functional components. The way a firm decomposes its product architectures will profoundly shape the way it builds and uses its knowledge in creating products. In essence, technical knowledge in an organization will tend to become clustered around the design, development, and improvement of the specific types of components that the organization commonly uses in its product designs (Henderson and Clark 1990).

The dotted arrows in Figure 11.1 represent the interactions between the functional components in a product architecture and specific activities in the process architecture for realizing each component and bringing all components together in the final product. In effect, for each component it uses in its products, a firm will have to have a corresponding process component for creating, producing, shipping, and servicing the component. The way a firm decomposes its product designs into functional components will therefore largely determine the kinds of processes a firm will follow in developing, producing, distributing, and supporting its products. Sanchez and Mahoney (1996) have expressed this impact of an organization's product designs on its process designs by arguing that although organizations ostensibly design products, at a more fundamental level "products design organizations."

Just as a firm's product-related knowledge becomes clustered around the components it uses in its product architectures, the process knowledge an organization develops will also become clustered around the component activities in its process architecture. Since the specific processes a firm must use to create and realize a product will be largely determined by the component structure of the product's architecture, both the content and the structure of an organization's *process* knowledge will also be greatly influenced by the *product* architectures the organization uses. Thus, a firm's choice of product architectures is not simply a technical matter, but rather is a strategically critical issue that will largely determine the content and structure of much of the knowledge that an organization develops.[1]

---

[1] The *content* and the *structure* of knowledge are inextricably interrelated concepts. The content of knowledge simply refers to what some bit of knowledge is about—i.e. its subject matter. The structure of knowledge refers to how the contents of the various bits of knowledge an organization has *are perceived within the organization* to be related or not related to each other. For example, suppose an organization that designs personal computers has knowledge of how to design both the microprocessor that executes applications programs and the power supply that powers the microprocessor. In one organization, the relationship between the two kinds of knowledge may be perceived as limited to determining the kind of electrical current the power supply must provide to enable the microprocessor to perform its function. Another organization, however, may understand that basic relationship, but also be aware that heat generated by the power supply (a new knowledge content) may interfere with the functioning of the microprocessor (a new relationship in the firm's knowledge structure). In this way, both the content and the structure of knowledge in the second organization are different from—and more elaborated than—the content and structure of knowledge in the first organization.

We can now define the concepts of *product architecture, process architecture,* and *knowledge architecture* (Sanchez 1999). These definitions will then serve as the springboards for our discussion of modularity and the role of modular architectures in knowledge management and organizational competence.

Product architecture

The decomposition of a *product design* into functional components and the specification of the component interfaces that govern how the functional components interact in the product to work together as a system.

Process architecture

The decomposition of a *process design* into functional components (activities) and the specification of the component interfaces that govern how the functional components interact in the process to work together as a system.

Knowledge architecture

The structure and content of an organization's knowledge about (i) decomposing product and process designs into functional components, (ii) how those components function, (iii) defining the interface specifications that govern the interactions between functional components, and (iv) assuring the ability of each of its process components to create and realize each of its product components (i.e. assuring the compatibility of its product and process architectures). An organization's knowledge architecture therefore fundamentally determines the product and process architectures the organization can create and realize.

MODULAR ARCHITECTURES

As system designs, the architectures of products and processes may be composed of either *tightly coupled* or *loosely coupled* functional components (Orton and Weick 1990; Sanchez and Mahoney 1996). The functional components in an architecture are tightly coupled when the ability of one component *design* to function properly depends on the use of a specific *design* for each component with which it interacts. Components are loosely coupled in an architecture when the proper functioning of one component design does not depend on its being used only with a single specific design for another component. In effect, loosely coupled components can function properly when used with a range of design variations in other components (Sanchez 1995).

Modularity is the property of an architecture in which a specified range of variations in loosely coupled functional components can be "substituted" into or "mixed and matched" within an architecture (Garud and Kumaraswamy 1993; Sanderson and

Uzumeri 1997). In essence, modular architectures enable the configuration of a range of variations in products and processes by assembling different combinations of "plug-and-play" compatible component variations.

The substitutability of a range of component variations within modular product and process architectures is suggested in Figure 11.2. In a modular product architecture, any component variation of a given component type can be mixed and matched with any of the component variations in other component types that the modular component interfaces have been specified to accommodate. Perhaps the most familiar example of a modular product architecture is again the personal computer, which makes possible the ready configuration of many different personal computer varia-

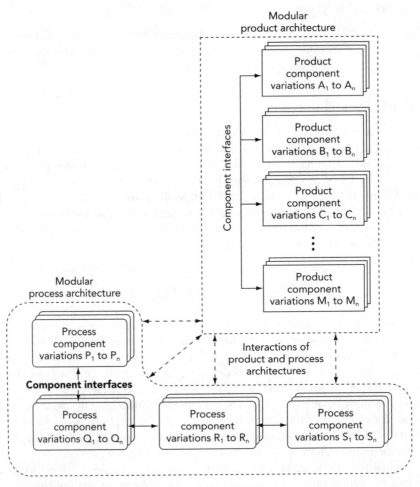

Fig. 11.2   *"Plug-and-play" component variations in modular product and process architectures.*

tions from various combinations of microprocessors, memory cards, hard disks, and other components within the same personal computer architecture.

Similarly, a modular process architecture is one that allows the flexible configuration of a number of process component variations within a stable process architecture. For example, in a modular process architecture, various kinds of development, production, distribution, and support activities may be performed by a firm's own functional groups or outsourced from external suppliers, but all providers of all activities can "plug-and-play" within the same process architecture. IKEA, the Swedish furniture manufacturer and retailer, has created a modular process architecture that provides plug-and-play compatibility among more than 2000 suppliers of furniture components around the world (Normann and Ramirez 1993; Sanchez 1999). All of IKEA's suppliers have been qualified to provide product component variations for IKEA's modular furniture architectures—for example, various table leg sets that can be combined with a number of table top variations. In addition, IKEA's suppliers have also been qualified to be plug-and-play compatible in IKEA's process architecture by following standardized process interfaces that define how orders will be transmitted from IKEA and confirmed by a supplier, how each type of component is to be packed in cartons and loaded into shipping containers, how transportation is to be provided to IKEA's facilities in Sweden, and so on. Qualifying its suppliers to function within its modular process architecture allows IKEA to place orders for product components with any of its suppliers while following a single way of working in coordinating its global network of suppliers.

Modular product and process architectures can bring a firm significant *strategic flexibilities*. Modular architectures enable firms to mix and match component variations to configure product variations to serve diverse market preferences. Modular architectures enable firms to improve product performance by "designing in" upgradability by directly incorporating technologically improved components in products as soon as they become available. Creating modular process architectures helps a firm to reconfigure its supply chains for developing, producing, and supporting products to meet a changing and diverse array of market demands (Sanchez 1995, 1996, 1999).

MODULAR ARCHITECTURES AND TECHNOLOGICAL KNOWLEDGE

Creating modular architectures imposes special demands on an organization's knowledge architecture. The nature of those special demands can perhaps best be understood by contrasting the conventional approach to creating a new product with the process that must be followed to create a modular product architecture (Sanchez and Mahoney 1996; Sanchez 2000).

In the conventional approach, development processes are typically focused on creating new component designs that often use new technical solutions intended to meet new performance or cost targets. The interface specifications that define how the new components will interact in a product design are generally allowed to evolve as component development groups explore and evaluate alternative designs for their individual components. In effect, the designs developed for individual components are allowed to "drive" the specifications of the interfaces between components. The architecture of a new product will therefore be determined by the set of component designs and their resulting interface specifications in the new product design that eventually *emerges* from the development process. This conventional approach to developing products also typically results in components that are tightly coupled in the product architecture—i.e. each component design can typically only be used with the other component designs in the specific product design that emerges from the development process.

By contrast, the creation of a modular architecture reverses the relative priority given to components and interfaces in the development process. A modular development process begins with the full specification of the interfaces between components and then standardizes or "freezes" the interface specifications for the duration of the development process (and often for the commercial lifetime of the product). Standardizing component interfaces has the important effect of constraining individual component development groups to develop component designs that will be compatible with the standardized interface specifications. Constraining development of each component to conform to standardized component interface specifications is the key to creating loosely-coupled component variations that are "plug-and-play" compatible with other component variations in a product architecture (Sanchez 1995, 1999).

The special demands that creating a modular architecture imposes on an organization's knowledge architecture derives from the high level of understanding of the *system behaviors* of the components in its products that an organization must have in order to fully specify modular "plug-and-play" component interfaces in an architecture *before* beginning actual development of components. The distinction between *know-how* and *know-why* forms of knowledge helps to explain this required higher level of understanding (Sanchez 1997).

Know-how knowledge is practical, "hands-on" knowledge of how a given system design currently works and can be maintained in its current state. Know-why knowledge is more fundamental, theoretical knowledge of why a given system works and is the form of knowledge required to create new designs of such systems. Establishing interfaces for a set of existing component designs in a conventional development process is largely a matter of practical, hands-on, know-how driven problem solving. Given a specific set of components emerging from individual component development processes, component developers need only be able to determine a set of interface specifications that will enable that specific set of component designs to work together acceptably. To specify modular component interfaces that will enable a range of different component variations (that are yet to be developed) to work together reliably, however, requires more in-depth, theoretical, know-why understanding of the essential forms of interactions among components in a system design that must be controlled through interface specifications.

When a firm attempts for the first time to fully specify modular interfaces for a range of loosely-coupled component variations in a product architecture, the limitations in the firm's technical knowledge about the system behaviors of the various types of components in its products will become much more apparent than when the knowledge in the firm is only being applied to defining workable interfaces for a single set of components in a single product design. In effect, trying to create modular architectures is a process that helps a firm understand more clearly what it knows—or does not know—not just about how its current products and processes work, but about how to create system designs for products and processes that have high levels of configurability. When a firm begins to realize that it has limited ability to specify modular interfaces for some of the components in its products or processes, organizational learning can be focused on improving its knowledge of those components and their system behaviors. In this way, efforts to create flexible system designs in the form of modular product and process architectures can become the driver of strategically important technological learning at the know-why level.

Furthermore, when a firm goes through processes intended to create modular product and process architectures, the interface specifications that the firm is able to create provide important insights into the current state of technological knowledge in the firm. Far from being merely a technical detail to be kept on file in the engineering department, the interface specifications a firm creates for its product and process architectures become a strategically important indicator of the level of knowledge the firm currently can apply to creating reliable, flexible system designs for its products and processes. In this regard, interface specifications may serve as both negative and positive indicators of the current state of a firm's strategically important knowledge and capabilities.

As a negative indicator, when a firm's current interface specifications constrain the firm to use only specific component designs in its product or process architectures, the inflexibilities in its component interfaces are likely to impose critical strategic inflexibilities on the firm. For example, a product component interface that requires use of a specific component design will limit the firm's ability to provide a product that meets various customer needs for the function provided by that component. Dependence on a single component design may also create a strategic dependence on a single supplier of that component. Similarly, an inflexible process component interface that locks a firm into using only its own internal processes in performing some activity can prevent the firm from considering outsourcing that activity to external suppliers. In effect, inflexibilities in a firm's current product and process component interfaces constitute "capability bottlenecks" that limit a firm's ability to respond to its competitive environment (Sanchez 2000).

As a positive indicator of firm capabilities, to the extent that the interfaces a firm creates bring it flexibilities to configure product and process variations, the range of product and process variations that the firm's interfaces can accommodate indicate the range of responses the firm is capable of making to changing markets, technologies, and industry conditions. In this sense, the flexibilities designed into the interface specifications of a firm's modular product and process architectures present a "balance sheet" of the organization's current ability to respond to a range of strategic demands and opportunities. Understanding both the constraints and the flexibilities inherent in the interfaces of a firm's product and process architectures is therefore essential to understanding the firm's *systemic flexibility* to respond to diversity and change in its competitive environment. When a firm's architectures include component types and interfaces that are standard within an industry, the firm may then benefit from the capabilities of suppliers and standard components. Thus, a firm's product and process architectures will also determine its ability to address technological knowledge and capabilities beyond its own boundaries.

MODULAR ARCHITECTURES AND MARKET KNOWLEDGE

Modular product and process architectures can improve the *breadth, depth,* and *speed* of a firm's processes for developing knowledge about its markets.

Developing broad knowledge of various customer preferences for a given kind of product requires observation and analysis of customer reactions to many different product variations. The more opportunities a firm has to interact with customers in its markets by offering more product variations for customers to react to, the greater the potential for the firm to understand the different sensitivities of various kinds of customers to the functions, features, and performance levels available in its products.

Figures 11.3(a) and 11.3(b) suggest how modular architectures can improve the breadth of knowledge a firm develops about the customer preferences that compose its markets. As suggested by the learning cycle in Figure 11.3(a), a firm that creates single products (or a limited number of related products) will have a limited number of opportunities for customers to interact with its products, to analyze various customer reactions to its products, and to create new products that serve customer preferences more effectively. By contrast, as suggested in Figure 11.3(b), a firm that can create modular product and process architectures that let it readily configure and bring to market a wide range of product variations can significantly broaden the scope of its interactions with its customers—and thereby improve the breadth of its knowledge of customer preferences for the kind of products it offers.

When modular product and process architectures are decomposed so that each function, feature, and performance level provided by a firm's product offers is "contained" within an individual modular component,[2] the ability to mix and match components in configuring modular product variations can help a firm learn about customer reactions to specific component-based functions, features, and performance levels in its products. The potential for this form of market learning is greatest when a firm can offer its customers menus of mix-and-matchable components that let individual customers configure the combination of components each would most like to have—as Dell Computer does in offering its customizable personal computers. In this regard, modular architectures not only make possible product e-business strategies of

---

[2] "Containing" product variety and change in specific components that deliver specific functions, features, or performance levels in a product is one of several *modular design principles* that enable modular architectures to be used as drivers of market exploration, technology development, and organizational learning (Sanchez forthcoming).

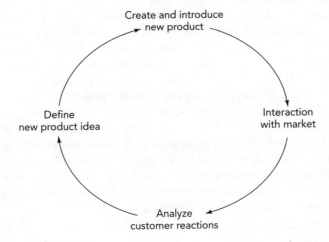

FIG. 11.3(a)   *Limited market learning through product-focused development processes.*

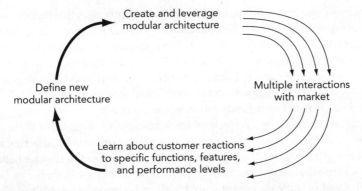

FIG. 11.3(b)   *Expanded market learning through architectural development processes.*

mass customization and product personalization (Pine 1992; Sanchez 1995, 1999), but enable a firm to develop much more fine-grained understanding of the characteristics of its products—at the component level—that customers most appreciate. As a firm develops deeper insights into which components in its architectures provide functions, features, and performance levels of greatest concern to customers, it can focus its organizational learning activities on improving those components.

The speed with which a firm learns about market preferences may also be accelerated when a firm can use fast, low-cost configuration of product variations to learn about market preferences in "real time." In real-time market research (Sanchez and Sudharshan 1993), rather than conducting time-consuming forms of traditional market research to determine which future product variations customers might prefer, a firm simply configures and brings to market small batches of product variations (ranging from a few to a few thousand units, depending on the product type) to test customer reactions in real time. Sony used modular architectures, for example, to configure more than 160 variations of its Walkman product for the USA market in the 1980s. By analyzing customer responses to a stream of product variations, Sony was able to discover which combinations of functions (e.g. single direction or auto reverse cassette drives), features (styling variations in plastic cases), and performance levels (Dolby noise reduction, bass enhancement) customers preferred in its new product concept. Today Nike explores evolving market preferences in real time through its Nike Town stores by introducing a changing array of new shoe variations based on "mix-and-match" combinations of soles, primary and accent materials, colors, and ties. By observing in real time which new products based on combinations of modular components elicit the strongest customer response, both Sony and Nike become fast, "real-time" explorers of evolving market preferences.

USING MODULAR ARCHITECTURES TO INTEGRATE TECHNOLOGICAL AND MARKET KNOWLEDGE

Many organizations have adopted long-term planning processes that include forward-looking assessments like market trend forecasting and technology roadmapping. What many firms continue to lack, however, is a clear framework for exercising the "corporate imagination" (Hamel and Prahalad 1991)—i.e. a framework that would help managers to integrate expected developments in markets and technologies into a vision of feasible future products and processes, and to identify new capabilities that would enable a firm to create future products and processes.

When market forecasting and technology roadmapping suggest that there are several possibilities for new technologies and future market preferences, selecting specific future products to develop often becomes quite problematic. On the one hand, very strong—and usually risky—assumptions about which future technologies and market preferences will become dominant would have to be made in order to identify the "most valuable" or "most promising" possibilities for future products. On the other hand, managers who are uncomfortable with making explicit assumptions about future outcomes may prefer to follow their "gut feel"—with the result that selection of future products for development often becomes *ad hoc*, arbitrary, and subject to undefined decision criteria that vary from manager to manager.

An alternative approach to strategic decision making under conditions of irreducible uncertainty about future markets and technologies is to refocus the attention of the firm on identifying and creating *strategic flexibilities* that will enable a firm to respond to a range of market and technology possibilities in the future (Sanchez 1993, 1995). The inherent flexibility of modular architectures to support configuration of many product variations offers a way out of decision-making dilemmas in product planning processes. Compared to asking managers to agree on specific products to develop when future market preferences and technology possibilities are uncertain, it is much more feasible for managers to discuss and agree on a *range* of future product variations to serve possible developments in market preferences and alternative technologies that managers consider most likely. When an organization's knowledge architecture enables it to create modular architectures for configuring a range of future product variations, a firm's long-term planning process can be redirected to defining and developing future-generation modular architectures that can respond to a range of future market and technology possibilities.

Moreover, much organizational learning and development of new capabilities takes place in product development projects. When a firm's long-term planning process is focused on individual products, project-driven organizational learning often builds unconnected islands of technical and market knowledge relevant only to specific future products. If the products a firm must create in the future change because of future developments in technologies or markets, the narrowly focused knowledge a firm has created in pursuing its original set of future products may not be readily applicable in creating a new set of future products. Organizational learning in projects to create future modular architectures that can support many product variations, however, will be inherently more deployable across a range of future product possibilities.

Some firms have recognized that processes for planning, creating, and leveraging modular architectures provide a powerful new framework for integrating a firm's evolving technical and market knowledge into effective product strategies (Sanchez 1995; Sanchez and Collins 1999). Figure 11.4 suggests some of the ways that modular architectures lead to a more integrative framework for leveraging an organization's current technological and market knowledge and for focusing organizational learning on creating new knowledge and capabilities with significant strategic benefits.

The objective in creating a next-generation modular architecture is to give a firm the broadest possible market coverage and the fastest possible upgrading of its products as technologically improved components become available. In essence, the objective for a next-generation modular architecture is to create a "platform" for responding effectively to a defined range of near-term market demands for product diversity and near-term opportunities for technological improvement. In effect, the next-generation architectures the firm creates will determine the *strategic options* the firm will have to bring product offers to its markets in the near term (Sanchez 1993, 1995). Creating next-generation modular architectures therefore provides a process for integrating identified near-term market opportunities with any new technological knowledge and capabilities the firm has created.

The leveraging of current-generation modular architectures consists of configuring product and process variations to explore markets and discover which configurations of products offer the best options for serving current market preferences. Leveraging current-generation architectures thus becomes the primary way a firm responds to both technology and market development opportunities in the near term. Technology development is focused on developing new component variations for the current-generation modular architecture. Market exploration then tries to determine which combinations of component variations are most effective in serving the current preferences of various customer groups. When marketing processes develop insights into

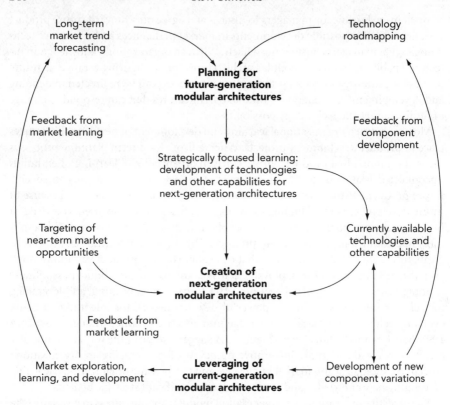

Fig. 11.4 *Planning, creating, and leveraging modular architectures as a framework for integrating technology and market knowledge.*

which component-based functions, features, and performance levels customers are most sensitive to, technology development efforts can be directed to creating a wider range of choices in those types of components and to developing higher performing versions of critical components.

Through its processes for exploring current market preferences, a firm may develop insights into possible evolutions of market preferences that become important inputs into a firm's long-term market forecasting. Similarly, the technical knowledge a firm creates in developing component variations to be used in next-generation and current-generation modular architectures can provide insights that improve a firm's technology roadmapping activities. For example, a firm's own experience in improving key components may help to form more accurate expectations as to future rates of technological improvement in those components, and such technological insights can improve a firm's planning processes for future-generation architectures.

IMPACTS OF MODULAR ARCHITECTURES ON ORGANIZATIONAL COMPETENCE

Sanchez, Heene, and Thomas (1996) proposed a working definition of organizational competence as "the ability to sustain the coordinated deployment of assets in ways that help a firm achieve its goals." As noted in the opening chapter of this volume, this simple definition incorporates the "four cornerstones" of the competence perspective:

1. The environment of a firm is *dynamic*. The normal state of affairs for most organizations is that both the markets they serve and the technologies that can be used to serve those markets are changing. An essential characteristic of the competent organization therefore is that it can sustain its ability to create value in its markets by responding advantageously to the market and technology dynamics in its environment.

2. Organizations are open systems that are embedded in larger "macrosystems" of industries and societies. Change in organizations is therefore *systemic* in nature and calls for approaches to managing change that can coordinate all the interacting elements of an organization in creating the new capabilities needed to respond to a changing environment. In effect, a key challenge in improving organizational competence is to increase the flexibility of the firm as an open system to respond effectively and quickly to the dynamics and diversity of its environment.

3. Managing systemic organizational change in a dynamic environment poses substantial *cognitive* challenges for managers. Much change in an organization's environment is uncertain, and the systemic adjustments needed in an organization to respond to various forms of change can be quite complex. The capacity of the human mind is constantly challenged by the complexity of the management task, and organizations must try to imagine and implement better approaches to managing complexity under conditions of dynamic uncertainty.

4. Managing organizations as systems in a changing and uncertain environment requires an understanding of the *holistic* nature of organizations. As open systems, organizations depend on ongoing flows of resources from many resource providers. As a result, the individual interests of many providers of essential resources intermingle in an organization. To continue to attract and access the best available resources in carrying out its processes, managers must recognize and provide adequate incentives and rewards to all providers of essential resources needed by the organization.

We now consider how learning to create and leverage modular product and process architectures can improve an organization's ability to manage its knowledge in ways that contribute significantly to each of these four dimensions of organizational competence.

Responding to environmental dynamics

Organizational competence requires the ability to respond advantageously to changes in both markets and technologies. Using modular architectures can significantly improve the responsiveness of a firm to both forms of change.

During the life cycle of a product, changes in market preferences typically evolve through several distinct stages (Sanchez 1995). When a new product concept is first introduced, potential customers who are unfamiliar with the new product concept are likely to be uncertain which "bundle" of functions, features, and performance levels they would prefer if they were to start using the new product. By creating a modular product architecture that can provide a range of product models based on different combinations of mixed-and-matched functional components, a firm may be able to stimulate initial trial of a new product by offering low-cost introductory product models that provide only the "core" set of functions, features, and performance levels essential to the new product concept. As adopters of a new product concept gain experience in using the product in their patterns of living, they may develop the ability to imagine the benefits to be derived from more fully featured, higher performing models, which the modular architecture may then be used to bring to market. As customers become more sophisticated in their understanding of the uses of the product, and as groups of customers begin to develop preferences for specific bundles of functions, features, and performance levels that best suit their individual lifestyles, modular architectures may be used to leverage a broad range of product variations to serve emerging market segments. In the most advanced stage of evolution of a market, some customers may come to understand how each component in a product contributes to the overall functionality and performance of the product. Modular architectures may then be used to present menus of component choices to customers that enable them to configure their own preferred, mass-customized product variation.

In this pattern of market evolution, it may be both necessary and desirable to create a succession of progressively more elaborate modular architectures to serve the increasingly sophisticated and diverse preferences of customers. Compared to trying to develop a growing range of individual product variations one at a time, however, creating modular architectures offers a much faster and more cost efficient way for a firm to investigate customer preferences as a market evolves (Sanchez 1999).

Used in this way, modular architectures can also help a firm use and develop new technological knowledge more effectively in serving evolving customer preferences. Changes in technology are normally embodied in either higher performing versions of current components or in wholly new kinds of functional product or process components. Anticipated technological changes—whether generated internally by the firm or adopted from external sources—may often be accommodated in modular architectures by "designing in" the flexibility to upgrade key product and process components as technologically improved components become available. Personal computer architectures, for example, typically use standardized component interface specifications that allow direct introduction of progressively higher performing components, such as the progressive upgrading of CD-ROM drives from 1X to 24X read speeds. Current generation personal computer architectures also have flexible interfaces for connecting computers to future-generation peripheral devices and complementary products. The FireWire port now designed into personal computers, for example, provides an interface for connecting computers to a growing number of new technology products like digital photograph and video cameras, audio systems, and televisions.

Beyond enabling a firm to leverage its current technical knowledge into product markets more effectively, modular architectures can also help a firm develop new technological knowledge that will be effective in serving evolving market preferences. By using modular architectures to explore market reactions to different combinations of component-based functions, features, or performance levels, a firm can more precisely direct its technological learning to improving components and creating new components that will provide the product characteristics most appreciated by customers.

Managing the firm as an open system

The "market test" of the competent organization is its ability to bring successful products to markets. Creating and realizing successful new products requires the ability to access and coordinate the best available resources for developing, producing, distributing, and supporting the products a firm brings to market. When a firm's knowledge architecture enables it to create modular product and process architectures, the firm can access a wider pool of resources for creating and realizing products, can coordinate those resources with reduced levels of financial and management inputs, and can accelerate the speed of its product creation and realization processes. The effect of these benefits is to give a firm more—and more valuable—*strategic options* to develop and realize products. Having more strategic options increases the *strategic flexibility* of the firm as an open system to respond advantageously to diversity and change in markets and technologies. Each of these elements in the new "strategic logic" of modular architectures deserves further explanation (Sanchez 1995).

First, let us consider how modular architectures make it possible for a firm to access a wider pool of resources for creating and realizing products. Recall from the discussion above the critical difference between conventional and modular development processes. In conventional development processes, the interfaces between functional components are determined by the designs of the individual components being developed and thus "evolve" during the component development process. Since individual component designs must work together in a product or process design, however, component designs must always be coordinated technically to assure that they will work together as a system. The investigation of alternative component designs by various component development groups therefore creates a constant stream of "interface issues" (Sanchez 2000). For example, when development groups for two interacting components create component designs that must subsequently be modified in order to work together, which group's component design should be modified, and in what ways? If design changes have to be made in one development group's component design because of a design change made by a second component group, which development group's budget should the cost of the design change be charged to? And how will such changes affect each development group's performance evaluations? Since resolving such issues may take a great deal of time and could become quite contentious if the component development groups are in different firms, conventional development processes are most commonly carried out within a single "authority hierarchy"—i.e. within the boundaries of a single firm—to enable managerial resolution of such issues (Sanchez and Mahoney 1996).

In contrast, by initially standardizing interface specifications for all components, the modular approach to creating product and process architectures essentially prevents such interface issues from arising and makes it much more practical for a firm to collaborate with component development resources beyond its own boundaries. When a firm's knowledge architectures enable it to define and standardize the interfaces between the components in its new product and process architectures before beginning development of new components, the firm effectively creates a well defined and stable technical environment for developing new components. The ability to define stable component development tasks that will not generate interface issues makes it much more possible for a firm to work with other firms in its own development processes. Thus, creating modular product and process architectures can make it possible for a firm to access a greatly enlarged pool of component development resources beyond its own boundaries, and thereby may greatly expand the number and range of products the firm can create and realize (Sanchez 1999).

Furthermore, establishing standardized component interfaces for a modular architecture creates an *information structure* that provides *embedded coordination* of component development tasks. Because standardized interface specifications effectively prevent interface issues from arising, modular development processes require much reduced levels of management inputs.[3] Alternatively, for a given level of management resources, modular architectures may let a firm greatly expand the range of products and processes it develops. When modular architectures improve a firm's ability to access development resources outside the firm, the financial resources a firm must directly invest to develop new products may also be reduced.

Modular architectures can also substantially reduce the time required to create and realize new products and processes. The key to accelerating product development is fully specifying—and then freezing—component interfaces to enable truly concurrent component development processes. When firms attempt to implement concurrent engineering practices, but do not fully define and standardize interface specifications governing interactions between components, the result is typically a form of "concurrent chaos" in which uncontrolled development of component designs quickly generates a complex and potentially paralyzing tangle of incompatible component designs. Firms that can fully define and standardize modular component interface specifications before beginning concurrent development, however, have reported 50 to 80 percent reductions in development time (and resources) required to design components for new products (Sanchez forthcoming).

---

[3] Although fewer management inputs will be required during development of components, increased management inputs will normally be required in processes for defining the interfaces in modular architectures. Moreover, those management inputs may be qualitatively different from the inputs normally provided by managers to development processes. Since the modular architectures the firm creates will effectively determine the strategic flexibility of a firm to respond to market and technology opportunities, a primary input required from managers is a clear strategic vision of the range of market and technology opportunities the firm will seek to respond to through its product and process architectures. (See Sanchez forthcoming.)

The strategic flexibility of a firm to respond to opportunities and demands can be expressed in concrete terms by the set of definable *strategic options* the firm has to bring specific products to market. The more component variations the interfaces in its architectures enable a firm to use, the more strategic options the firm will have to configure product variations that can respond to change and diversity in markets and technologies. Because modular architectures may also enable a firm to draw on a wider base of development resources, to coordinate those resources with fewer management and financial resources of its own, and to use concurrent design of components to bring new products to market faster, a firm that learns how to create modular product and process architectures may create more strategic options—and thus greater strategic flexibility. Moreover, to the extent that a modular-capable firm creates its strategic options at lower costs and can exercise those options (i.e. bring new products to market) faster than other firms,[4] each of its strategic options will also be more valuable than it would otherwise be. Used in this way, modular architectures can increase the strategic flexibility of a firm as an open system to respond advantageously to change and diversity in its environment.

Managing cognitive processes

Sensemaking is a fundamental activity of organizations. Managers must "make sense" of the organization as a system, of the change and complexity in the organization's competitive environment, and of the best prospects available to an organization for survival and success. The primary way that a firm seeks to survive and succeed in its environment is through creating and realizing products. When managers think in terms of developing individual products as the way to respond to environmental change and diversity, the ability of managers to develop a clear, coherent strategy for a firm may be overwhelmed by the large number of product variations needed to serve diverse market demands and keep up with competition. The cognitive complexity of managing change and diversity in competitive markets can be significantly reduced, however, when managers begin to think in terms of creating modular architectures that can serve a range of market demands and can support significant extensions and renewals for a range of products.

The concept of logical incrementalism (Quinn 1978) helps to clarify the way in which modular architectures can simplify the cognitive processes involved in managing competitive dynamics and complexity. The basic notion of logical incrementalism is that organizational change can be managed more effectively when it is undertaken in incremental steps that progressively and logically lead to new organizational activities.

---

[4] The value of an option increases with the length of time during which an option can be exercised. However, when the value of the underlying asset (the asset that can be claimed by exercising the option) can be expected to decrease or "erode" over time, the optimal time to exercise an option may be sooner rather than later. When a firm has a strategic option to bring a new product to market, but the potential value of that opportunity is decreasing with the passage of time because other firms can be expected to bring competing products to market, a firm's ability to bring a new product to market faster (i.e. to exercise its option sooner rather than later) will increase the value of that option (Sanchez 1993).

In essence, the best approach to managing an organization in a changing environment is likely to be continual, progressive adjustments of its products and processes in ways that are readily understood by everyone in an organization.

The usual interpretation of logical incrementalism is that decomposing change into small increments is generally beneficial, because small adjustments are easier to accomplish in organizations than radical, "big bang" transformations. What an architectural perspective on managing change helps us to understand, however, is that trying to manage change by making "too many" incremental adjustments that are "too small" can generate its own form of organizational complexity. In particular, trying to make large numbers of incremental changes in individual products in an effort to keep up with high rates of market change can create organizational complexity that makes it difficult for managers to maintain clear direction and focus in an organization's market strategies. Given the dynamics and diversity in market demands that many firms face today, developing individual products is often simply too small an incremental adjustment to sustain coherent, manageable, strategically focused organizational processes. Even if a firm that develops individual products manages to sustain high levels of product development activity in many projects, its managers may lose a clear understanding of where all its development activities are headed, and why.

Modular architectures, however, offer a larger unit of incremental adjustment that is more appropriate for conceptualizing and managing a firm's response to dynamic competitive environments. By offering managers a feasible basis for thinking in terms of making incremental adjustments that can cover a range of current and future market possibilities, modular architectures offer a more comprehensible—and thus more cognitively feasible—unit of incremental adjustment in formulating an organization's strategies for responding to high levels of change and diversity in product markets.

Managing organizations holistically

Organizations are communities of convergent—but not identical—interests. The interests of key resource providers to an organization will necessarily have something in common—namely, a desire to see an organization succeed, at least in ways that can help individual resource providers achieve their goals. But the differences in goals that typically exist across individuals suggest that there will rarely be perfect alignment of interests among all individual resource providers to an organization. To attract and maintain the best possible flows of essential resources, the competent organization must understand what kinds and levels of rewards it must distribute to all individual providers of essential resources. The concept of managing organizations holistically is therefore not a simplistic communitarian notion, but rather a concept that recognizes the importance of defining, measuring, monitoring, and rewarding the contribution that each resource provider makes to the overall ability of an organization to create value through its product offers.

Developing new products in the conventional way—i.e. by letting component interfaces be driven by component designs—inherently creates a tight coupling between component development activities. When component development groups are not constrained to honor standardized component interface specifications, design decisions made in one development group are very likely to affect the suitability of the component design decisions made in other development groups. This technical interdependence between component designs creates two conditions of tight coupling. Both the performance of a given component in the product and the performance of each component development group in designing their component will depend on decisions made by other development groups. Since both modes of performance depend on factors beyond the control of any development group, the tight coupling of component development processes in conventional development processes makes it virtually impossible to determine the relative performance of individual component development groups in the overall development of a product. When the relative performance of component development groups cannot be ascertained, determining an appropriate distribution of rewards to development groups becomes problematic.

When a firm follows a modular approach to creating and realizing products, however, the standardizing of component interface specifications before component development begins means that design decisions made in one component development group will not be affected by design decisions made in another development group, as long as all development groups honor the standardized component interface specifications applicable to their component. Component development activities therefore become loosely coupled, and this makes it more feasible for a firm's managers to assess the relative performance of each component development team in carrying out its design task, and to distribute rewards accordingly.

Adopting modular process architectures brings a similar improvement to the evaluation of groups in performing activities in a process architecture. When the interfaces that define the inputs and outputs of process activities are not fully specified and standardized, variations in the outputs of one process activity may have disruptive impacts on the downstream process(es) it provides inputs to. When a group responsible for a process activity is subjected to inadequately controlled variations in inputs that affect its ability to perform its task well, it is difficult if not impossible to fairly assess that group's performance and to allocate appropriate rewards. When an organization has a modular process architecture, however, the well defined and standardized input and output interfaces between activities creates a loose coupling between activities. The loose coupling of activities in a modular process architecture makes it more feasible to assess and reward the relative performance of each work group in carrying out its process activity. Having well defined processes and interfaces also improves the ability of a firm to benchmark the practices and performance levels of its work groups against those in other organizations.

CONCLUSION

Compared to current practices in most organizations, the use of modular architectures requires a higher degree of definition of an organization's current knowledge and capabilities and a more disciplined approach to learning through product creation and realization processes. Making the transition to a more defined and disciplined modular way of working, however, can help an organization understand and manage some fundamental—but at first counterintuitive—aspects of organizations. We conclude this discussion of modular architectures in organizational competence by summarizing two counterintuitive ways that the definition and discipline inherent in modular architectures can improve organizational flexibility and creativity.

In our usual perceptions of the product creation process, we observe new products emanating from organizations and therefore are likely to surmise that "organizations design products." Viewing the product creation process from an architectural perspective, however, helps to reveal the profound impact that an organization's product architectures have on the way an organization is structured and functions—i.e. the fundamental ways in which "products design organizations." Without the benefit of this architectural perspective, efforts to improve an organization's competence in creating new products are likely to be focused on improving the way the organization currently works. Such efforts usually try to add new coordination procedures, more communication links between development groups, more reporting or oversight responsibilities, and so on. In a basic sense, however, trying to improve product creation competence by improving conventional development practices is tantamount to treating the symptoms of a dysfunction rather than correcting the underlying cause of the dysfunction. The architectural perspective helps us to understand that significant improvements in an organization's product creation competence must begin with improvements in the architectures of the products the organization creates. Improved organizational flexibility in product creation will not be attainable unless an organization's product architectures become more flexible, and modular architectures are the quintessential flexible architecture.

Another common perception is that generating "creative" new products requires a "creative" organizational environment, which is often assumed to be an essentially unstructured, unfettered environment in which "creative" people may freely try out all kinds of new product ideas and ways of doing things. As a consequence, many people would consider an environment that requires disciplined adherence to a well-defined process structure to be inimical to creativity. What the architectural perspective makes plain, however, is that disciplined adherence to a well-defined *modular* development process can enable many new configurations of products and processes to flourish.

Music offers an instructive analogy. The tonal scales of notes in music are a well-defined but flexible structure for inventing virtually unlimited new combinations of notes. Creativity in music can be expressed both by inventing new kinds of music architectures for arranging notes (sonatas, blues, bebop jazz) and by composing new combinations of notes within existing architectures. It would be difficult to argue that accepting the discipline of working within the tonal scale structure compromised the creativity of Amadeus Mozart or Miles Davis in creating and using music architectures. On the contrary, the discipline of following the tonal scale structure has enabled the creation of many music architectures that facilitate an endless stream of creative improvisation. In an analogous way, learning to work in a well-defined and disciplined modular process can help organizations create architectures that enable creative, improvisational configuring of new products and processes that work effectively together. Creating and using modular architectures may well become an essential capability of those organizations that know how to be both creative and effective in meeting the market test for competence.

REFERENCES

GARUD, R. and A. KUMARASWAMY (1993). "Changing competitive dynamics in network industries: An exploration of Sun Microsystems' open systems strategy," *Strategic Management Journal*, 14 (5), 351–69.

HENDERSON, R. and K. B. CLARK (1990). "Architectural innovation: The reconfiguration of existing product technologies and the failure of established firms," *Administrative Science Quarterly*, 35, 9–30.

HAMEL, G. and C. K. PRAHALAD (1991). "The corporate imagination and expeditionary marketing," *Harvard Business Review*, 69 (4), 81–93.

NORMANN, R. and R. RAMIREZ (1993). "From value chain to value constellation: Designing interactive strategies," *Harvard Business Review*, 71 (July–Aug.), 65–77.

ORTON, J. D. and K. WEICK (1990). "Loosely coupled systems: A reconceptualization," *Academy of Management Review*, 15 (2), 203–23.

PINE, J. D. (1992). *Mass Customization: The New Frontier in Business Competition.* Boston: Harvard Business School Press.

QUINN, J. B. (1978). "Strategic change and logical incrementalism," *Sloan Management Review*, 20 (1), 7–16.

SANCHEZ, R. (1993). "Strategic flexibility, firm organization, and managerial work in dynamic markets: A strategic options perspective," *Advances in Strategic Management*, 9, 251–91.

—— (1995). "Strategic flexibility in product competition," *Strategic Management Journal*, 16, 135–59.

—— (1996). "Strategic product creation: Managing new interactions of Technologies, Markets, and Organizations," *European Management Journal*, 14 (2), 121–38.

—— (1997). "Managing articulated knowledge in competence-based competition," in R. Sanchez and A. Heene (eds.), *Strategic Learning and Knowledge Management.* Chichester: John Wiley, 163–87.

—— (1999). "Modular architectures in the marketing process," *Journal of Marketing*, 63 (Special Issue 1999), 92–111.

—— (2000). "Modular architectures, knowledge assets, and organizational learning: New management processes for product creation," *International Journal of Technology Management*, 19 (6), 610–29.

—— (forthcoming). *Modularity, Strategic Flexibility, and Knowledge Management.* Oxford: Oxford University Press.

—— and R. P. COLLINS (1999). "Competing in modular markets," working paper #IMD 99-7, IMD—International Institute for Management Development, Lausanne, Switzerland.

—— and J. T. MAHONEY (1996). "Modularity, flexibility, and knowledge management in product and organization design," *Strategic Management Journal*, 17 (Winter Special Issue), 63–76.

SANCHEZ, R. and D. SUDHARSHAN (1993). "Real-time market research," *Marketing Intelligence & Planning*, 11, 29–38.

—— A. HEENE, and H. THOMAS (1996). *Dynamics of Competence-Based Competition*. Oxford: Elsevier Pergamon.

SANDERSON, S. W. and M. UZUMERI (1997). *Managing Product Families*. Chicago: Irwin.

Index

Index